ROBERT MENZIES' FORGOTTEN PEOPLE

Judith Brett was born in Melbourne in 1949. She studied philosophy and politics at the University of Melbourne, and anthropology at Oxford. She completed a Ph.D. on psychoanalysis and literature at the University of Melbourne, where she subsequently taught Australian politics. She edited *Meanjin* from 1982 to 1987 and was the literary editor of the *Times on Sunday* during 1987. She currently teaches Australian politics and biography at La Trobe University. She has contributed articles, reviews and essays to a wide range of publications. *Robert Menzies' Forgotten People* is her first book.

ROBERT MENZIES' FORGOTTEN PEOPLE

JUDITH BRETT

MACMILLAN
AUSTRALIA

First published 1992 by Pan Macmillan Publishers Australia
a division of Pan Macmillan Australia Pty Limited
63-71 Balfour Street, Chippendale, Sydney

Copyright © Judith Brett 1992

All rights reserved. No part of this book may be reproduced
or transmitted in any form or by any means, electronic or
mechanical, including photocopying, recording or by any
information storage and retrieval system, without prior
permission in writing from the publisher.

National Library of Australia
cataloguing-in-publication data:

Brett, Judith Margaret, 1949- .
Robert Menzies' forgotten people.
Bibliography.
ISBN 0 7329 0761 6.

1. Menzies, Sir Robert, 1894-1978. 2. Menzies, Sir Robert, 1894-1978 - Psychology. 3. Prime ministers - Australia - Biography. 4. Australia - Social conditions - 20th century. 5. Australia - Politics and governement - 1939-1945. 6. Australia - Politics and government - 1945-1956. I. Title.

994.042092

Typeset in 13/15 pt Bembo by Midland Typesetters, Australia.
Printed in Australia by Australian Print Group

CONTENTS

Acknowledgements	vii
Chronology	ix
THE WORDS OF MR MENZIES	1
'The Forgotten People'	5
I PUBLIC LANGUAGE	29
THE FORGOTTEN PEOPLE	31
Labour and non-labour	31
'We don't have classes here'	38
Women at home	51
The independent virtues	59
THE COMMUNISTS	74
Ambivalent commitments	74
Trouble on the waterfront	82
Paranoid politics	92
A fraudulent document	98
John Stuart Mill and Lady Macbeth	108
II PRIVATE LANGUAGE	127
ENGLAND	129
An imagined place	129
Centre and periphery	143
'*My England*'	150
INLAND BORN	156
Jeparit	156
Germans and Aborigines	165

KNOWLEDGE, CULTURE, EXPERIENCE	174
An instinctive conservative	174
The sorry tale of the Royal Academy of Australian Art	179
Literary aspirations	187
A hollow man?	195
FATHERS	199
Ambitions and ideals	199
James and Kate Menzies	201
A family romance	212
The men of England	215
THE ELEVATED SELF	225
Inferiors	225
Superiors	233
The narcissistic wound of colonial birth	239
CHURCHILL AND THE MEANING OF 1941	244
War-time London	244
Return and resignation	251
Recovery	258
Lord Warden of the Cinque Ports	266
CORRESPONDENCES	270
Notes	275
Bibliography	300
Index	308

ACKNOWLEDGEMENTS

My first and greatest debt in writing this book is to the late Alan Davies, who taught me to approach politics with the fullest imaginative and intellectual range I could muster, and whose writing has been a continual source of inspiration and wisdom for my own. He read some of my early work on Robert Menzies, but died before it was properly under way. I also owe an enormous debt to two colleagues of his and mine, Graham Little and Angus McIntyre, both of whom generously read and commented on the completed manuscript. Various other people discussed my work on Menzies with me and I would particularly like to mention Hugh Stretton, the late Vincent Buckley, Paul Carter, Amanda Lohrey, Janet McCalman, Hilary McPhee, Don Watson and Jim Davidson, as well as the students in the course on political biography which I teach at La Trobe University with Angus McIntyre. I would also like to thank my husband, Graeme Smith, for his helpful suggestions on the manuscript and for his unfailingly calm support.

Helen O'Shea and Susan Lever both provided me with hospitality on my numerous trips to Canberra to consult Menzies' papers in the National Library of Australia where the staff of the manuscript reading room were always helpful. I would also like to thank Kevin Perkins for generously allowing me to listen to interviews he recorded with Frank Menzies and Isabel Green in the 1960s; and Mark Cranfield in the Oral History section of the NLA, the staff of the National Film and Sound Archive, Deborah Richards of the ABC and Peter Allen of the *Sydney Morning Herald* for assistance with locating audio and visual material on Menzies. (The author and publisher would be pleased to hear from any copyright holder we have been unable to locate.) Robert Menzies' daughter, Mrs Heather Henderson, kindly gave me permission to quote from her father's published and unpublished writings and speeches. The Victorian Ministry of the Arts assisted the project in its early stages by providing a grant towards my research expenses at a time when I was without paid employment.

CHRONOLOGY

1894	20 December: Robert Gordon Menzies born to James and Kate Menzies in Jeparit, Victoria. He was their fourth child.
1899-1907	Attended state schools in Jeparit and Ballarat.
1908	Topped State Scholarships Examinations, continued schooling at Grenville College, Ballarat.
1910	Family moved to Melbourne, Robert attended Wesley College.
1913-16	Studied law at University of Melbourne.
1916	Graduated with first-class honours in law and won Bowen Essay Prize.
1918	Admitted to the Bar where he read with Owen Dixon.
1920	Successfully argued the Engineers' Case before the High Court. Married Pattie Leckie.
1928	Entered Legislative Council (Upper House) of Victorian Parliament as member of Nationalist Party.
1929	Appointed King's Council. Won seat in Victorian Legislative Assembly (Lower House).
1932	Minister for Railways and Attorney-General in Stanley Argyle's government.
1934	Contested and won the Federal seat of Kooyong. Appointed Attorney-General and Minister for Industry in Joseph Lyons' United Australia Party government.
1935	First trip to England as member of party attending King George V's Silver Jubilee celebrations. Appeared before Privy Council.

1939	Lyons died suddenly of heart attack. Menzies became leader of the UAP and Prime Minister, despite trenchant opposition from Country Party leader Earle Page. War was declared.
1941	January-May: Menzies made 4-month visit to Middle East, Britain, Canada and United States, extending his stay in Britain three times.
	August: Menzies resigned as Prime Minister; Country Party leader Arthur Fadden became Prime Minister.
	October: Fadden's government defeated when two independents crossed the floor. ALP, led by John Curtin, formed government. Menzies resigned from leadership of UAP; replaced by Billy Hughes.
1942-43	Made series of radio broadcasts, of which 'The Forgotten People' was one.
1943	Again elected leader of the UAP. UAP suffered devastating electoral defeat.
1944	Called conferences in Albury and Canberra to discuss formation of a new non-labour party. Liberal Party of Australia formed with Menzies as federal parliamentary leader.
1946	Election at which Liberal Party improved position.
1949	Liberal Party won federal election, defeating Ben Chifley's Labor government.
1950	Communist Party Dissolution Bill introduced.
1951	Referendum proposals to ban Communist Party of Australia defeated.

1954	Soviet diplomat Vladimir Petrov defected on eve of federal election. Liberal Party won election.
1955	ALP split.
1963	Menzies appointed Knight of the Order of the Thistle.
1966	January: Retired as leader of the Liberal Party and as Prime Minister of Australia.
	July: Installed as Lord Warden of the Cinque Ports.
1978	15 May: Died.

THE WORDS OF MR MENZIES

... grand and magnificent, and the best man of his time.
SIR JOHN BUNTING

Pig Iron Bob is Dead!
WORKERS' WEEKLY NEWS, OBITUARY, 18 MAY 1978

'There'll always be a Menzies
While there's a BHP'
STUDENT SONG, SUNG TO THE TUNE
'THERE'LL ALWAYS BE AN ENGLAND'

AMONG AUSTRALIANS who remember Menzies, opinions are divided into one of three positions. To some he was the supreme twentieth-century Australian statesman and politician, presiding with ease over the post-war boom and representing Australia abroad with dignity and aplomb. He spoke well, looked good and stood for clear, solid values – hard work, independence, family life, Parliament and the Queen. This Menzies is the grand old man of the Liberal Party, who brought non-labour back from the wilderness of the war years and kept the socialists from power, his bulky presence guaranteeing Australia's domestic security.

Then there is the Menzies of the left who first showed his true colours in the 1930s when, as Federal Attorney-General, he tried to prevent the anti-fascist activist Egon Kisch from landing on Australian shores, and who, on the eve of World War II, fought the waterside workers over the shipment to Japan of pig iron, which, they claimed, was destined for the Japanese war machine. Returned to office in 1949, he swam happily with the McCarthyist tide, introducing the Communist Party Dissolution Bill in 1950 and pulling a Russian defector, Vladimir Petrov, out of the hat on the eve of the 1954 election. He won the election and precipitated a disastrous split in the Australian Labor Party (ALP). Authoritarian despite his professed liberal beliefs, he kept the ALP from office for seventeen years through a combination of unscrupulous opportunism, remarkable good luck, and the gullibility of the Australian people.

These first two views of Menzies are based in the party political conflicts of the day. The third view is generationally based, held by those like myself who were young in the 1950s and 1960s, and for whom Australian cultural life then seemed frozen by smugness, fear and indifference, and dominated by the values and assumptions of a bygone age. Menzies in full evening dress, greeting Queen Elizabeth in 1963 with the lines 'I did but see her passing by, And yet I love her till I die', was a ludicrous anachronism, holding Australia back from the bright new decade of youth, damming her energy and creativity behind a solid wall of cautious conservatism. This view drew on the demonology of the old left, but its main complaint against Menzies was that he was still there, 'a frozen Edwardian', as Donald Horne described him in *The Lucky Country*, who seemed determined to freeze the culture with him. Among the generation who came of age in the 1960s, the mere mention of his name is still sufficient to express one's distance from the conventional values of the past, of middle Australia, and to signal the superiority of the politically, sexually and culturally sophisticated world to come.

In revenge perhaps for his political longevity, Australians to date have not been much interested in revising the political representations of Menzies current during his lifetime, freezing him as some felt he once froze the culture. These frozen representations of Menzies are part of a much more general reluctance to think hard about the politics and culture of the last fifty years. From the perspective of the old left, there has been a refusal to see that conservatism is as deeply rooted in Australian experience as the radical egalitarianism in which they had placed their faith. From the perspective of the Liberal Party there is the expected glorifying of their origins, a reluctance to dwell on past mistakes and a nostalgic wish to repeat them. For the sixties generation, there is the difficulty of integrating the suburban family-centred people many of us have become with our past view of ourselves. Our image of Menzies reassures us that some things, at least, have changed.

My interest in Menzies was sparked by reading his wartime radio broadcast 'The Forgotten People'. To me it bespoke a much more complex and more interesting politician than was captured in any of the popular representations. I was attracted to its praise for the family and the home-centred life and its defence of a realm of values irreducible to the material and utilitarian; yet there was a hard, unforgiving quality to much of the imagery, an infuriating refusal to recognise the values which animated labour politics, and a general air of defensive self-satisfaction and smug sanctimoniousness about its paraded virtues. And although the speech smacked of the authoritarian moralising of headmasters' addresses and Sunday sermons, Menzies' obvious skill with language was impressive. Reading the speech today, when the language of many of our prominent politicians is garbled or aggressively evasive, and when even the most articulate of them employ speechwriters, one cannot help but feel there has been a decline in the standard of public men. Neither the left nor the right nor the sixties youth could give an account of Menzies and his place in Australian politics and culture which included both his strengths and his weaknesses, both the values he stood for and those he denied.

'The Forgotten People' is Menzies' richest, most creative political speech and one of his most influential. In it Menzies makes his most direct address to the Australian middle class, the people he calls 'the forgotten people', who will return him to power in 1949 and keep him there till his retirement in 1966. It gave non-labour images with which to recreate and enlarge its constituency and has continued to be an important source of inspiration for the Liberal Party, particularly recently when the party has been looking again for a way out of the doldrums of opposition.

I have returned again and again to this speech in my attempts to understand the dynamics of Australian conservatism and Menzies' place in it. Circling over its themes and images I have tried to discern its rhetorical and emotional strategies, its organising values and ideals, as well as its patterns of evasion and denial; and I have tried to understand the relationship it embodies between the Australian middle class and its most successful representative. For this speech marks not just a turning point in the fortunes of non-labour in Australia but a turning point in Menzies' own political fortunes. It marks the break between the old and the new Menzies, between the aloof, ambitious politician of the 1930s, too clever by half, who came such a cropper in 1941, and the wiser, humbler, more mature Menzies of the second prime ministership. The speech can be read for its biographical strategies and allusions as well as for its political meanings, and it seems to me, after many readings, to hold clues to the means by which Menzies effected this change.

The Forgotten People

From R.G. Menzies, *The Forgotten People*, pamphlet published by Robertson & Mullens, 1942

*Q*uite recently, a Bishop wrote a letter to a great daily newspaper. His theme was the importance of doing justice to the workers. His belief apparently was that the workers are those who work with their hands. He sought to divide the people of Australia into classes. He was obviously suffering from what has for years seemed to me to be our greatest political disease; the disease of thinking that the community is divided into the rich and relatively idle, and the laborious poor, and that every social and political controversy can be resolved into the question: WHAT SIDE ARE YOU ON?

Now, the last thing that I want to do is to commence or take part in a false war of this kind. In a country like Australia the class war must always be a false war.

But if we are to talk of classes, then the time has come to say something of the forgotten class - *The Middle Class* - those people who are constantly in danger of being ground between the upper and the nether millstones of the false class war; the middle class who, properly regarded, represent the backbone of this country.

We don't have classes here as in England, and therefore the terms don't mean the same. It is necessary, therefore, that I should define what I mean when I use the expression 'the middle class.'

Let me first define it by exclusion: I exclude at one end of the scale the rich and powerful; those who control great funds and enterprises, and are as a rule able to protect themselves - though it must be said that in a political sense they have as a rule shown neither comprehension nor competence. But I exclude them because in most material difficulties the rich can look after themselves.

I exclude at the other end of the scale the mass of unskilled people, almost invariably well-organized, and with their wages and conditions safeguarded by popular law. What I am excluding them from is my definition of the middle class. We cannot exclude them from the problem of social progress, for one of the prime objects of modern social and political policy is to give to them a proper measure of security, and provide the conditions which will enable them to acquire skill and knowledge and individuality.

These exclusions being made, I include the intervening range, the kind of people I myself represent in Parliament – salary-earners, shopkeepers, skilled artisans, professional men and women, farmers, and so on. These are, in the political and economic sense, the middle class. They are for the most part un-organized and un-selfconscious. They are envied by those whose social benefits are largely obtained by taxing them. They are not rich enough to have individual power. They are taken for granted by each political party in turn. They are not sufficiently lacking in individualism to be organized for what in these days we call 'pressure politics.' And yet, as I have said, they are the backbone of the nation.

The Communist has always hated what he calls 'the bourgeoisie' because he sees clearly that the existence of one has kept British countries from revolution, while the substantial absence of one in feudal France at the end of the 18th century and in Czarist Russia at the end of the last war made revolution easy and indeed inevitable.

You may say to me: 'Why bring this matter up at this stage when we are fighting a war, in the result of which we are all equally concerned?'

My answer is that I am bringing it up because under the pressures of war we may, if we are not careful, if we are not as thoughtful as the times will permit us to be, inflict a fatal injury upon our own backbone.

In point of political, industrial and social theory and practice there are great delays in time of war. But there are also great accelerations. We must watch each, remembering always that whether we know it or not, and whether we like it or not, the foundations of whatever new order is to come after the war are inevitably being laid down now. We cannot go wrong right up to the Peace Treaty and expect suddenly thereafter to go right.

Now, what is the value of this middle class, so defined and described?

First: It has 'a stake in the country.' It has responsibility for homes – homes material, homes human, homes spiritual.

I do not believe that the real life of this nation is to be found either in great luxury hotels and the petty gossip of so-called fashionable suburbs, or in the officialdom of organized masses.

It is to be found in the homes of people who are nameless and unadvertised, and who, whatever their individual religious conviction or dogma, see in their children their greatest contribution to the immortality of their race. The home is the foundation of sanity and sobriety; it is the indispensable condition of continuity; its health determines the health of society as a whole.

I have mentioned homes material,
       homes human,
          and homes spiritual.
Let me take them in their order: What do I mean by 'homes material'?

The material home represents the concrete expression of the habits of frugality and saving 'for a home of our own.' Your advanced socialist may rage against private property even whilst he acquires it; but one of the best instincts in us is that which induces us to have one little piece of earth with a house and a garden which is ours, to which we can withdraw, in which we can be among our friends, into which no stranger may come against our will.

If you consider it, you will see that if, as in the old saying, 'The Englishman's home is his castle,' it is this very fact that leads on to the conclusion that he who seeks to violate that law by violating the soil of England must be repelled and defeated.

National patriotism, in other words, inevitably springs from the instinct to defend and preserve our own homes.

Then we have *homes human*: A great house, full of loneliness, is not a home. 'Stone walls do not a prison make' nor do they make a house; they may equally make a stable or a piggery. Brick walls, dormer windows and central heating need not make more than an hotel.

My home is where my wife and children are; the instinct to be with them is the great instinct of civilized man; the instinct to give them a chance in life is a noble instinct, not to make them leaners but lifters.

If Scotland has made a great contribution to the theory and practice of education, it is because of the tradition of Scottish homes. The Scottish ploughman, walking behind his team, cons ways and means of making his son a farmer, and so he sends him to the village school. The Scottish farmer ponders upon the future of his son, and sees it most assured not by the inheritance of money but by the acquisition of that knowledge which will give him power, and so the sons of many Scottish farmers find their way to Edinburgh and a University degree.

The great question is: 'How can I qualify my son to help society?' and not, as we have so frequently thought: 'How can I qualify society to help my son?' If human homes are to fulfil their destiny, then we must have frugality and saving for education and progress.

And, finally, we have *homes spiritual:* This is a notion which finds its simplest and most moving expression in 'The Cotter's

Saturday Night' of Burns. Human nature is at its greatest when it combines dependence upon God with independence of man.

We offer no affront, on the contrary we have nothing but the warmest human compassion, for those whom fate has compelled to live upon the bounty of the State, when we say that the greatest element in a strong people is a fierce independence of spirit.

This is the only *real* freedom and it has as its corollary a brave acceptance of unclouded individual responsibility.

The moment a man seeks moral and intellectual refuge in the emotions of a crowd, he ceases to be a human being and becomes a cypher.

The home spiritual so understood is not produced by lassitude or by dependence; it is produced by self-sacrifice, by frugality and saving.

In a war, as indeed at most times, we become the ready victims of phrases. We speak glibly of many things without pausing to consider what they signify. We speak of 'financial power,' forgetting that the financial power of 1942 is based upon the savings of generations which have preceded it.

We speak of 'morale' as if it were a quality induced from without, created by others for our benefit, when in truth there can be no national morale which is not based upon the individual courage of men and women. We speak of 'man power' as if it were a mere matter of arithmetic, as if it were made up of a multiplication of men and muscles without spirit.

Second: the middle class, more than any other, provides the intelligent ambition which is the motive power of human progress. The idea entertained by many people that in a well-constituted world we shall all live on the State is the quintessence of madness, for what is the State but *us* – we collectively must provide what we individually receive.

The great vice of democracy, a vice which is exacting a bitter retribution from it at this moment, is that for a generation we have been busy getting ourselves on to the list of beneficiaries and removing ourselves from the list of contributors, as if somewhere there was somebody else's wealth and somebody else's effort on which we could thrive.

To discourage ambition, to envy success, to hate achieved superiority, to distrust independent thought, to sneer at and impute false motives to public service, these are the maladies of modern democracy, and of Australian democracy in particular. Yet ambition, effort, thinking, and readiness to serve are not only the design and objectives of self-government but are the essential conditions of its success.

If this is not so, then we had better put back the clock, and search for a benevolent autocracy once more.

Where do we find these great elements most commonly?

Among the defensive and comfortable rich?

Among the unthinking and unskilled mass?

Or among what I have called 'the middle class'?

Third: The middle class provides more than perhaps any other the intellectual life which marks us off from the beast; the life which finds room for literature, for the arts, for science, for medicine and the law.

Consider the case of literature and art. Could these survive as a Department of State? Are we to publish our poets according to their political colour? Is the State to decree surrealism because surrealism gets a heavy vote in a key electorate? The truth is that no great book was ever written and no great picture ever painted by the clock or according to civil service rules. These things are done by *man*, not men. You cannot regiment them. They require opportunity, and sometimes leisure. The artist, if he is to live, must have a buyer; the writer, an audience. He finds them among frugal people to whom the margin above bare living means a chance to reach out a little towards that heaven which is just beyond our grasp.

It has always seemed to me, for example, that an artist is better helped by the man who sacrifices something to buy a picture he loves than by a rich patron who follows the fashion.

Fourth: This middle class maintains and fills the higher schools and universities and so feeds the lamp of learning.

What are schools for?

To train people for examinations?

To enable people to comply with the law?

Or to produce developed men and women?

Are the universities mere technical schools, or have they, as one of their functions, the preservation of pure learning, bringing in its train not merely riches for the imagination but a comparative sense for the mind, and leading to what we need so badly – the recognition of values which are other than pecuniary?

One of the great blots on our modern living is the cult of false values, a repeated application of the test of money, of notoriety, of applause.

A world in which a comedian or a beautiful half-wit on the screen can be paid fabulous sums, whilst scientific researchers and discoverers can suffer neglect and starvation, is a world which needs to have its sense of values violently set right.

Now, have we realized and recognized these things, or is most of our policy designed to discourage or penalize thrift, to encourage dependence on the State, to bring about a dull equality on the fantastic idea that all men are equal in mind and needs and deserts, to level down by taking the mountains out of the landscape; to weigh men according to their political organizations and power, as votes and not as human beings?

These are formidable questions and we cannot escape from answering them if there is really to be a new order for the world.

I have been actively engaged in politics for fourteen years in the State of Victoria and in the Commonwealth of Australia. In that period I cannot readily recall many occasions upon which any policy was pursued which was designed to help the thrifty, to encourage independence, to recognize the Divine and valuable variations of men's minds. On the contrary, there have been many instances in which the votes of the thriftless have been used to defeat the thrifty. On occasions of emergency, as in the depression and during the present war, we have hastened to make it clear that the provision made by a man for his own retirement and old age is not half as sacrosanct as the provision which the State would have made for him had he never saved at all.

We have talked of income from savings as if it possessed a somewhat discreditable character. We have taxed it more and more heavily. We have spoken slightingly of the earnings of interest at the very moment when we have advocated new pensions and social schemes. I have myself heard a Minister of power and influence declare that no deprivation is suffered by a man if he still has the means to fill his stomach, to clothe his body and to keep a roof over his head!

And yet the truth is, as I have endeavoured to show, that frugal people who strive for and obtain the margin above these materially necessary things are the whole foundation of a really active and developing national life.

The case for the middle class is the case for a dynamic democracy as against a stagnant one. Stagnant waters are level and in them the scum rises. Active waters are never level; they toss and tumble and have crests and troughs, but the scientists tell us that they purify themselves in a few hundred yards.

That we are all, as human souls, of like value cannot be denied; that each of us should have his chance is and must be the great objective of political and social policy.

But to say that the industrious and intelligent son of self-sacrificing and saving and forward-looking parents has the same social deserts and even material needs as the dull offspring of stupid and improvident parents is absurd.

If the motto is to be:

> 'Eat, drink and be merry for to-morrow you will die, and if it chances you don't die, the State will look after you; but if you don't eat, drink and be merry, and save, we shall take your savings from you' –

then the whole business of life will become foundationless.

Are you looking forward to a breed of men after the war who will have become boneless wonders? Leaners grow flabby; lifters grow muscles. Men without ambition readily become slaves. Indeed, there is much more slavery in Australia than most people imagine.

How many hundreds of thousands of us are slaves to greed, to fear, to newspapers, to public opinion – represented by the accumulated views of our neighbours? Landless men smell the vapours of the street corner. Landed men smell the brown earth and plant their feet upon it and know that it is good.

To all of this many of my friends will retort: 'Ah, that's all very well, but when this war is over the levellers will have won the day.'

My answer is that, on the contrary, men will come out of this war as gloriously unequal in many things as when they entered it. Much wealth will have been destroyed; inherited riches will be suspect; a fellowship of suffering, if we really experience it, will have opened many hearts and perhaps closed many mouths. Many great edifices will have fallen, and we will be able to study foundations as never before, because war will have exposed them.

But I don't believe that we shall come out into the overlordship of an all-powerful State on whose benevolence we shall live, spineless and effortless; a State which will dole out bread and ideas with neatly regulated accuracy; where we shall all have our dividend without subscribing our capital; where the Government – that almost deity – will nurse us and rear us and maintain us and pension us and bury us; where we shall all be civil servants, and all presumably, since we are equal, heads of departments!

If the new world is to be a world of men we must be not pallid and bloodless ghosts, but a community of people whose motto shall be *'to strive, to seek, to find, and not to yield.'*

Individual enterprise must drive us forward. That doesn't mean that we are to return to the old and selfish notions of laissez faire. The functions of the State will be much more than merely keeping the ring within which the competitors will fight. Our social and industrial obligations will be increased. There will be more law, not less; more control, not less.

But what really happens to us will depend on how many people we have who are of the great and sober and dynamic middle class – the strivers, the planners, the ambitious ones.

We shall destroy them at our peril.

'Certainly a radio scoop has been scored by the Macquarie Network in engaging the former Prime Minister (Mr Menzies) to give an exclusive commentary on international affairs at 9.15 p.m. every Friday,' wrote the weekly radio guide *The Listener-In* in January 1942 when Menzies began the series of broadcasts of which 'The Forgotten People' is one.[1] His host radio stations in the two main capital cities were the popular commercial stations 3AW in Melbourne and 2UE in Sydney, and the speech was also broadcast on a range of regional stations. Menzies continued the series till April 1944.[2] When the weekly broadcasts began, Menzies followed the Tailwaggers' Series, but by May this had been replaced by a better tone of programme. Those listening to him on 22 May when 'The Forgotten People' was broadcast would have heard a programme of plantation melodies before they turned their attention to his well-modulated voice with its full vowels and clearly enunciated consonants, the sort of voice which conveyed education, confidence and respect for England. Despite the latter, it was an unmistakably Australian voice, the voice of the Australian managerial and professional classes in the middle decades of this century.[3]

Out of power since his humiliating resignation from the prime ministership the previous August, Menzies was determined not to stay out of sight on the opposition backbenches. These weekly broadcasts kept him before the public eye; and they gave him the chance to reflect on his political ideas and values. He complained to his brother Frank that he found them a bit of a chore, but added that he was pleased to find there was a political philosophy in them.[4] At stake in these broadcasts was both Menzies' own political future and the future of post-war Australia. In 1942 the ALP occupied the government benches and there seemed little prospect of their defeat in the near future. A year before Menzies had been

Prime Minister, leading the country at war and sitting on Churchill's war cabinet. Menzies had succeeded Joseph Lyons as Prime Minister in 1939 after Lyons' death in office, but he had never had the whole-hearted support of his government. He was distrusted by many as arrogant and ambitious, particularly by his Country Party colleagues, and had been subjected to a blistering attack by the Country Party leader Earle Page when he became Prime Minister. Not only did Page accuse him of having contributed to Lyons' death by his ambition but said that a man who had failed to serve in World War I was unfit to lead a country on the brink of a second. Menzies replied to the accusations with dignity, but they show the depths of distrust with which many viewed him.[5]

Five months after Menzies became Prime Minister war broke out. Australia was ill-prepared and the government's response was muddled and indecisive. During an extended trip to England in the first part of 1941, intrigue against Menzies mounted, and within a few months of his return he had resigned as Prime Minister. Country Party leader Arthur Fadden became Prime Minister but was unable to hold the support of the two independents on whom the governing parties depended. He was defeated on the floor of the House and the ALP leader John Curtin was invited to form a government. Menzies resigned from the leadership of the United Australia Party and his humiliation was completed when Billy Hughes, the veteran of World War I conscription debates, was elected as his replacement.[6]

Menzies was widely regarded as finished in Australian politics at this time. The political journalist Alan Reid remembers standing at the foot of the stairs leading to the press gallery when Menzies came out of his office and walked slowly and alone along the government lobby towards King's Hall. The lights were out and he watched Menzies vanish into the darkness. In an article at the time he wrote, 'And so Menzies disappeared into the shadows for all time. For there is no way back in Australian politics.'[7] The United Australia Party's days also seemed nearly over. It had lost all sense of political direction and could provide no effective challenge to the ALP. The extra-parliamentary organisation was in disarray and rival non-labour organisations were proliferating. The 1943 election returned an ALP government with a landslide victory which confirmed the depths of the UAP's problems.

The pundits were wrong about Menzies, and he re-emerged from the shadows of the backbench to become Australia's longest serving prime minister. By September 1943 he was again leader of the UAP after a bitter Billy Hughes had finally stepped aside. The UAP's days were numbered, however, and in October 1944 a conference was called to discuss the formation of a new non-labour party. In December of that year the Liberal Party of Australia was formed with Menzies as its leader, and by 1949 Menzies and the newly formed Liberal Party were in power.[8]

In order for Menzies to swing non-labour's fortunes around, ideological as well as organisational work was needed. Not only had a new non-labour organisation to be built to match the strength of labour's mass-based party, but labour's socialist values had to be challenged and individualist values and symbols given a new life relevant to a society changed by the experience of war and depression. During the war-time emergency, people were prepared to accept centralised control over the economy. The question was whether they would continue to accept it in peacetime; whether they would have become convinced of the public benefits of greater government regulation of social and economic life, or whether they would accept Menzies' call for a post-war society centred on the values of individual enterprise. The ALP made several attempts to extend the central government's increased powers into the post-war period, but all were defeated. A referendum in 1944 to extend war-time powers for five years after the end of hostilities was defeated, as was another in 1948 for government control of prices and rents. It also met massive resistance to its attempt to nationalise the trading banks. The ALP's vision of post-war Australia was finally and decisively defeated in 1949 when the coalition parties won the election and began their twenty-two years of government. The political values of the forgotten people had won.

Speaking of the importance of the home in the nation's life, Menzies' confident, well-modulated voice came into those homes through the radio sets which had spread throughout Australia during the previous decade. Official radio broadcasting had begun in Australia in 1923 and, as with later domestic technologies, Australians had taken it up with enthusiasm, accepting the advertisers' assertion that the radio set was not a luxury but a necessity for the modern home, and absorbing it into the rituals of their family life. By the late 1930s there were wireless sets in two out of every three Australian homes and a radio audience of about five million.[9] Radio brought the outside world into the home, to the family gathered around the set; and it got politics off the streets and into the kitchens and respectable lounge rooms of the nation.

Radio stations had begun broadcasting speeches at public meetings in the 1920s when they relied heavily on outside broadcasts to fill their programmes. This was a particular boon to women who could now 'listen in' to the rowdy political meetings and rallies they rarely attended.[10] While radio continued to be an important medium for the transmission of non-radio events, like election rallies, it also quickly developed its own forms of political discourse. During the 1930s, radio became more intimate and informal, with broadcasters entering listeners' ordinary, everyday lives and speaking directly and personally to each one.[11] Franklin Roosevelt's 'fireside chats' to depression America showed the potential of this for politicians. As one admiring listener wrote, 'You feel the President is really speaking to you alone... That he's really standing in your own home, not telling... but explaining.'[12] Politicians now needed to supplement the techniques of voice projection and crowd control required for the hustings with the cultivation of a quieter, more informal mode of political address, learning to talk to the public about politics as if talking a matter over with a group of friends.[13]

Menzies was quick to see the potential of radio for the politician. He was not as enthusiastic about television, although under pressure from the party organisation, he did learn to use it for electioneering.[14] At the 1963 federal election he moved Australian political campaigning into a new era by presenting the Liberal–Country Party coalition policy to a nationwide audience in a forty-minute prerecorded telecast. The traditional rally in his Kooyong electorate was held the following night.[15] Again the tone was intimate and friendly; as the *Age* said the next day, 'He wanted it to appear that he was in your living room, reasoning with you.'[16]

Menzies brought to his use of the new communication media attitudes to political language developed when political meetings and rallies were the prime sites of communication between politicians and their publics, and when Parliament could still be imagined to be the centre of political life. This was well before speechwriters and advertising men had transformed the public face of the politician into an image. For Menzies politics was, in good part, public theatre, with politicians as the key actors on the public stage. At the centre was the theatre of Parliament, its debates harking back to the golden age of British parliamentary politics when skilled orators like Edmund Burke could sway the Commons. Around this central theatre were the clubs, private side-shows to the main arena where public men could perform for each other in more relaxed and informal modes, listening to each other's after-dinner speeches and swapping well-turned anecdotes. Beyond were the constituents of a democratic politics: the various political parties and organisations with their continual demands for speakers; and the audiences at the mass meetings and political rallies. Here a man's oratorical skills were really put to the test. Speaking in the open from hastily erected platforms or in large, draughty public halls, one needed a voice which could hold a crowd's attention and the presence of mind to deal with disruptions; it was not always easy to be heard above the noisy interjectors.

Menzies was adept in the performance requirements of all these venues; he combined prowess with language with a quick mind, a commanding physical presence and an actor's sense of timing. An outstanding parliamentary debater in the rather lacklustre Australian Parliaments of his day, when he finally visited England in mid life he was gratified to find he was able to hold his own there too. He spoke in Westminster Hall, 'in the presence of the shades of Edmund Burke and Fox and Sheridan' and received a standing ovation.[17] And he shone in the side-shows. He was an accomplished and much sought after speaker for public and private functions, able to construct a speech deftly around a few key points, light anecdotes and quotations from nineteenth-century English poets. Often all he had to go by was a couple of roughly pencilled points.[18] Similarly, he took the public rallies in his stride and was undaunted by a hostile crowd, being as prepared to face striking New South Wales coalminers as a Liberal Party election rally.[19] He relished sparring with the ever-present hecklers and many of his most renowned lines come from such exchanges: to the woman waving an umbrella who shouted 'I wouldn't vote for you if you were the archangel Gabriel' he retorted, 'If I were the Archangel Gabriel, madam, you wouldn't be in my constituency.'[20]

Language mattered to Menzies and his skill with it was his single most important asset in his successful career. The scholarships which enabled him to continue his secondary education and to study law at the University of Melbourne were awarded on the basis of his success in the language-based humanities, and after he became a lawyer his formidable skills as an advocate quickly earned him a successful practice. As a politician he is remembered as much for his mellifluous voice and his command of the Queen's English, his speeches and his quick wit, as he is for substantive policy initiatives. One thing nearly all the respondents to his 1963 policy speech agreed on, no matter what their political loyalties, was his eloquence.[21]

But language for Menzies was more than a means to his success and a chance for self-display; it was central to the way he conceived of democratic politics. In the essay 'Politics as an Art', Menzies answers the question What is politics? with the proposition that 'the art of politics, in relation to public affairs, is to provide exposition, persuasion, and inspiration'.[22] The politician's task, as Menzies saw it, was to convey ideas to others and to argue for them, to appeal to the noble and humane passions and rally them behind political action, and the best way of doing this was by the politician speaking directly to his audience. A politician's speech-making, as he called it, was his prime means of presenting himself to his public and attempting to win their support:

'... the essence of a speech is that it should reach the hearts and minds of our immediate audience. It must therefore be made *to* them and not merely in their presence.' In this essay Menzies deplored two 'modern devices' as having an adverse effect on good public speech: amplification by microphone, and the politicians' practice of distributing their speeches to the press before they are spoken. Both these devices divided speakers from their audience, thinning the communication and diminishing the human bond between them.

The microphone, wrote Menzies, 'eliminates the curiously moving quality of the human voice, directly heard', and destroys 'the old intimate contact between speaker and audience'.[22] Menzies was a connoisseur of political oratory, and his published descriptions of other politicians generally include a comment on their voice and oratorical style: Stanley Baldwin's voice 'with a masculine music in it, revealed a cultivated simplicity'; Joe Lyons 'spoke easily with a rare combination of dignity and simplicity'; much out-of-doors speaking had left Ben Chifley with 'a gravelly voice. He aspired to none of the arts of oratory'.[23] The politician's voice was both one of his political tools and part of his public presence, capable of conveying his origins, political history, personality and moral calibre.

For Menzies the spoken word took precedence over the written in the relationship between politicians and their publics; the written was properly only a record of a speech *after* it had been delivered, such as one finds in Hansard, where the primary act is the delivery of the speech to the assembled members of Parliament to attempt to win their support. To read a speech, or worse still to distribute it beforehand, was to deprive the audience of any real function in the performance, to drain their presence of any significance.

> The speech ceases to be the obvious expression of the speaker's personality and ideas, since anybody may have written it. The speaker himself misses the stimulus which comes from addressing a living meeting, the impact upon his own mind which a good audience can procure. His speech loses flexibility. It all too frequently ceases to persuade because persuasion depends upon the creation in the mind of the listener of a feeling that the speaker is addressing him, man to man, and is dealing with the point that is troubling his mind.[24]

The audience was thus transformed from participant into spectator. Although Menzies did not develop this point, one can easily see the changed relationship between politicians and their audiences which Menzies was describing here as symptomatic of more general changes which were taking place in the politics of liberal democracies. As politicians were becoming managers of national economies rather than leaders of national polities, their attention turned from ideological conflict and the task of persuading people to particular ways of thinking and feeling to the mastery of technical problems. Admiring spectatorship is all such politician managers require of their publics.

Menzies continually exhorted his audiences to remember their responsibility as citizens in a democracy, to take their political decisions seriously, and he spent time attempting to persuade them to particular ways of thinking and feeling about public issues. For Menzies, political leadership implied moral leadership. One of the politician's tasks, as he saw it, was to 'temper the frequently absurd asperities of political conflict by seeking to stir up only noble and humane emotions, since ignoble passions, so easily aroused, can in the nature of things produce only ignoble policies and unfair administration'.[25]

Politicians and commentators of today sometimes say of Menzies that he spent too much time making speeches and not enough time worrying about the nation's economy, implying that making speeches was a trivial pastime. Such a comment is a mark of the shrinking of public politics since Menzies' day, even though the business of government has grown exponentially. Today's politicians are for the most part absent to their publics, communicating with them indirectly, through speechwriters, journalists and television cameras. Menzies spoke to audiences as if it mattered what they thought, and regarded it as an insult to an audience to use a speechwriter. If he was asking the public for support, it was him they should hear and be able to judge.

Menzies took great care with his own speeches. Not only did he prepare and write them himself, but he treated their delivery as a performance. Although some were written out beforehand, most were not.

> I invariably write memorial lectures, since I have what is, as yet, a not completely defeated hope that some day somebody may wish to read them.
>
> I write important formal statements for the House. All this writing I do in long hand, with a lead pencil! But I do not write debating speeches or public political speeches (except, of course, a Policy Speech), or social speeches. I do a lot of preparation of facts and ideas, and make highly summarized notes and headings; but I never prepare the actual language.[26]

Liberal MP Edgar Holt reported that 'for a few hours before an important speech he was unapproachable, as the speech took shape inside his head';[27] and his sister, Isabel Green, described how keyed up and nervous he was before even relatively minor speeches.[28]

The importance Menzies attached to his speech-making helps to explain why he became such a powerful political and cultural symbol. Menzies made no secret of what he stood for. Through his speeches he offered himself and his values to the public, but this offering was shaped in interaction with the public's anticipated response. Successful politicians always exist in a symbiotic relationship with their supporters. Without supporters they are nothing but discontented aspirants to greatness; with them they become important men and women, enjoying power and influence, fame and fortune, and having a chance to write their names in history. A political leader needs a constituency, a group who will take him or her as their representative, as one who knows their fears and hopes and recognises their worth and in whom they can recognise themselves. There is, of course, something essentially duplicitous in this relationship; the politician who speaks for the plain, ordinary man or woman, reflecting back to them their ordinary anxieties and aspirations, is doing this so that they themselves can become anything but ordinary. Mrs Thatcher speaking of the housewife's experience with the family budget, Ronald Reagan pretending to have a war record, any of them talking of the importance of family and a quiet life, are presenting themselves as representatives of ordinary experience even as they strive for goals quite different from the ones they purport to represent. Because of the tension between the desire for power and the means of acquiring it in democracies, accusations of inauthenticity and duplicity haunt our politicians.

Political language is first and foremost public language, the chief means by which an aspiring politician reaches out to potential supporters. As public language, it is conventional, cliched and redundant, using images and arguments that are quickly recognisable to its audience and able to be deployed easily by its speakers in the heat of debate. Its purpose is to convince particular groups in society to see, feel about and act in the political world in certain ways, and to win support for the speaker as the representative or defender of those ways of seeing and feeling. The arguments and images used have histories in these groups' past social and political experience and ways of understanding them, and a skilled politician will be able to create from these past histories convincing political language to fit the present circumstances.

Some politicians will be much better at this than others, much better at using the available public political rhetoric of the day to fit changing political circumstances. This is not just a matter of skill, but of the personal connections the politician has forged with the language used and the group or cause represented. Political language faces two ways: outwards to the audience being addressed and the support being wooed; inwards to the politician's own emotions and biographical experience. The challenge for the reader of political language is to find the connections between the two, the chains of private meaning and association which link the politician's personal history and experience with the public political language, the points through which personal emotions and desires can flow through into the public ideological forms of the day.

The image of the 'forgotten people' is one such point of connection in Menzies' language. His transformation of the forgotten *class* of non-labour ideology into the forgotten *people* is a key move in shaping Australian post-war history. It is also a key move in Menzies' own political fortunes, a ploy at the nadir of his political career to prevent himself from ever being forgotten again. If the forgotten people would take him as their rememberer, then he himself would be saved from oblivion. Deeper and more personal than this, the forgotten people also have associations which go back into

Menzies' childhood in the small Wimmera town of Jeparit and the strategies he developed there for negotiating his relationship with his parents.

This book has a dual focus: the first is on the public face of Menzies' language, exploring themes in Australian culture which he came to represent; the second is on its private face and the reasons why he was the one to play out for Australians certain aspects of themselves writ large. The order in which they are presented is the order in which they were written, as I slowly worked from the detailed, close reading of Menzies' public language through to my understanding of its private, biographical meanings.

I
PUBLIC LANGUAGE

THE FORGOTTEN PEOPLE

LABOUR AND NON-LABOUR

LABOUR AND non-labour are the two poles around which most Australian political thought and action are organised.[1] Each constructs an image of itself and what it stands for in contrast to the values and characteristics it attributes to its opponents. The labour movement, both the Australian Labor Party and the trade union movement, sees itself as representing the interests of ordinary working Australians and non-labour as serving the interests of the rich and powerful; the main non-labour party has seen itself, in contrast to the sectional Labor and Country Parties, as the only truly national party, drawing support from across all classes and sections and so able to develop policies to benefit the whole community. The images each party holds of its opponents rarely meet. When particular policies are being debated, arguments and figures are matched with arguments and figures, but the further one moves towards general statements of party philosophy the more one has the sense of the parties talking quite past each other. Their representations of the social world and of the other party's designs on it hardly seem to connect. This is not surprising, for these representations are one of the central fields of party conflict.

Politics always involves struggle over definition, over how particular events or situations are to be represented. The manner in which a situation is defined affects the way we respond to it, the actions and feelings which seem appropriate. A strike can be described as a threat to the economic life of the country, a selfish and unwarranted disruption of the public's convenience. Such descriptions evoke a social whole in which we are all working together for a common good and in which no person or group should press their claims above the interests of the whole. If, by contrast, the same strike is described as part of the workers' struggle, it is put in the context of the history of the labour movement and trade unions' long struggle for better wages and conditions. It suggests there is an irreconcilable conflict of interests between workers and bosses in which workers have had to fight hard for the conditions they now enjoy. Behind the first description is the ideal of a harmonious social consensus, behind the second a model of social relations in which conflict between capital and labour is inevitable.

Politics involves a struggle over definitions in two main ways. The central concepts of politics, like class, freedom, power, democracy, and even politics itself, are 'essentially contested concepts'; that is concepts which do not have, in principle, one clear, well-defined meaning, but which carry a range of meanings which can be differently weighted in political arguments.[2] Hence arguments about the meaning and range of application of the central concepts of politics are a central and inevitable part of the political life of a society. In 'The Forgotten People' Menzies can attempt to define the concept of class in a particular way because of the complex and contradictory range of meanings it carries.

Politics also involves attempting to convince people to accept certain definitions of themselves and their experiences as the basis of their political actions and to exclude others. Individuals have complex and often contradictory experiences of themselves in society, and politics involves a struggle over which of these will be the basis of their political identifications. Groups and individuals do not come to political action with already well-formed demands and interests, but have their demands and interests shaped by their participation in politics. In 'The Forgotten People' Menzies is attempting to create a constituency for non-labour by persuading people to define their political interests in one way rather than another. Addressing the family listening around the radio, he tries to persuade its members to make their private and domestic experiences the basis of their political identification, rather than their experiences as workers or as members of an economically defined class. Here, as they are in their lounge room or kitchen, should be the site of their political identity, not the factory floor or the public politics of mass action.

Menzies' argument in 'The Forgotten People' has its roots in the debates between liberalism and Marxism, as well as in the political struggles which these different positions helped articulate. The people listening around the radio who responded to his praise for their home-centred independent individualism, and those who rejected this appeal as an attack on the collectivist solidarity of working-class politics, would have had different degrees of understanding of the philosophical and historical backgrounds of their responses. For the most part their responses would have been part of their commonsense understanding of the world and their place in it, backed up by moral judgements about such things as the value of work and the importance of duty on the one hand, or the need for people to stick together in hard times, on the other.

Such commonsense understandings and moral values have histories in the changing historical experience of social groups and their changing understandings of these experiences. Antonio Gramsci was the first Marxist to argue for the need for Marxists to understand ordinary people's view of the world.³ He discriminated between the different levels at which a dominant ideology operates: the relatively formal and articulated system of meaning, values and beliefs argued about by intellectuals are very different from the mixed, confused and inarticulate consciousness of most people. Yet they are not unconnected. The great philosophical systems and debates of the past leave their traces in common sense, even though those who now bear those traces know little or nothing of that past.

To view common sense through its history, however, is only half the story. No matter what the history of the beliefs people hold, they hold these beliefs now, and use them to understand and order their contemporary experience. To understand people's social and political beliefs one must take those beliefs seriously as attempts to make sense of the contemporary world; one must get inside them to understand the way they make sense of experience to those who hold them, even if from other standpoints that sense is both partial and partisan, an imaginary representation only of real experience which denies as much of experience as it includes. To attempt this implies a rejection of earlier Marxist notions of false consciousness.⁴ It also, less obviously, implies understanding the psychological and emotional as well as the cognitive structure of people's beliefs, although most of those who have argued for taking ideology seriously have shown little interest in this.

The philosophies of political parties stand halfway between systematic political philosophy and common sense. More worked up than the political views of most people, the philosophies of political parties are still contradictory and fragmentary compared with the order and coherence for which philosophy aims. Political historian Peter Loveday has commented on the ambiguity and generality of the themes which run through the philosophy of the Australian

Liberal Party and its predecessors. There are a few linking notions – individual, bureaucracy, socialism – but the main themes are vague, allowing the politician without any particular philosophical skill to use them as the political occasion demands. The party's philosophy, he concludes, is integrated, not by a few fundamental propositions or concepts, as a philosophical system would be, but by its anti-Labor rhetoric.[5]

Since Menzies' death the terms of conflict between the Australian Labor Party and the non-labour parties have shifted, and the two parties' views of the social world are no longer as different from each other as they were during the middle of this century. Although the need for opposition continues, competition between them is now more about economic management skills than values and ideas. In the 1930s, '40s and '50s the ideological differences between the parties were far sharper. In his 1949 policy speech, Menzies expressed his belief that politics is a high and real conflict of principles, and presented the Liberal Party and its Labor opponent in terms of its opposition to and support for socialism.

> This is our great year of decision. Are we for the Socialist State, with its subordination of the individual to the universal officialdom of government, or are we for the ancient British faith that governments are the servants of the people, a faith which has given fire and quality and direction to the whole of our history for 600 years?[6]

For the ALP, socialism essentially meant a limited commitment to nationalisation or public ownership when private ownership was deemed grossly oppressive and exploitative. It did not mean the revolutionary overthrow of existing social relations, nor even workers' control and industrial democracy, but state or publicly owned activities replacing some private or individual ones.[7] Anti-socialist rhetoric could thus effectively be directed against the growth of the bureaucratic state as well as against the aspirations of the lower orders.

'The Forgotten People' is Menzies' most powerful and coherent expression of the opposition between socialism and individualism. Looking back on it with the hindsight of non-labour's domination of the 1950s and 1960s, it is easy to miss its urgent argument and to forget that at the time it was made there was no certainty that its arguments would win. In danger of being forgotten himself, Menzies is not reflecting here from the security of office but arguing passionately for values that seem about to be eclipsed, attempting to persuade people to certain political identifications to the exclusion of others, in particular those attributed to the ALP and the wider labour movement.

Opposition is the fundamental figure of Australian party rhetoric and provides its underlying structure.[8] For both labour and non-labour, images and arguments line up as pairs of opposites – the positive assigned to oneself, the negative attached to the other side. In debating an issue like bank nationalisation, for example, labour will oppose private selfishness and greed to public good; non-labour will oppose individual freedom to state regulation and control. What matters in deploying party rhetoric is that one knows which opposition to invoke, not that one has a coherent grasp of unifying philosophical arguments.

Underlying 'The Forgotten People' is non-labour's way of constructing the opposition between labour and non-labour. The meaning Menzies attaches to the two political positions emerges from a series of oppositions:

individual	mass
people	class
the home	work-place/bureaucracy
liberal individualism	Marxism
unity	conflict
harmony	division
individual	state
freedom	socialism
ordinary language	jargon/technical language
independent	dependent
country	city
youth	old age
life	death
savings	wages
work	idleness
agent/subject	object

I have listed these oppositions in no special order, and although one could no doubt attempt to locate the more fundamental pairs, to use such a set of opposing terms effectively one does not need to be able to do so. Such a set of terms clearly marks for both speakers and listeners the side of the fence to which images and arguments belong; one can move easily between the pairs, always sure of one's political position, without any clear idea of the relations the opposing pairs have to each other, and without being troubled by any apparent contradiction between them. Exactly what the relationship is between the oppositions of youth and old age and savings and wages does not matter so long as one can recognise to which side of the fence they belong and can employ whichever suits the argument at the time.

These oppositions have histories: they are partial and contested oppositions, formed in conflict and aimed at persuasion, which draw on a long history of social and political conflict. The traces of past controversies are carried in their imagery, as well as more recent social experiences. While some of the oppositions, such as that between youth and age, have a natural obviousness, others like that between savings and wages are embedded in complex practices for maintaining inequality.

Reading 'The Forgotten People', I am interested in both the political-historical and the psychological structures of its arguments and images: in the historical and social experiences carried by particular images and arguments and in the psychological uses these had for the people who regarded them as speaking for themselves. Gramsci stressed the fragmentary nature of people's social and political beliefs and values; yet there will be a psychological consistency in the issues politics raises for a particular person and in the characteristic ways they resolve them. In 'The Forgotten People' the main psychological issue is the opposition between independence and dependence and the emotions embraced and excluded by the choice of one rather than the other.

'WE DON'T HAVE CLASSES HERE'

What are the conditions that buttress and that create and that preserve all the beautiful things that we envisage when we say or write the word 'home'?
The Woman, 20 April 1933

MENZIES' CENTRAL argument in 'The Forgotten People' is with a class-based understanding of politics and he begins by eschewing the relevance of class to a society like Australia. 'In a country like Australia the class war must always be a false war... We don't have classes here like in England.' The irrelevance of Old World class divisions to a new country is a familiar theme in Australian non-labour rhetoric. Its plausibility depends on understanding classes as relatively fixed status groups.[9] The potential social mobility of individuals in the New World, it was argued, made such a conception of class irrelevant: Australia did not have fixed status groups hence it did not have classes.[10]

That said, Menzies proceeds to employ class language:

> But if we are to talk of classes, then the time has come to say something of the forgotten class – *The Middle Class* – those people who are constantly in danger of being ground between the upper and nether millstones of the false class war; the middle class who, properly regarded, represent the backbone of the country...
>
> Let me first define it by exclusion: I exclude at one end of the scale the rich and powerful; those who control great funds and enterprises, and are as a rule able to protect themselves – though it may be said that in a political sense they have as a rule shown neither comprehension nor competence. But I exclude them because in most material difficulties the rich can look after themselves.
>
> I exclude at the other end of the scale the mass of unskilled people, almost invariably well-organized, and with their wages and conditions safeguarded by popular law. What I am excluding them from is my definition of the middle class. We cannot exclude them from the problem of social progress, for one of the prime objects of modern social and political policy is to give them a proper measure of security, and provide conditions which will enable them to acquire skill and knowledge and individuality.

> These exclusions being made, I include the intervening range, the kind of people I myself represent in Parliament – salary earners, shopkeepers, skilled artisans, professional men and women, farmers, and so on. These are in a political and economic sense the middle class. They are envied by those whose social benefits are largely obtained from taxing them. They are not rich enough to have individual power. They are taken for granted by each political party in turn. They are not sufficiently lacking in individualism to be organized for what in these days we call 'pressure politics'. And yet, as I have said, they are the backbone of the nation.

The middle class is the middle term in a three-part scheme: on top are the rich, beneath is organised labour. Notice that in the third paragraph Menzies provides space for the acceptance of the legitimacy of some social welfare programmes. After the large-scale unemployment and poverty of the Depression and the sacrifices people were making during the war, non-labour was starting to realise that the government had to guarantee people 'a proper measure' of social security. But, as this speech demonstrates, they were deeply uneasy about the implications of this sort of government action for self-reliant individualism.

Menzies' description of the middle class as forgotten echoes an earlier one by his predecessor in the seat of Kooyong, John Latham, almost word for word:

> It seems to me that the middle class is too often left out of it in political matters; though it is one of the most valuable in the whole community. It is not rich, but it is not poor, and it is often forgotten. It includes nearly all professional men, most farmers and rural producers, a tremendous

number of shopkeepers, a large number of clerical employees, a considerable proportion of manual workers, especially the skilled and more particularly the highly skilled artisans, and all kinds of people working on their own account.[11]

Menzies' shift for the speech's title from the familiar appeal to the forgotten class to the forgotten people is a brilliant rhetorical move, making explicit what has always been implicit in non-labour's view of the middle class – that it is not just an economic class but a moral category whose members are defined by their political values, social attitudes and moral qualities as much as by their social and economic position. Describing his own social origins in an interview after his retirement, Menzies said:

> If social classes are, as they sometimes are, based upon the possession of money, then I was in the lowest possible social stratum in Ballarat as a boy; but if classes depend on something else, some personal qualities, then people like myself and my parents did not feel they were in any way out of it.[12]

Menzies does allude to the social position of the middle class during the speech, with references to the ability to afford private secondary and university education; but for the most part he is concerned to elaborate the class's moral virtues rather than dwell on its economic position. This is part of the speech's general strategy of defining politics in terms of a clash of values and ideals rather than a conflict of economic interest. Nothing at all is said of the bourgeoisie's entrepreneurial role – nothing of the importance of independent enterprise for the economy, for example, nor the importance of market freedoms, and Menzies' list of groups comprising the middle class does not even include Latham's 'all kinds of people working on their own account'. Although he makes the traditional claim that the middle class is the dynamic class, he fails to give this dynamism any substantive economic role.

The middle class is, for the most part, defined by its members' possession of superior moral qualities. Crucial to the logic of the speech is members' possession of these virtues as *individuals* rather than as members of a class. As a moral category the middle class has no material economic boundaries; anyone can belong to it through identifying with the values associated with it. The Marxist way of classifying people in terms of their position in the economy is clearly rejected in favour of a classification of people according to their individual moral qualities and personal characteristics. This has a wide commonsense appeal; it both seems more humane and it is the way we most often experience people we know, and more importantly, ourselves. In an interview in 1988, Jennifer Cashmore, then a Liberal Member of Parliament in South Australia, gave a typical response in her description of her political education.

> My interest in politics really started around the family dinner table. From the time I was old enough to listen and comprehend, I remember vigorous debates between my elder sister and my father on the Communist Party Dissolution Bill. My parents were firmly in support of Menzies and there was much criticism of Ben Chifley, but I never remember Ben Chifley being derided because he was an engine driver. It really galls me when I hear people deride Liberals because they are allegedly rich farmers. To my mind it's not what a person does, it's what a person is that counts.[13]

'It's not what a person does, it's what a person is that counts.' Embedded in such a statement is a rejection of the very notion of social classification. The middle class is a category caught in Bertrand Russell's paradox: it is the class of people who have no class – the class of individuals. The middle class is not opposed to some other class but opposed to the very idea of class. In Menzies' image of the middle class ground between the millstones of a false class war, the middle class is an unwilling victim but not itself a protagonist. Rather, as the speech progresses, it becomes society's integrating centre – the class which is not a class, which holds society together, and which is able to include anyone who shares its values and its sturdy moral qualities, no matter what their economic position.[14]

One of the speech's organising figures is the contrast between 'backbone' and 'spineless'. Early in the speech the middle class is described as 'the backbone of the country' and the listener is warned of the danger of inflicting 'a fatal injury upon our own backbone'. They do not want to live 'spineless and effortless on an all-powerful state': 'Are you looking forward to a breed of men after the war who have become boneless wonders? Leaners grow flabby, lifters grow muscles.' Menzies' use of this image again reveals the class's paradoxical nature: the image of the backbone refers not so much to the class's collective strength as to the strength its individual members possess as individuals. The working class collapses into an amoebic mass in which neither the class as a whole nor its individual members has any backbone.

Although social classification is rejected, moral classification is enthusiastically embraced; the praise bestowed on the middle class has its other side in the blame heaped on those who do not participate in its virtues. In a 1954 speech, 'Democracy and Management', Menzies gave one of his clearest statements of the moral opposition he was invoking when he praised the virtues of the middle class: 'Attempts to create "class" hatred in a nation whose only true classes are the active and the idle are in truth attacks upon democracy'.[15] Active and idle, leaners and the lifters, the spineless and those with backbone, Menzies divides society into two parts. The three-part scheme with which 'The Forgotten People' begins, the very rich, the middle class and the organised poor, collapses into a two-part scheme with the rich and the organised poor together in the same category as idle, spineless leaners, and the middle class as the active, dynamic class. 'The case for the middle class is the case for a dynamic democracy as against a stagnant one. Stagnant waters are level and in them the scum rises.'

The idea of the middle class Menzies is working with here stretches back to the nineteenth-century English reformers' faith in middle-class values to temper the effects of the extension of the franchise, and forward to today's pervasive identification with middle-class life style. Menzies presents the opposition between the middle class and the working class not as one based on differing economic positions but as an opposition between two different ways people can understand their position in society. In one, people understand themselves as individuals; in the other, through embracing such impersonal categories as class to make sense of their social existence, their individuality disappears. They become, from Menzies' perspective, an anonymous mass.

One of the aims of social progress, he says, is to give to the *mass* of unskilled people 'skill, knowledge and *individuality*' (my emphasis). The working class's lack of individuality is made clearest by their exclusion from the speech's key image of individuality – the home. The supreme value of the middle class, Menzies says, comes from 'their stake in the country' and he amplifies this in terms of their 'responsibility for homes – homes material, homes human and homes spiritual'. He associates frugality and patriotism with 'homes material', ambition for one's children with 'homes human' (the absence of any reference to family conviviality and tenderness is striking), and independence with 'homes spiritual'.

> I do not believe that the real life of this nation is to be found either in great luxury hotels and the petty gossip of so-called fashionable suburbs, or in the officialdom of organized masses.
>
> It is to be found in the homes of people who are nameless and unadvertised, and who, whatever their individual religious conviction or dogma, see in their children their greatest contribution to the immortality of their race.

At first glance it seems that Menzies is going to elaborate his three-part class scheme in terms of the dwelling places appropriate to the different classes. The rich live in great luxury hotels, with their suggestion of sexual licence, or waste their lives in petty gossip in fashionable suburbs; the nameless and unadvertised middle class have their family-centred homes; but when we come to the working class a cog slips. Where we would expect to find working-class dwelling places – rented rooms or over-crowded slums perhaps – we have 'the officialdom of the organized masses'. The domestic space the series opens up for the working class is side-stepped and the class is defined instead in terms of the relations of the work place.

It is as if the working class do not also have wives and homes and children; or rather, in as much as they do have them, they are invited to see themselves as middle class. Menzies' apparent lapse of logic here reveals the deeper logic of the oppositions with which he is working between incompatible ways of understanding the individual's relations to society. The home is the site of people's experience of themselves as individuals and Menzies implies that those who understand their place in society primarily through their place in the economy or at work lose their individuality. It is as if he is arguing that one cannot be both an individual and a member of a class.

The home stands in general opposition to the outside world – to the world of work and by extension to the economy, politics and the law and the way they represent individuals. In contrast with home and children, work is presented negatively. 'Organization', 'mass', 'level', 'officialdom' form a cluster of associations around work which represent it as an anonymous, dull and routine world in which the chances for individual achievement and satisfaction are few. The opposition Menzies is working with here is between the home as the seat of the individual's sense of dignity and worth and work as a place where one is anonymous, hemmed in by rules and regulations. Thus people are invited to identify their political interests with their private and domestic rather than their economic roles, and a space is created for non-labour which can accommodate manual workers and factory managers, the owners of businesses and their clerical employees and, most importantly, the wives of them all. Attempting to shift the terrain of politics away from the work place and the conflicts of the economy towards the home and the consensual symbols of the domestic sphere, Menzies is arguing for a view of politics which excludes all those images and issues which were so difficult for non-labour in the 1930s, and includes all the benefits which post-war affluence was to bring.

As a symbol of a full and rich experience of individuality, the home stands in opposition not just to the depersonalised world of work but to all aspects of modern life which seem to diminish the individual's sense of agency. Liberalism's belief in the value of the individual and in individuals' power to control their lives is, like most beliefs, part truth and part illusion. It is true of the way people experience themselves most of the time as freely acting and choosing individuals, but it is illusion from the perspective of the constraints within which people choose and act. People are both agents in and products of the social world and the difficulty of negotiating this dual focus runs right through twentieth-century social and political thought, from debates about free will and determinism to Marxists' arguments about the need to intervene in history. Whereas individualism greatly exaggerates people's freedom, understanding people in terms of class or some other sociological abstraction can seem to greatly diminish it, and to reduce people's subjective experiences of agency to illusion.

These differences in the way individual experience is represented are set within a changing social world in which some changes seem to increase people's freedom, others to decrease it. People look for ways of representing and understanding these changes, and one of the chief causes of social change, capitalism's search for profit, is often unmentioned in non-labour rhetoric, yet non-labour must still deal in some way with the anxieties change induces and the sense many people have that the forces which control their lives are outside their control. The championing of the home has been one part of its strategy; another has been to attach negative symbols of modernisation to the labour movement and its support for increased state power. Because non-labour denies the extent to which both contemporary society and social change are outside conscious control, Marxism, communism and by extension the ALP could become bearers of the imagery of mechanical and inhuman social forces.

When Menzies represents the working class as the 'organized masses', in contrast with the homes of the middle class, not only is he denying the working class a domestic life, but he is attaching to them and to the labour movement negative images of both the impersonal modern world and its impersonal organisations, in particular bureaucracy. Towards the end of the speech there is a hint, too, of the production line, that supreme symbol of the fragmentation and alienation of modern life, when Menzies describes the dangers of an all-powerful state which 'will dole out bread and ideas with neatly regulated accuracy'. The image recognises the production line's reduction of a person to a cog in a machine, but associates it with the individual's relationship with the state, rather than with the production line of industry.

One way of understanding modernisation is as increasing rationalisation.[16] Different areas of human activity become organised according to impersonal criteria like profitability, efficiency, or bureaucratic rationality, and people's participation in these areas is understood in terms of abstractions like economic role or legal or bureaucratic status. Such abstractions, of necessity, reduce the complexity of individual experience by breaking it into components relevant to different social systems; but when faced with an abstract version of themselves, individuals often feel diminished and resentful. This is clearest in the widespread hostility towards bureaucracy. Designed in part to ensure equality of treatment, bureaucratic rationality is often experienced as uncaring impersonality. The messiness of life and the impossibility of devising rules in advance to cover every possible case mean that there are inevitable breakdowns in the adequacy with which bureaucracies deal with people, and when such breakdowns do occur they are met with anger, hurt and a sense of injustice. Because of the ALP's commitment to state-owned enterprises and increased state regulation, anti-labour rhetoric was able to draw on this resentment of bureaucracy.

In contrast to the rationalisation and abstraction which govern people's participation in the institutions of the economy and the state, the home is a place of face-to-face relations conducted in ordinary language. It can seem untouched by the regimentation and depersonalisation that characterise modern life. In the ideal home, it is people's moral and personal qualities that matter and there is the time and the interest to know a person in all their complexity. The home, too, is the place of childhood. At various points in the speech Menzies rejects abstract understanding of social relations in favour of understanding in terms of individual motives and actions.

> We speak glibly of many things without pausing to consider what they signify. We speak of 'financial power' forgetting that the financial power of 1942 is based upon the savings of the generations which preceded it... We speak of 'manpower' as if it were a matter of arithmetic, as if it were made up of a multiplication of men and muscles without spirit.

And he rejects policies designed 'to weigh men according to their political organisation and power, as votes and not as human beings'. Here Menzies is contrasting the commonsense language of everyday understanding, which is the language of the home, with the abstract language of modern politics and economics, and rejecting the latter as diminishing the individual. This is a characteristic move of Menzies, as is his attribution of this abstract language to the left. In the Communist Party Dissolution Bill Second Reading Speech, Menzies apologises for the terms 'proletariat' and 'bourgeoisie'. 'Honourable members are familiar, of course, with the jargon of Marxist writers. They talk about the bourgeoisie and the proletariat. Indeed, they seem to be incapable of saying things in what we would regard as a simple way.'[17] Thus Menzies directs attention to the language in which the left couches its arguments and ignores the arguments.

Sociology developed to try to understand the transition from traditional societies to modern society with its complex specialisation of labour, continual social change and large, integrated political and social organisations. Non-labour has rejected Marx's sociological understanding of people almost as fervently as his political message. To understand is often to forgive, and increased sociological understanding has greatly increased society's forgiveness of deviants of all kinds. This sits uneasily with individualism's belief in responsible moral agents, as well as with the satisfaction many people get from apportioning moral blame. The refusal to understand society in terms of class is also in part a refusal to entertain sociological abstractions which seem to diminish the individual's dignity, a refusal to see people in terms of their social, political or economic positions. That this refusal greatly reduces the ability to understand and forgive people is, of course, part of the point.

Sociology did not cause the social developments it tries to understand and which it has described in its various abstract and technical languages. Through Marxism, the labour movement took on a partial sociological understanding, embracing concepts like class to help it understand relations between people in rapidly industrialising capitalist societies. Because the working class bear the brunt of technological change and have little control over the day to day circumstances of their working lives, sociological understanding is not as discordant with their everyday experience of themselves as it is for the self-employed professional or the middle-class housewife. So often treated as objects in their everyday lives, they are not as resistant to explanations which seem to minimise their conscious control over their lives.

In opposition to the negative images of modernity associated with the labour movement, Menzies associates the middle class and the home with a simpler, pre-modern life. This is another of the speech's strategies for dealing with the anxieties engendered by modernisation and is implicit in the description of the middle class as forgotten – one does not have to respond to the changes happening around one but can simply continue to be oneself and wait to be rediscovered. The middle class is described, anachronistically, as 'feeding the lamps of learning', and Menzies cites Burns's 'The Cotter's Saturday Night' with its idyllic picture of pre-industrial family life to illustrate the values of homes spiritual. He refers to the Scottish ploughman walking behind his plough, and towards the end of his speech he contrasts urban and country dwellers: 'Landless men smell the vapours of the street corner. Landed men smell the brown earth and plant their feet upon it and know that it is good.' Most of the people Menzies was addressing were city dwellers, but this would not have prevented them from recognising the opposition he was evoking between the virtues of the simple, family-centred country life and the corrupt modern city. The dream of an independent yeoman farmer underlay many an Australian suburban home.[18]

WOMEN AT HOME

WHILE MENZIES identifies the middle class such that most people can identify with it through the values which shape their private aspirations, his representation of experience speaks more to people in some social locations than others; in particular it speaks to women in their traditional social location. The home is women's social space. In elaborating the political values of the middle class in terms of the home, Menzies was elaborating them in a way which would particularly appeal to women and draw them into politics. As radio made politics accessible to women, enabling them to follow it from their kitchens and lounge rooms, so defining politics in terms of private and domestic concerns made it relevant to them.

A decade earlier, *The Woman*, the official organ of the influential conservative women's organisation the Australian Women's National League, described women's political demands thus:

> What then does the good woman want in economic life, in politics and in legislation, and in the administration of public affairs?
>
> She wants – above all things – first and last and all the time – all those conditions that make for the stability of the home, and for its serenity, refinement, sweetness and purity. These, of course, are the ideals of every good citizen, but they are preeminently the life impulses of the average woman.[19]

Australian non-labour parties have, until recently, drawn more support from women than men,[20] and women's political conservatism has been widely discussed. Generally it has been explained negatively, in terms of the limitations of women's experience. Their isolation in the home has been seen as depriving them of knowledge of the affairs of the world, making them insecure in their judgements, and excluding them from the associations of the work place which are the basis of working-class politics.[21] While such arguments may explain the conservatism of some women, they fall too easily into the left's familiar habit of ascribing false consciousness to a group whose political behaviour seems out of line with its interests. And they are no help in understanding politically active conservative women: anyone less anxious and insecure than Enid Lyons, the formidable wife of Joe Lyons, would be hard to imagine.

Women have been the organisational mainstay of non-labour parties, both here and in Britain.[22] A Liberal Party woman interviewed in the middle 1960s said, 'All the strength of the organisation, really, comes from the women's side.'[23] Women did most of what is generally described as the political housekeeping for the non-labour parties – canvassing and the distribution of pamphlets and how-to-vote cards. To describe this as political housekeeping, however, underplays the ideological importance of women to non-labour parties. Canvassing door to door and providing speakers for interested groups, politically active conservative women were building and maintaining a mass base for non-labour through their promulgation of non-labour ideology in its consensual, domesticated version. Like the middle class, women could be represented as a stabilising force in the community whose voice had to be heard if harmony and moral values were to prevail; they too were described as 'the backbone of the nation'. The women who joined organisations like the Australian Women's National League or the women's branches of the various non-labour parties were not politically ignorant and incompetent, but actively working for values they believed in.

The home was both the centre of such women's social experience and the basis of their political values. Commentators on politically active conservative women have often noted the contradictions between the values they espouse – the importance of the home and of womens' roles as wives and mothers – and their own active political lives. This contradiction is more apparent than real, for the advocacy of the home is more about the primacy of certain values than about where women should spend their days.

In her autobiography Enid Lyons describes the way in which she softened Joe's class-based politics with the values of the home.

> Often our views were at variance and Joe tried to teach me the art of argument. The chief fault of women, he pointed out, was their tendency to make a personal issue of every point in dispute. I thought it over and knew that he was right. For women generally, the objective view was hard to achieve.
>
> But if I altered so did he. The Wild Irishman I had married had mellowed with the years. In politics his republican leanings had given place to a convinced support of monarchy. He regarded the American system that required the Head of State to struggle in the miry arena of party politics as lessening the dignity of the State itself, and tending to lessen the respect in which its laws were held. A symbol of State set apart and above the common things of everyday life had become his ideal. His early dreams of socialism were tempered now by awareness of the dangers to individual freedom that lay within it. For Australia he wanted the things we most desired for our children, and he pictured it always as leading the world in humanitarian legislation, a model for democratic governments: a land whose citizens were truly free; where a man could keep a straight back, and look every other man in the eye.
>
> Tolerance was now part of him. A few years earlier, when the older children had begun to read beyond the limits of school requirements, I had suggested that we cancel our subscription to the *Australian Worker*, journal of the AWU, to which

he had been devoted all his adult life. I thought it too bitter in its denunciations, far too intolerant and biased in the expression of its views. I did not want the children to cut their political milk teeth on a diet tinctured with the poison of class hatred. Joe had acquiesced. He agreed that we could not teach them love and hate together. If religion mattered at all, it mattered in every department of life.[24]

In this marital exchange of qualities, the woman must learn that the norms governing relations with friends and family are inadequate for understanding relations within society at large, and the man that they still have an important place. Radical politics is banished from the home because its language of conflict is deemed inappropriate in that consensual sphere, and because its concern with people's social and economic role, with the objective view, rather than with their individual moral qualities challenges the very basis of familial relations.

Outside the spheres governed by the norms of technical rationality, women's daily lives in the home are spent dealing with people as individuals; women do not have to make decisions in terms of impersonal criteria like profitability, class position and solidarity, or bureaucratic regulation, but rather deal with people face to face, equipped with moral and emotional concepts like selfishness, duty, hope and love. They understand people and society in ordinary language. Women's often remarked political individualism arises not just from their unorganised social existence and the consequent difficulties they have in forming a sense of collective political interests, but from their daily experience of dealing with people as individuals. Their conservatism is not just a negative consequence of the limitations of their social experience, but a positive affirmation of the values in which that experience is grounded.

Much of 'The Forgotten People' seems particularly addressed to women. While a passage like the following no doubt speaks to many men whose working lives have brought them few satisfactions, it speaks primarily to women in their roles as homemakers and mothers. 'The real life of the nation is to be found in the homes of people who are nameless and unadvertised, and who... see in their children their greatest contribution to the immortality of the race.'

Prima facie the forgotten people Menzies was addressing were the middle class, but they were also women whose particular interests and problems had generally been forgotten by a politics organised around the conflicts of the economy and the work place. In elaborating the virtues of the home as central to non-labour ideology, Menzies was elaborating the virtues of women's traditional social space. While this could be seen as reinforcing women's traditional role, it also made it easier for the needs of women in the home to be articulated as political demands, for the problems of the private and domestic sphere to become political. A generation before the women's movement, Menzies was politicising the non-political.

In 'The Forgotten People' the appeal to women is implicit rather than explicit, in the use of symbols and arguments which are central both to many women's understanding of their experience and to the political beliefs of conservative women's organisations like the Australian Women's National League. Trying to shift non-labour away from its links with big business towards a renewed mass base, Menzies shifts it closer to the way women, who have been so important in maintaining that mass base, see the social world. The implicit appeal to women in 'The Forgotten People' became explicit once the Liberal Party was formed. This was no doubt partly due to the role played by the Australian Women's National League in the formation of the Liberal Party. Of the non-labour organisations which buried their identities in the new party, the AWNL was reputedly the largest with over 40,000 members.[25] Its assets financed the embryonic Liberal Party in its first six months, in exchange for which it extracted concessions in terms of equal representation of women in the organisation of the new party. It no doubt also brought home to Menzies the importance of women's ideological contribution to non-labour politics. In his closing address to the conference in Albury at which the new Liberal Party of Australia was formally constituted, Menzies stressed the role women had to play in the new organisation, and the important role they had played in the past: 'In the educating of the electorate in liberal ideas they have for many years been an effective force.'[26]

Menzies' 1946 federal election policy speech included a direct appeal to women:

> May I say that this speech is addressed not only to men but to women. Indeed, even more to women than to men! For, during the war, even the most unimaginative of men must have been acutely conscious of the incalculable importance of the work done by women in industry, in the Services, and in the home. Upon our wives and mothers has fallen the main burden of the dreadful anxieties of war, of every civil restriction, of every shortage, of the standing in queues, of the cessation of the home delivery of goods, of the sharp reduction in domestic help, of the housing shortage, of gas and power rationing when strikes are on. Women, even more than men, have been responsible for the family saving that has done so much to fill our war loans.

> It is the women of Australia who most eagerly seek those policies which will build homes, will banish the fear of depression, will hold out the hope of advancement for husband or son or daughter; who want a better system of education; who know that lower taxes would brighten the future and bring more contented work and more goods and services.[27]

While women's role in industry and the services is mentioned, it is their role in the home that is elaborated and seen as carrying the main burden of the anxieties of war. The middle-class virtues of frugality and aspiration for one's children are now explicitly ascribed to women, and to them a new one is added – the eager consumer of the future.

Menzies' 1949 policy speech also has a supplementary statement on women's special problems.[28] By comparison, Chifley's policy speech for the same election shows just how much more conscious Menzies was of the need to speak to women's experience. Chifley dwells on the memory and lessons of the unemployment of the Depression.

> So far as it can humanly contrive, never again will the dole queues be seen in this country. Never again will competent workmen stand idle for months and years while limitless work remains to be done. Never again will young men drift hopelessly from town to town and from State to State, searching for jobs, which in all this wide land, did not exist for them.[29]

Chifley's reminders here of the dole queue, and elsewhere in the speech of thousands of ill-clad and under-fed breadwinners queuing at factory gates, of the fear of the sack and the right of every man to receive a fair return for his labour, enterprise and initiative, all speak primarily to men's experience of the work place. Men are asked to vote as workers and although the term 'breadwinners' does imply wives and children, they are entailments; the particular experiences of women during the Depression are unmentioned. If Menzies had wanted to remind people of the Depression, he would have spoken of mothers living on tea to feed their children, of their difficulties maintaining a home as they shifted endlessly between rented rooms, and he would have evoked the suffering of wives watching helplessly as their husbands' spirits were broken by the futile search for work.

THE INDEPENDENT VIRTUES

MUCH OF the strength of 'The Forgotten People' is in the historical richness of the symbols Menzies is deploying against labour. Layer upon layer of historical experience has built up the symbol of the home as Menzies is using it here: the political struggles over the role of class in politics; the alienating experience of much modern work; the anxieties engendered by modernisation and rapid social change; the increasingly bureaucratic regulation of life; the place of women as the custodians of moral and emotional life. Linking the home with frugality, Menzies brings into play another layer of historical experience – Protestant religious beliefs. Homes material are the concrete expressions of 'the habits of frugality and saving for "a home of our own"'; homes human fulfil their destiny through parents' 'frugality and saving for education and progress'; homes spiritual are produced 'by self-sacrifice, by frugality and saving'. The emphasis on frugality in this speech is extraordinary: the words 'frugal'/'frugality' appear five times; the words 'thrift'/'thrifty' three; and the words 'save'/'savings' eight.

Represented here by the virtue of frugality is a whole complex of attitudes which is central to Menzies' attack on the ALP's commitment to socialism.

True to the speech's general strategy of locating all political values in the private realm, money appears mainly as saved money, rarely as earned money. Even when Menzies is talking about the dependence of present wealth on the past, it is from the savings, not the work or labour of the past that the future grows ('the financial power of 1942 is based upon the savings which have preceded it'). Savings are represented here as the private actions of individuals, the result of personal decisions and strength of character. The word 'work' scarcely appears in the speech. Both work and saving involve the renunciation of pleasure, but Menzies gives no direct weight in this speech to the renunciation involved in work. This absence of work is part of the speech's general strategy of shifting political attention away from public, economic activity, in which conflicts of interests are hard to avoid, to the private realm of domestic activity. It is also testament to the strength of the labour movement's grip on the symbols of work and worker within the oppositional structure of Australian party rhetoric. There is a tension here, however. Although Menzies wants to shift attention away from economic activity and so from work and the central symbols of the labour movement – in particular its championing of the dignity and rights of the workers – work has a central place in Protestant experience and he does not want to imply that only the working class work.

In his 1954 election policy speech, Menzies made an attempt to capture the symbol of work from the ALP and give it the same kind of consensual meaning he earlier gave to middle class, claiming 'We are the true workers' party':

> Some wage-earners say, 'I vote Labour [sic], because I am a worker.' But how many are not workers? Is a man who works with his hands a worker, and another man who works with his head not a worker? Are our wives workers? We need workers with hand, heart and head, if we are to become a great nation...
>
> The 'workers' of Australia are not a special section; we are the overwhelming majority. No policy can be a workers' policy unless it seeks justice for all – employers, employees, housewives (the hardest workers of all), self-employed in shop or office or farm.[30]

The attempt failed. Menzies' claim that we're all workers did not enter into Liberal Party ideology in the way his construction of the middle class did. It would have brought it too close to labour's central symbols and may have led to considerations of the very different degrees of control different types of 'workers' have over their working lives and its monetary rewards.

Capital accumulation and entrepreneurial activity have been the bourgeoisie's prime economic tasks. Menzies' stress on saving includes the former of these (he is far less comfortable with the latter). In *The Protestant Ethic and the Spirit of Capitalism*, Max Weber showed how this capital accumulation was impregnated with religious meanings.[31] The Protestant ethic had two contradictory attitudes to money: on the one hand its accumulation was a visible sign of the accumulator's salvation and of the divine approval of his dedication to his chosen calling; on the other, it was not to be spent on comfort or enjoyment. The result of an otherworldly asceticism expressed through hard work and self-denial was compulsory saving.

The strength of the labour movement's hold on the symbol of work was clearly very frustrating for Menzies. Work does appear in the speech, but in other guises – as effort, public service, activity, enterprise or contribution – and some of these can as easily refer to monetary savings as to labour. Perhaps the speech's extraordinary emphasis on saving is because saving must refer to the self-discipline and effort involved in both saving and work: because the latter can not be mentioned, saving must stand for the renunciation involved in both.

Most of the religious significance of Calvin's doctrines had faded from Protestants' commitment to work and renunciation by the middle of the twentieth century, but some of the habits of character remained, together with the sense that such habits were divinely sanctioned. Independence, a central value of individualism, could be seen as the hallmark of a godly man. Menzies introduces homes spiritual as finding their most moving expression in Burns's 'The Cotter's Saturday Night'. This poem was very popular among Presbyterians, an inspiration to family piety with its image of the simple labouring family gathered together for their supper of milk and porridge and for worship around the family Bible.[32] 'The Cotter's Saturday Night' was regularly read to the young Menzies and his siblings by their father.[33] Menzies uses the poem here not so much to emphasise piety as independence: 'Human nature is at its greatest when it combines dependence upon God with independence of man... the greatest element in a strong people is a fierce independence of spirit.'

In his 1946 policy speech, Menzies contrasts 'a society which seeks salvation in the rules and regulations of the bureaucratic state with a society which seeks salvation through the divine restlessness and ambitious enterprise of the individual'.[34] Residual in such an argument against socialism was the fear that socialism would deny individuals the chance to manifest their salvation through work. Most of Menzies' audience would have had little interest in their eternal salvation, but many would still have responded to the argument that their work was the chief manifestation of their character and that socialism might deny them the chance to prove its superiority. Similarly, they would have held little sympathy for those whose character manifested itself in sloppy, half-hearted work, or even worse, in idleness. Something remained of the sense that one's damnation as well as one's salvation could be manifest in one's attitude to work. John Bunting, who worked closely with Menzies as Secretary of the Prime Minister's Department in the 1960s, reports the disdain with which Menzies in later life treated those who were less than fully dedicated to their work;[35] by contrast he regularly stressed how hard he himself worked during his life.[36]

In 'The Forgotten People', after a rather half-hearted gesture towards universal humanity, Menzies makes his views clear on the differing deserts of the active and the idle.

> That we are all, as human souls, of like value cannot be denied; that each of us should have his chance is and must be the great objective of political and social policy.
>
> But to say that the industrious and intelligent son of self-sacrificing and saving and forward-looking parents has the same social deserts and even material needs as the dull offspring of stupid and improvident parents is absurd.

By the 1920s, Protestants had crossed the threshold into a post-doctrinal age and their religious ideas had generally become rather vague.[37] Still, one can hear echoes of earlier doctrinal differences in Brian Lewis's account of his

Presbyterian family's religious life in Melbourne during World War I: 'we think Methodists rather hysterical, always holding revivals and trying to save souls. We would prefer souls to look after themselves and not crowd out heaven with people we don't really want to meet.'[38] Brian Lewis, who was later Professor of Architecture at Melbourne University, went to Wesley where his older brothers knew Menzies; his sister, Phyllis, was briefly engaged to him.[39]

Calvinism was carried on most fully in Presbyterianism, and Weber comments on the harshness of its adherents towards the sins of their neighbours and their lack of understanding or forgiveness of another's weakness. The world was divided between the elect and the rest whom the elect held in contempt.[40] Menzies displays something of that harshness here as he unhesitatingly visits the sins of the fathers on their children and hardens the difference between the deserving and the rest with the contrast between 'offspring' and 'son'. Much more was at stake here than the maintenance of social difference. The passage continues:

> If the motto is to be: 'Eat, drink and be merry for tomorrow you will die, and if it chances you don't die, the State will look after you; but if you don't eat, drink and be merry, and save, we shall take your savings from you' – then the whole business of life will become foundationless.

This passage is interesting, for despite its conclusion it betrays the cracks in the system, the huge costs of the renunciation of instinctual pleasures. Of course the attractiveness of these pleasures will be rigorously denied, but fantasies of the spendthrift's indulgence will lurk behind the pursed, disapproving lips of the frugal. The Victorian's terms for sexual abstinence and ejaculation – saving and spending – easily fit this emotional structure of pleasure denied. While saving (renunciation) is presented as 'the whole business of life', Menzies recognises that pressure is needed to keep people up to the mark, that eating, drinking and being merry do have their attractions. The pressure behind most people's saving was fear of impoverishment from sickness, unemployment, death of a spouse, or old age, and it was just these pressures that the ALP's welfare programmes were designed to alleviate. The danger, as Menzies saw it then and as critics of the welfare state continue to see it, is that without such fears people will collapse into indolence and dependency.

As well, the commitment to equality inspiring social welfare policies is regularly presented by its critics as motivated by envy. The middle class, says Menzies, is 'envied by those whose social benefits are largely obtained by taxing them'. Political programmes calling for a redistribution of property are seen as an expression of the envy of the have-nots for the haves, their passion directed towards taking wealth away from those who have earned it rather than to the creation of more wealth. In such arguments about the social role of envy, the haves usually get off rather lightly.

Envy is a destructive emotion. Unchecked, its anger at and wish to destroy another's possession and enjoyment will eat away at its bearer's self-esteem and pleasure in life; all experience will be blighted by the desire for the envied object. As traditional beliefs about the evil eye testify, fear of envy is often as powerful a social and psychological motivator as envy itself.[41] Those who locate envy mainly on the left and in the working class, focus envy on material goods. But one can envy experience as well as possessions. Neglected by such conservative critics is the envy of those with a little, dearly bought, for the imagined pleasures of others, often with less. The middle class to whom Menzies spoke would have known the value of respectability. It was an essential qualification for much white-collar employment, but one nevertheless which required immense self-discipline. The young bank clerk forbidden to marry till he reached a suitably senior position, who had continually to display his sober and diligent nature in his lifestyle and choice of friends if he wanted advancement, could well envy the less respectable their pleasures, even as they may envy his salary.[42]

Despite his praise for their sturdy independence, Menzies' forgotten people seem rather timid folk – anxious about the future and about getting on. Historian Stuart Macintyre writing of the same groups calls them 'the anxious class'.[43] In 'The Forgotten People' Menzies focuses their anxiety on their sense of unwarranted neglect; the modern age does not sufficiently appreciate their virtues; it sees only their rewards and not their sacrifices: 'To discourage ambition, to envy success, to hate achieved superiority, to distrust independent thought, to sneer at and impute false motives to public service, these are the maladies of modern democracy, and of Australian democracy in particular.'[44]

There are two classic accounts of the psychology of the lower middle class: Max Scheler's *Ressentiment* and Svend Ranulf's *Moral Indignation and Middle Class Psychology*.[45] These are both based on the European petit bourgeoisie, the small shopkeepers and business people who must be industrious, thrifty, sober and chaste if they are not to be reduced to beggary. Scheler's thinking is deeply aristocratic, and he expounds the psychological costs of an open society which make it difficult for people to accept what he sees as the natural differences between them. Ranulf's book is more sociological, focusing on the reasons for the strength of the disinterested tendency to inflict punishment among the lower middle classes, in their interest in the denigration and condemnation of the faults of others, even when those faults do not impinge on them directly. He notes that these are almost non-existent in societies without a middle class and tend to disappear as the middle class acquires a certain standard of wealth and prestige. The charitable virtues – generosity, compassion, forgiveness – are all missing from the psychology of the lower middle class. Ranulf argues that this disinterested desire to inflict punishment, found almost exclusively among the lower middle classes, results from the extraordinarily high degree of social restraint and repression they are forced to live under. Moral indignation, he argues, is a kind of resentment fuelled by repression of the instincts.

These authors help us to identify the air of resentful self pity that pervades 'The Forgotten People'. Both link the psychology of the lower middle classes to feelings of weakness and impotence: resentment is found in those unable to express openly their antagonism to a social system which demands such high costs from them; instead, they have a sense of powerlessness, of being out of touch with dominant trends, of being neglected, left out, forgotten.

This resentment and denigration is always socially structured and directed. In the nineteenth and early twentieth century Europe Scheler and Ranulf were describing, it was directed against the pursuit of pleasure by both the aristocracy and the working class. Menzies' three-term class system repeats this: he gestures towards the middle class's historic disdain for the idle rich with its rich living in hotels and gossiping in fashionable suburbs; but most of his attention is on the idleness below. The political purpose of Menzies' speech is not to argue against government policies which would benefit the rich, but against those which will benefit the poor – the sons and daughters of 'stupid and improvident parents'. Menzies presents the tide of political events as moving with labour's socialist policies and the interests of the working classes, playing on the middle class's resentful sense of weakness and neglect, even as he praises them for their strength.

Although the forgotten people to whom Menzies spoke might feel their sacrifices were insufficiently appreciated, many could not contemplate life without them. If they did eat, drink and make merry with no thought of tomorrow *then the whole business of life would become foundationless* (my emphasis). Socialism threatened to rob life of its purpose: Menzies frequently referred to socialism as 'dull', 'dreary', 'dismal', 'deathly'. Some of the life-and-death urgency Menzies ascribed to the struggle against socialism was the historical residue of the desire to see one's eternal salvation manifest in one's worldly activity; but its contemporary urgency derived more from the psychological structures to which these beliefs had contributed than from the beliefs themselves. For the psychological heirs to Protestantism's belief in predestination, the struggle and competition of the world could seem the whole business of life; the need to strive, to seek, to find and not to yield was (and is) so deeply embedded in their sense of self and of life's purpose that without it life seemed empty.

In the 1946 policy speech Menzies contrasts the ALP's concern with security with the Liberal Party's commitment to development. Although he recognises that some form of the welfare state is here to stay in the form of such things as old-age and widows' pensions, he argues that the ALP is too concerned with security at the expense of progress and development. He develops the contrast in terms of youth and old age: the Liberal Party's policies are appropriate to 'a young country' and 'a virile growing community'.

> I want to say to Australia that if we are to grow to our full strength, we must not sit at home huddling about ourselves the garments of mere safety.[46]
>
> ... I want to say to this young man's country that the greatest goal that we can have in the years

to come is that of development and growth. But development is the result of initiative; of risk-taking; of ambition.[47]

The appeal is to an image of an independent, youthful masculinity which proves itself through competition. Although both ambition and enterprise are presented as characteristics of the individual, they require a competitive social organisation for their enactment. The most potent image of competition, the market, is missing from 'The Forgotten People'; when one looks to see where the ambition which Menzies praises so highly is to express itself, it is in education. Elaborating on the great instinct of civilised man to give his children a better start in life, Menzies says:

> If Scotland has made a great contribution to the theory and practice of education, it is because of the tradition of Scottish homes. The Scottish ploughman, walking behind his team, cons ways and means of making his son a farmer, and so he sends him to the village school. The Scottish farmer ponders upon the future of his son, and sees it most assured not by the inheritance of money but by the acquisition of that knowledge which will give him power, and so the sons of many Scottish farmers find their way to Edinburgh and a University degree.

In 'The Forgotten People' ambition is presented as the pursuit of individual progress within a relatively stable status system based on education. A more open, entrepreneurial, adventurous spirit is of little interest. The restriction of Menzies' interest in competition to competition limited by already secure conventions is an important clue to Menzies' personality, to be taken up later.

The virtues Menzies stresses in this speech are the virtues of independence – the manly virtues of self-reliance, courage and ambition – and it is these virtues which socialism is seen to threaten. He contrasts those forced to live on the bounty of the State with the fierce, independent spirit of a strong people:

> ... the greatest element in a strong people is a fierce independence of spirit. That is the only *real* freedom and it has as its corollary a brave acceptance of unclouded individual responsibility. The moment a man seeks moral and intellectual refuge in the emotions of a crowd, he ceases to be a human being and becomes a cipher. The home spiritual so understood is not produced by lassitude or by dependence; it is produced by self-sacrifice, by frugality and saving.

In his 1954 policy speech the message is even clearer:

> We believe in the individual, in his freedom, in his ambition, in his dignity. If he becomes submerged in the mass, and loses his personal significance, we have tyranny ... the dull, unproductive, Socialist philosophy is merely the definition of stagnation and death.'[48]

Being one of a crowd for Menzies represents not comfort or strength or solidarity, but death: one's self disappears when the only thing that gave it a sense of life – its difference from others formed and displayed through competition – is irrelevant. We see here the psychological underpinning to non-labour's rejection of objective sociological categories like class. Such categories not only affront one's subjective sense of agency; they threaten the very ground of a sense of self based on one's proven and established *difference* from others. To be an individual, a person, one must have the chance to earn one's individuality in competition with others.

The dependence on the state which socialism would foster is linked to dependence on the mother and to sexual impotence. 'Are you looking forward to a breed of men after the war who will have become boneless wonders? Leaners grow flabby, lifters grow muscles.' To increase the state's power is to reduce its citizens to children. Under socialism – 'the overlordship of an all powerful State', 'the Government – that almost deity – will nurse us and rear us and maintain us and pension us and bury us'. The state Menzies projects is not labour's state – the creative expression of the interdependence of members of society, a co-operative solution to their common problems – but a threatening, suffocating state, like a mother who won't let her children grow up. The threats posed are different for sons than for daughters: sons will lose their sexual potency while daughters will have their role usurped, as the Women Who Want to be Women will later complain.

Menzies' stress on the independent virtues represents both a political philosophy and a psychological-cum-moral position. It has its roots both in liberal individualism's conceptualisation of society as composed of separate and fully formed individuals set in conflict with each other by their natural needs and desires, and in the sense of self formed through the social relations which this conceptualisation of society legitimises. As such it is opposed both to the socialist understanding of the individuals' relationship with society, which sees individuals as formed in and through their relations with others, and to a psychological-cum-moral position which emphasises the emotions and virtues which bind rather than those which separate.[49] To the virtues of independence we can contrast the virtues of charity – compassion, sympathy, generosity, trust, gratitude – those virtues in which the self is opened out to others and which express a sense of fellow feeling and implication with others; to the pleasures and strengths of independence we can contrast the pleasures and strengths of dependence – of recognising, celebrating and drawing sustenance from people's interdependence with each other.

What I am calling the virtues of charity are all missing from the emotional register with which 'The Forgotten People' works. While this speech is concerned to bring out the strengths and pleasures of the virtues it celebrates, these virtues have a darker side and can be seen as defending against certain human experiences, even as they celebrate others. In particular, they defend against the dangers of vulnerability to others. To be open, to be interdependent, is to be vulnerable. Others can drag you down with their insatiable demands, or they can fail you just when you need them most. Better to neither a lender nor a borrower be and rely solely on oneself, however lonely and neglected that may leave you. The description 'forgotten' captures well the dangers of self-reliant individualism. If you give little or nothing to others, even though you ask for nothing in return, others are unlikely to recognise your virtues and to come to your aid when you are in difficulty. Your virtues will be unappreciated and your difficulties ignored. So Menzies, like the defenders of the middle class before him, praises it for its strengths and its social contribution, even as he plays on its fears.

'Good fences make good neighbours' argues Robert Frost's New England neighbour; but the poet is not so sure.

> *Before I built a wall I'd ask to know*
> *What I was walling in or walling out,*
> *And to whom I was like to give offense.*

Walls protect and keep safe and the emphasis in 'The Forgotten People' is on elaborating the virtues and the meaning of the experiences inside the walls of the home. But walls can exclude as much or more than they protect:

> ... one of the best instincts in us is that which induces us to have one little piece of earth with a house and a garden which is ours, to which we can withdraw, in which we can be amongst friends, *into which no stranger may come against our will.* (my emphasis)

The virtues of the forgotten people have a defensive edge, and the balance can easily shift from the values and experiences celebrated and enjoyed to the values denied and the experiences excluded. The danger is that the walls will keep out and exclude so much that there will be little left to protect and the homes of the forgotten people will become safe but empty.

THE COMMUNISTS

AMBIVALENT COMMITMENTS

IF THE forgotten people carried the values Menzies represented in politics, the communists stood for all he opposed. They were not, however, legitimate opponents like the ALP, which Menzies was always careful to describe as socialist rather than communist. Where the ALP had chosen the parliamentary road to socialism, the communists' commitment to the revolutionary overthrow of capitalism and parliamentary democracy took them outside the bounds of legitimate political conflict. In the early 1950s Menzies attempted to ban the Communist Party of Australia. Although he was ultimately defeated, his actions at this time sat uneasily with his oft-professed commitment to civil liberties and have supported the left's depiction of him as fundamentally authoritarian, if not downright fascist. His critics can point to other incidents to support their position, in particular his involvement as Attorney-General in the 1930s with prohibiting the entry into Australia of anti-fascist activist Egon Kisch. Historian Robin Gollan sees Menzies' role in the Kisch case as giving 'full expression to the fundamental authoritarianism which lay behind the facade of liberalism and respect for human liberties he so constantly proclaimed'.[1]

Prima facie, such actions of Menzies seem at odds with the strong commitment to civil liberties manifest at other points in his political career. He frequently made clear, strong statements of support for the traditional liberal values of freedom of thought and speech and the importance of open debate in a democracy. At the outbreak of World War II, for example, he reaffirmed the central values of a liberal democracy:

> We do not seek, however long the war may last, a muzzled opposition. Our institutions – Parliament, all liberal thought, free speech and free criticism – must go on. It would be a tragedy if we found that we have fought for freedom, free beliefs and the value of every individual's soul, and won the war, but lost the things for which Australia was fighting.[2]

And he acted on such beliefs: as Attorney-General in the 1930s he eased the administration of Australia's book censorship laws[3]; and as Prime Minister at the outbreak of war he initially resisted pressure from the military and the intelligence organisations to declare the Communist Party illegal – he did not want measures taken which would infringe the rights and civil liberties of innocent persons.[4] Similarly, immediately after the war when many on the conservative side of politics were calling for the banning of the Communist Party, Menzies declined to join in. During the 1946 election campaign when Arthur Fadden, the leader of the Country Party, was demanding its banning, Menzies defended the CPA's right to exist, arguing that in time of peace it is 'a very serious step to prohibit the association of people for the promulgation of any particular views',[5] and 'that it must not be thought that they are such a force in political philosophy that we cannot meet them'.[6]

By 1949 Menzies had changed his mind.

> The day has gone by for treating Communism as a legitimate political philosophy. Our attitude has been one of great tolerance. We conceded freedom and were rewarded with a series of damaging industrial disturbances with no true industrial foundation... The Communists are the most unscrupulous opponents of religion, of civilised government, of law and order, of national security... Communism is an alien and destructive pest. If elected we shall outlaw it. The Communist Party will be declared subversive and unlawful, and dissolved.[7]

They were elected and they did, as promised, introduce legislation to outlaw the CPA.

The Communist Party of Australia was established in 1920 in the wave of radicalism that followed the Bolsheviks' victory in Russia. Established with the approval of the Comintern, it maintained close links with the Soviet Union.[8] During the war both the party membership and its strength in the union movement increased sharply, though both fell rapidly after the war.[9] By 1949, the membership had fallen from its war-time peak of 23,000 to 12,000, and the party had abandoned the policy of maintaining a united front with the ALP, which it had pursued during the war, and was engaged in a bitter struggle for control of the union movement with both the ALP's industrial groups and B.A. Santamaria's Catholic Social Movement.[10]

The CPA's increasingly belligerent attitude to the ALP was a reflection of the rapid cooling of relations between the Soviet Union and her war-time allies. Country after country in Eastern Europe fell under Soviet control and in

1948 the Western allies were denied land access to Berlin. In 1949 the Nationalist Government of Chiang Kai-shek collapsed and Mao Zedong's forces won control of China. For Australians this fused the fear of communism with their longer-standing fear of the Asian hordes, and the Korean War which broke out in mid-1950 confirmed fears of communist expansion in Asia. Attacking the Communist Party early in 1949 Menzies linked the enemy without with the enemy within:

> The Communist Party is not organised for social purposes, but for high treason. The only difference between the aggression and march of Hitler in 1938-39 and that of Stalin today is in terms of colour.
>
> Does anybody believe that, if we were forced into war, there would be no Fifth Column in Australia?[11]

Menzies explained his change of attitude towards the banning of the CPA by the worsening international situation. Just three weeks before making the above statement, Menzies had called an urgent Premiers' Conference on Defence, claiming 'We have not a day more than three years to get ready' for possible war with Russia.[12] Introducing the legislation in Parliament he described it as 'a law relating to the safety and defence of Australia'.

> Let me say at the outset that it will be without avail for any honourable member to point out, as can be done quite readily, that for some years I and other persons resisted the idea of a Communist ban on the ground that, in time of peace, doubts ought to be resolved in favour of free speech. True, that was my view after the war, and it was the view of many others. But events have moved. We

are not at peace today, except in a technical sense. The Soviet Union – and I say this with profound regret – has made perfect the technique of the 'cold war'.[13]

The passage of the legislation through Parliament was slow, the ALP, which still controlled the Senate, being divided as to how to respond.[14] It was eventually passed and immediately challenged in the High Court by the Communist Party and ten powerful unions. The High Court upheld the challenge, seeing the legislation as an invasion of the normal civil and contractual rights of citizens. Although such an invasion was allowed under the Commonwealth government's defence powers during war, the court rejected the government's argument that the times were equivalent to those of war. The government then put the matter to a referendum which was narrowly defeated.[15] After this, Menzies and the Liberal–Country Party Government accepted defeat and gave up trying to outlaw the Communist Party. Australia succumbed neither to an invasion from a communist power nor to civil disorder.

The operative measures of the Bill were that the Communist Party of Australia and any affiliated organisations were to be dissolved and a receiver appointed for their property; no one was to attempt to carry on any activities connected with the organisation under threat of imprisonment. A person who had been a member or officer of an unlawful association between 10 May 1948 and the day the legislation was proclaimed, or was a communist, and so likely to engage in activities prejudicial to the security of the Commonwealth, could be declared by the Governor-General. (This date was the last date of the National Congress of the Communist Party of Australia.) The Bill defined 'communist' very broadly as 'a person who supports or advocates the objectives, policies, teachings, principles or practices of communism as expounded by Marx and Lenin'. Once declared, a person could appeal to the High Court and attempt to prove that they were innocent of the charge, but the onus of proof was with them. This was justified by the need to protect the security service who were to be the main providers of the information on which a person was declared. A declared person was disqualified from employment with the Commonwealth government or any of its instrumentalities, and from holding office in any trade union involved with a declared vital or key industry.[16]

Most of those opposing the Bill and the subsequent referendum were also opposed to communism, but they disputed the means used to meet the threat. Arguments against the legislation were of two main types. The first questioned the need for it and its likely effectiveness. Chifley, for example, argued that there were already sufficient legislative powers to deal with subversive activities;[17] others argued that banning the party would be ineffectual, or counter-productive, perhaps even increasing the party's popularity.[18] The second group of arguments focused on the implications of the legislation for civil liberties. Chifley pointed out that the policy Menzies had announced in his election speech had been to ban organisations which were declared unlawful; the legislation, however, allowed for individuals as well as organisations to be declared.[19] People were to be denied certain rights, not because of anything they had done but because of beliefs they held and actions which might be expected of them on the basis of those beliefs. The traditional onus of proof clause was to be reversed and the legislation was to be retrospective, people being charged with offences which were not illegal at the time of committal. Replying to Menzies' Second Reading Speech, Chifley attacked the legislation as opening the door 'for the liar, the perjurer and the pimp to make charges and damn men's reputation'.[20]

As well, the legislation's very broad definition of 'communist' threatened to embrace many on the left, including members of the ALP. The legislation presented the teachings of Marx and Lenin as if they were a unified body of doctrine, without internal contradictions or possibilities for different interpretations. Supporting Marx's general arguments about the nature of social relations in capitalist society does not imply supporting immediate violent revolutionary action, but the legislation offered no recognition of such a possibility. Marx's writings as a complex and sometimes contradictory body of thought were treated as a simple body of unarguable dogma. The crucial consideration for many who opposed banning the Communist Party was just how sharply communists could be distinguished from many other members of society, particularly among left liberal intellectuals. This was an argument the government and its supporters seemed unable to grasp. The pamphlets setting out the Yes case stressed that 'No non-communist person or organisation can come within its scope',[21] as if communists were a discrete class of persons and who was and who was not a communist could never be a matter of serious dispute.

The debates over both the initial Bill to ban the Communist Party and over the referendum were bitter. The basic, divisive question was whether the threat posed to the Australian state and society by Australian communists was sufficient to justify the state defending itself by suspending the normal civil liberties of some of its citizens. Menzies, along with many others, argued it was: on the grounds of the communist doctrine of the revolutionary overthrow of the bourgeois state; on the grounds of the international conflict between the Soviet Union and the Western allies which turned Australian communists into a fifth column;

and on the grounds of the communists' strength within the trade union movement.

Most political divisions in Australia are over economic issues, groups and individuals taking positions in terms of their immediate interests, and the normal political processes of compromise giving some satisfaction to both sides. With the proposal to ban the Communist Party no compromises were possible. It raised questions of fundamental political philosophy: questions about the importance of social order, the power and nature of the state, and the rights of individuals. How should conflicts between the state and the individual be resolved? What are the limits of a society's tolerance of people who challenge its fundamental legitimations? The beliefs people hold about such questions will express not just their economic interests but the way they have resolved fundamental psychological questions.

What sense are we to make of Menzies' ambivalent commitment to civil liberties? Was he pushed into his campaign against the communists by his Country Party colleagues; was he lured by the easy political pickings it offered as an issue which confused and disabled the opposition; or was he convinced that communists and communism posed a deadly threat to Australian society? The answer is probably all three, but the one I am interested in is the third – the patterns of conviction anti-communism held for Menzies; or to put this slightly differently, the patterns of conviction Menzies was able to make anti-communism hold for himself. Here, it is not so much a matter of assessing how realistic Menzies' response to communism was – how real a threat the Communist Party of Australia actually posed to Australia's security and civil order – as in exploring the particular shape Menzies gave to anti-communism, how this fitted with his ideas about civil liberties, and what it reveals about how he imagined both society and Australia. This imagining has both a public and a private face. When Menzies embarked on his attempt to ban the Communist Party he had a tradition of Australian anti-communist rhetoric on which to draw, yet he drew on it in a partial and distinctive way.

TROUBLE ON THE WATERFRONT

> The idea of society is a powerful image. It is potent in its own right to control or to stir men to action. This image has form; it has external boundaries, margins, internal structure. Its outlines contain power to reward conformity and repulse attack. There is energy in its margins and unstructured areas. For symbols of society any human experience of structures, margins or boundaries is ready to hand.
> Mary Douglas, *Purity and Danger*[22]

> Parliament has declared its policy and reinforced – if I may use the expression – the right of every civilised country to control the terms upon which foreigners shall enter it. We have, as an independent country, a perfect right to indicate whether an alien shall or shall not be admitted within these shores.
> Menzies as Attorney-General justifying to Parliament on 14 November 1935 the refusal to allow Egon Kisch to land.[23]

ON 2 November 1934 the *Strathaird* docked at Fremantle with the German-speaking, Czech anti-fascist writer Egon Kisch on board. Kisch had been invited to address a peace conference organised by the Congress Against War and Fascism. The conference was to be held from 10–12 November, dates which made clear its challenge to the symbols of Anzac and Empire which would be celebrated in the Armistice Day celebrations of November 11.[24] Although Kisch had been issued with a visa, government officials at Fremantle informed him that he had been declared a prohibited immigrant and refused him permission to land. Protests began immediately. At Adelaide the ship was met by a great crowd, including Germans from the wine-growing villages.

At Melbourne the police cordoned off the pier to prevent Kisch receiving visitors and delegations, but as other passengers on the boat were allowed visitors it was not hard for Kisch's supporters to obtain the passenger list. Lawyers for Kisch challenged the power of the ship's captain to detain Kisch and the ship waited at Station Pier for the verdict. There was a crowd of Kisch's supporters on board, dock workers on the pier, and red-flagged boats carrying anti-fascist youth on the water. As soon as the message came through by phone that the judge had rejected Kisch's case the ship prepared to leave; but with a yard of water between the ship's side and the pier, Kisch jumped. He broke his leg and was immediately arrested and returned to the ship, which sailed on to Sydney with Kisch's leg untreated.

The incident went badly for the government. Kisch's spectacular leap assured huge public interest and a degree of public sympathy, for his pluck if not his political views. Legal action was undertaken on Kisch's behalf and Mr Justice Evatt of the High Court found against the government's action in refusing Kisch permission to land. Kisch was subsequently arrested again by the Customs Department and charged with illegal entry. Under the Immigration Act of 1901 a person wanting to enter Australia could be required to pass a dictation test in a European language. Nervous of Kisch's reputation as a linguist, the authorities gave him a test in Scottish Gaelic. Again appeal was made to the High Court, which found that Scottish Gaelic was not a European language within the meaning of the Act, causing no end of upset to Scotsmen.

Menzies, who had recently replaced John Latham as Attorney-General, defended the government's action and its right to decide who should be admitted to Australia's shores. Just as those suffering from certain diseases and those associated with crimes were prohibited, so were those advocating the overthrow by force or violence of the established government of the Commonwealth. Pressed for the grounds on which Kisch had been declared a prohibited immigrant, Menzies appealed to the government's special knowledge, the sources of which, unfortunately, he could not reveal. His arguments here were of a pattern he was to repeat in the post-war campaign against the Communist Party. Kisch had been denied entry to Britain, said Menzies, and this was surely argument enough:

> I do not need to indicate to any honourable member of this House that the standard of tolerance which exists in the United Kingdom is very high. If the British Government has thought fit to exclude this man from Great Britain, there can be little room for wonder that a Minister of the Crown in Australia should, in turn, make a declaration which has the effect of excluding him from Australia.[25]

Throughout the parliamentary debates Kisch's foreignness was stressed continually. He was called 'Herr Kisch'. Minister for Customs Tommy White, describing him as 'this alien pseudo-author who comes to our shores', challenged those supporting his entry 'to name a single book that Kisch has written. Not a single publication by Kisch has been translated into the English language.'[26] The political and ethnic complexities of central Europe were completely beyond Country Party member Archie Cameron, who confidently elaborated in the Federal Parliament on Kisch's excessive foreignness.

> Does it not strike honourable members as strange that Herr Egon Kisch who, according to the Adelaide newspapers, and according to statements

ABOVE: Menzies' ability to stand up and speak on any occasion, to any audience, was one of his greatest political assets. During his political career he made thousands of speeches. Here he speaks at the official launching of HMAS Warrego in 1940. AUSTRALIAN WAR MEMORIAL
BELOW: Visiting Australian troops in the Middle East in 1941 on his way to England, Menzies banters with the men. It was a new experience for him to be taken as a national rather than a partisan figure and he 'was never so moved' in his life. AUSTRALIAN WAR MEMORIAL

I take the material Recitals in their order:-

1. " AND WHEREAS THE AUSTRALIAN COMMUNIST PARTY, IN ACCORDANCE WITH THE BASIC THEORY OF COMMUNISM, AS EXPOUNDED BY MARX AND LENIN, ENGAGES IN ACTIVITIES OR OPERATIONS DESIGNED TO ASSIST OR ACCELERATE THE COMING OF A REVOLUTIONARY SITUATION, IN WHICH THE AUSTRALIAN COMMUNIST PARTY, ACTING AS A REVOLUTIONARY MINORITY, WOULD BE ABLE TO SEIZE POWER AND ESTABLISH A DICTATORSHIP OF THE PROLETARIAT: "

I have before me a copy of the Constitution of the Australian Communist Party. It is, on the face of it, a fraudulent document, for it piously claims that the Party is a firm supporter of the United Nations, believes in world peace, and does not aim at establishing a totalitarian State, and even professes to adopt the democratic method, i.e., the winning of a majority of the Australian people.

"LOOK LIKE THE INNOCENT FLOWER, BUT BE THE SERPENT UNDER IT"

These things are SO INCONSISTENT with the BELIEFS OF RUSSIAN COMMUNISM that it seems remarkable that in the same document the Australian Communist Party has in words put itself "in line with the great teachings of Marx, Engels, Lenin and Stalin".

ABOVE: *Backed by a grim-looking front-bench, Menzies argues in Parliament for the Communist Party Dissolution Bill, May 1950.* SYDNEY MORNING HERALD

BELOW: *His reading notes for the speech guided rather than determined his delivery. On this page he has pencilled in a quotation from Shakespeare's Lady Macbeth which he used to illustrate the Communists' duplicity.* NATIONAL LIBRARY OF AUSTRALIA

ABOVE: *Leaving an election rally at the Malvern Town Hall in 1954, Menzies accepts the applause of his middle-class supporters.* HERALD & WEEKLY TIMES

BELOW: *One of Menzies' political achievements was to make the political values of women in the home central to non-labour ideology. Here he speaks with some admirers in the early 1960s.* AGE

ABOVE: *Menzies was in his element addressing large public meetings, which were the lifeblood of public politics before television. Here Menzies addresses an attentive, respectably dressed lunch-time meeting in the Sydney Town Hall.* SYDNEY MORNING HERALD

BELOW: *Menzies was as prepared to address a hostile or sceptical crowd as a sympathetic one.* SYDNEY MORNING HERALD

In forming and leading the Liberal Party of Australia, Menzies brought stability and success to non-labour politics. CANBERRA TIMES

With his parents, James and Kate Menzies, after he has become Prime Minister in 1939. The strength of James's personality is still apparent in his straight, challenging demeanour.
FAMILY PHOTO

Menzies' elevated self, photographed by Dickinson Monteath Studio, Melbourne, 1940. *La Trobe collection*, STATE LIBRARY OF VICTORIA

With cane, cigar and homburg hat, Menzies glows with charm and pleasure after a private luncheon at which he and the King of Norway (on right) were the guests of honour, London, 1941. SYDNEY MORNING HERALD

made in the House this afternoon, is a citizen of the newly founded state of Czechoslovakia, should carry the German designation 'Herr' instead of 'Monsieur' which is used in Czechoslovakia? He publishes writings in German and lives in France. He comes to Australia in order to carry on propaganda in behalf of a foreign constituted organisation.[27]

He was so foreign he was foreign even in his own country.

Communism was a threat to the social order of capitalist society. Its central tenet, that the present social and economic order is based on the systematic exploitation of one class by another, challenged all rhetoric of unity with that of division. To the unifying symbols of nation, crown and the parliamentary system, communism again and again opposed the inevitable conflict between those who own and control the means of production and those who must live by the sale of their labour; and it argued that this conflict would eventually lead to the end of the capitalist system and a new social order. Whether communists believed this change would come as a result of the working out of historical forces, or whether they believed history needed a little help, the beliefs themselves, irrespective of the actions they inspired, challenged the social order's inevitability, permanence and inherent justice. For communists argued that the existing way of organising the world was not the only way; that the deprivations and injustices suffered by some groups at the hands of other groups could be changed; and that all talk of social unity was to be treated with suspicion.

In such arguments communism was taking on powerful forces, for it had to vanquish not just those with vested interests in certain social, economic and political arrangements, but the commitment to social unity itself and the bonding of the members of the group with each other. Although at times Australian anti-communist rhetoric did meet communism's challenge directly by arguing for the common interest of capital and labour and the justice of existing distributions of political and economic power, it generally avoided such close engagement with its arguments which might, after all, suggest that there was indeed a case to be answered. Australian anti-communist rhetoric did not generally invoke the details of a particular social order but social order itself.

Eric Campbell, leading figure in the vehemently anti-communist New Guard, recalls that the New Guard's hatred and fear of communism was not based on any detailed understanding of communist ideology: 'the philosophy of Karl Marx was literally a sealed book. Communism, anarchism, and the IWW were to most of us all of one kidney, their outstanding common characteristic being disloyalty with a capital D.'[28] Members of the New Guard enthusiastically gathered information on people of doubtful loyalty. 'It was not difficult to run to earth anyone of doubtful loyalty. In some cases enthusiasm led to the other extreme. More than one harmless eccentric was the object of grave suspicion and only reluctantly crossed off the danger list.'[29] Historian Michael Cathcart's book on the secret armies of the same period also documents the ease with which many Australians could be mobilised against the communists by calls for loyalty. The world view which informed the secret armies, he argues, cannot be understood solely in terms of class and the conflict between capital and labour; it depicted society as a united body of loyal individuals threatened by hostile influences in their midst.[30]

The social anthropologist Mary Douglas has looked at the way different societies represent the social whole and the boundary between what is inside and what is outside society. The human body is a particularly rich source of imagery for the understanding and organisation of social life. The body's margins and internal divisions, along with images of bodily pollution and integrity, provide ways of thinking about threats to the social order – the body politic – and means of combating them.[31] Much anti-communist rhetoric has drawn on bodily imagery: the imagery of sickness and disease (a social cancer) and the anal erotic imagery of the attack from behind (rooting rats out of holes). There are occasional uses of such imagery by mainstream Australian non-labour politicians like Menzies, but they are surprisingly few. Although the body is a particularly rich source for imagery of social unity, as Douglas makes clear, any bounded unit will do; and whatever unit chosen, there will be a preoccupation with margins, entrances and exits.

The image of society as a bounded unit most often evoked in Australian anti-communist rhetoric and practice was not the body but the image of the island continent. For Australian anti-communists the margins of Australia were the shores of the continent and the exits and entrances those perennial trouble spots, the ports, docks and wharves of the waterfront. Until the development of air travel, dangers came to Australia on ships: the diseases to weaken her agriculture and people; cheap manufactured goods to compete with her own; cheap labour to threaten her workers' jobs; non-white immigrants to contaminate the race; seditious, blasphemous and obscene books to corrupt the minds of her citizens; and political agitators to undermine the state. There is energy at the boundaries of society and the docks were places of excitement and possibility; but the excitement at the margins has its darker side in the threats posed to the social order by those who are different and do not accept its rules. In all societies non-conformists are found at the margins, however those margins are defined. The notoriety of the men who worked on the waterfront attached not just to their undoubted power to disrupt economic activity by refusing to load and unload ships, but to their symbolic power as men on the margins.

Between the wars both sides of politics shared the image of Australia as a socially orderly, politically harmonious and racially homogeneous society co-extensive with the island continent of Australia. Aboriginal Australia was not seen as part of Australian society, and ethnic communities like the Chinese or Italians were small enough to be treated as anomalies. Communism and communists were presented as alien intruders to the shores of this harmonious society and the Immigration Act was the first line of defence, as it was against threats to Australia's racial purity.

The first concerted attack on communism was sparked by the 1925 Seamen's Strike. The strike was violent, with riots, shootings, and assaults on the police, and it dominated Australian politics while it lasted. Prime Minister Stanley Bruce responded by amending the Immigration Act to increase the Commonwealth's power to deport troublemakers.[32] Supporting the amendment, Bruce reiterated the people of Australia's determination 'to maintain their racial purity', to remain 'more British than the British'. As well as dealing with threats to racial purity, the Bill dealt with threats to political purity. It was necessary, said Bruce, that 'we should have the power to rid ourselves' of persons of 'alien race' who do not recognise our ideals.[33] Such people, unsocial and unAustralian, Bruce suggested, were responsible for the industrial troubles of the times: 'If there were in Australia none of these alien agitators, we should not have half the trouble we are experiencing today.

These disturbances are not caused by the Australian born, but are due to the doctrines and atmosphere introduced by aliens.'[34]

Not surprisingly, industrial unrest increased during the Depression, and socialist ideas became more convincing to many seeking explanations for the misery of unemployment and their apparent lack of control over their lives. But even as radical ideas became more popular, so they were more likely to be seen as a cause of rather than a response to social and economic problems.

Some Labor Party members could see this, and argued that communists were the symptom not the cause of disorder and strife, and that the best defence of governments against revolution was to remove the suffering and want that lead to revolutionary politics.[35] Later, Chifley argued, against the Communist Party Dissolution Bill, that the best method for combating communism was to make democracy work as a system benefiting no classes or groups but benefiting all members of the population.[36]

In the 1920s and 1930s, anti-communism was non-labour's main ideological response to growing industrial unrest and possible economic breakdown. Social order, however, was threatened not so much by the handful of members of the Communist Party (in 1931, just before Lyons launched his offensive against them, the Communist Party had 1,116 members[37]), but by the difficulties capitalism was experiencing, and by the various secret right-wing militias. Richard Hall estimates that at their peaks the various right-wing armies had a membership of 130,000 men ready to combat the communist menace.[38] In a deflection of responsibility characteristic of the defenders of capitalism, those who described the conflict were accused of causing it and so became the focus of its solution.

When the Lyons government was elected in 1932 it pledged it would deal with the communist menace and instituted a number of repressive measures against communism, including further amendments to the Immigration Act to increase the government's power to restrict the immigration of people with criminal convictions.[39] The censorship of books was also intensified, particularly books regarded as seditious, and communist literature was prevented from circulating through the post. Banned books were treated as prohibited imports and so fell under the authority of the Minister for Trade and Customs, Tommy White, whom Peter Coleman describes as one of the most determined censors in the history of Australian customs.[40] Under White the interpretation of sedition was broad, and distinctions were not always drawn between books advocating revolution and communist ideas and those which simply referred to or discussed the place of communist ideas in history and contemporary events. Australians were prevented from reading works on the history and economy of the Soviet Union as well as works by Marx, Lenin and Stalin. White's zeal led to the formation of the Victorian Book Censorship League which was successful in 1935 in having the responsibility for censorship transferred to the Attorney-General, Robert Menzies, who assured the league that the administration of the law would be relaxed. Some of the previously banned books started to appear soon afterwards.[41]

In drawing the boundaries around Australia, the sharp distinction was between who was inside and who out, and not too much care was taken to distinguish between different grounds for exclusion. Supporting the Lyons government's amendments to the Immigration Act, White unconcernedly ran together the criminal and the non-white.

> It is only by keeping the White Australia policy inviolate that we shall preserve the honesty and loyalty of our people and the integrity of our political institutions. We must preserve the honesty and loyalty of our people by excluding from our midst men of a criminal type.[42]

White added to the list of those who must be kept out: 'aliens with Russian sympathies'; those 'imported agitators who, by their insidious teaching are undermining the working men of Australia', and 'red-anting the trade union movement by becoming its leaders'; and those 'whose standards are distinctly unBritish'. To be excluded from Australia were the non-British, the disloyal, the subversive and seditious (communists), and the criminal. For White, threats to Australia from communism and from racial contamination through non-British immigration were both threats to Australia's purity – political or racial – coming from aliens. That alien communist agitators were often British and hence racially acceptable did not stop the sliding back and forth between one sort of threat to the purity of the nation and the other. Those defined as unAustralian, whether because of their race or political beliefs, were tainted by each other: hence non-British were expected to have unacceptable political beliefs and those with unacceptable political beliefs were expected to be non-British. There were only two categories: Australian and non-Australian; the firm line was between them and little care was taken to distinguish between different ways of being non-Australian.

Racism and anti-communism are two powerful sets of beliefs about the integrity of society, each with its distinctive history and emphasis on the reasons for exclusion and on the fundamental characteristics of society which are to be protected. Racism has always tapped sexual fears, the purity of the race carrying images of its opposite in miscegenation and competition for women with more sexually potent and aggressive men. Anti-communism is much more overtly concerned with the protection of property and a social order that maintains a certain distribution of power. In Australian anti-communist rhetoric of the period there were, however, substantive connections with British racism. According to widely held beliefs, a nation state's political and social institutions were manifestations of its inhabitants' inherited racial characteristics. So the virtues of the Westminster political system represented British racial superiority and, conversely, those attacking contemporary political institutions and arrangements were manifesting their unfitness to participate in and their alienness from that racial superiority.[43] The compatibility between racism and anti-communism is, however, deeper than can be explained by tracing shared substantive beliefs. It is in the formal characteristics they share – in their preoccupation with the boundaries of the social group and their intolerance of difference and ambiguity – that we see the habits of mind which underlie them both.

PARANOID POLITICS

COMMUNISM RAISED deep fears about the vulnerability of society. These fears were allayed by drawing the boundaries around society tighter, paying more attention to what was inside and what outside, policing who got in more vigilantly, and trying to rid society of unwanted elements already in. Australia's legislative attempts to deal with communism can all be understood in this way. Such a tightening of society's boundaries entailed a hardening of the categories in which individuals were seen; those who were outside were seen as sharing very little with those who were in.

Belief in communism was not seen as one attribute of a communist among others, nor was it considered that there might be significant differences among communists. Rather, communists were defined by their communism, lifted out of ordinary social life and emptied of their individuality by their political beliefs. So anti-communists spoke of 'the communist mind', and 'the communists', as if people who held communist beliefs were members of another species which could be sharply and easily distinguished from the rest of society.

This belief in the complete difference between communists and non-communists was central to the anti-communists' inability to meet many of the arguments civil libertarians brought against their attempt to ban the Communist Party. Anyone who was not a communist had nothing to fear from this legislation, they kept reiterating. To them it was inconceivable that a communist could be confused with a non-communist; it would be like confusing a rat with a rabbit or, perhaps more to the point, a white man with a black or yellow man. To them the differences were obvious and the boundaries clear. The world was split between communists and the rest and in them no good was to be found. It was just such beliefs which many of the opponents of various anti-communist measures saw as posing a fundamental threat to civil liberties. It was not hard for the category 'communist' to become all those who are not like us, particularly when, as Eric Campbell of the New Guard made clear, many anti-communists had very little idea what it was that communists believed anyway, except that, whatever it was, it was a threat to the social order. The fears of many intellectuals that they would be easy targets in the climate of general suspicion created by such legislation were, as it turned out, quite justified. ASIO files of the period reveal that a close watch was kept on many intellectuals and writers who were suspected of communist sympathies, whether or not they were ever members of the Communist Party.[44]

The mechanisms with which the society responds to perceived threats mirror the psychological mechanisms individuals use to deal with their own vulnerability to threat. Psychological terms like 'paranoid' and 'hysterical' have been regularly applied to anti-communism, both by its opponents, in an attempt to dismiss it, and by observers. Such terms are part of the everyday vocabulary of the modern world and, while many who use them would disavow Freud, they draw on psychoanalytic understandings. 'Hysterical' generally means that a response is out of proportion and so out of control; its use recognises the irrational at work. The everyday use of 'paranoid' refers not just to the presence of the irrational but to the content of the irrational belief in an unwarranted conviction of threat and persecution. It recognises that there is a psychological component in the readiness with which people perceive threats in the external world, although it implies that those too quick off the mark are out of touch with reality. Of course this is not always the case. Those less aware of the aggressive impulses in themselves may be less responsive to them in others and so fail to act in time in the face of real threats. The misjudgement so many made in the 1930s of the threat posed by Hitler was fresh in people's memories in the early 1950s, and the Western allies did not want to make the same mistake again. It is often difficult to tell, until after the event, just how realistic the perception of any particular threat was.

While some adults are more alert to threat than others, we have all, in our infancies, passed through a period when our psyche was organised primarily to defend itself against threat, and this remains a permanent possibility in our psychological experience. Melanie Klein is the psychoanalyst who gives the clearest account of this stage of psychological life, and she shows the deep link between the preoccupation with threat and the maintenance of hard, clear boundaries between what is good and what is bad in both the world and the self. In early infancy, says Klein, we have only very primitive means for organising experience, and understand the mother, the source of all our gratifications, as alternatively good and bountiful when she is present, and hateful and threatening when she is absent. We do not understand at this early stage that the good mother and the bad mother are one and the same person, and so hate and want to kill the bad mother with passionate intensity, while adoring the good mother equally passionately.[45] The contrast in so many traditional fairy tales between the ugly wicked witch or stepmother and the beautiful, good mother or fairy godmother draws on this early split experience of the mother, as does the difference between the Virgin Mary and the whore in some Christian belief.

This splitting of the world is also a splitting of the self in which bad, hostile or unacceptable parts of the self are projected onto objects in the external world where they can be punished. The gain is that the self can maintain the illusion that it is good and pure and that the sources of danger are all external; the loss is an increased sense of threat and persecution as one's own projected aggression returns to haunt one. Projection is clearly seen in racism, where the characteristics attributed to the racial outgroup, like rampant sexuality, inordinate avarice, or wanton sloth, are just those which the dominant group most vehemently denies in itself. Klein calls this the paranoid schizoid position, emphasising its two interdependent characteristics – the splitting of the world between good and bad and the experience of the bad as persecutory.

When the child does realise that the good and the bad mother are one and the same person, it enters into a more complex emotional and psychological position, which Klein calls the depressive. No longer can the bad mother be hated and her death wished for, for she is the source of nourishment and pleasure as well as of anger and frustration. To harm the bad mother will also harm the good. In this realisation the possibility of paradise is lost, along with the possibility of innocence. The child must start to own its emotions, to recognise itself as a source of anger and hate and to see the consequences of its own destructive wishes. Guilt becomes possible and the child begins to confront the complexities and ambiguities of human experience, the intermingling of pleasure and pain, joy and suffering, the inevitability of loss, and the ambivalence which accompanies all human experience.[46]

Whatever one thinks of Klein's theory as an account of infantile emotional development, the two psychological positions she characterises are powerful tools for understanding adult emotional life. She describes them as positions, not phases or stages, thus emphasising that although one passes through them, they remain permanent possibilities in the adult psyche. It is always possible to regress to the paranoid schizoid position, and it is particularly possible when one is experiencing threatening situations in adult life. Then, the desire to understand the perpetrators of the threat as all bad can be overwhelming; the effort of keeping their humanity in focus impossible. In war, when both sides have projected a wholly hateful and destructive enemy, paranoid phantasies match and the perpetrator of the threat really is to be feared for one will be treated by the enemy as wholly hateful and destructive and killed.

Its central concern with the management of aggression gives much in politics an affinity with paranoia; there are times, however, when paranoid political beliefs capture the allegiance of large numbers of people and come to dominate the politics of a collectivity. There is a long history of such belief systems and they have a remarkable similarity.[47] The American political historian Richard Hofstadter argues that the anti-communism of the United States in the 1950s was the heir to a series of beliefs in powerful conspirators for evil in American politics: Jesuits, Freemasons, international capitalists and international Jews. The belief system stayed essentially the same, only the identity of the enemy changed.[48] The central image of the paranoid style, as Hofstadter describes it, is of a vast, sinister conspiracy to undermine and destroy a way of life. The enemy has access to an especially effective source of power, so that even if their numbers are small the danger is not, and is so absolutely evil that no compromise is possible. Ordinary political processes cannot deal with this enemy; thus extraordinary measures are needed and needed urgently, for time is fast running out.

There are many obvious similarities between the political style Hofstadter describes and Australian anti-communism – particularly in the centre-piece of a worldwide conspiracy emanating from the Soviet Union, in the idea of a fundamental threat to a way of life, and in the belief that the communists had special powers and hence extraordinary measures were needed to deal with them. But there are differences too. Australian anti-communism was never as lurid as its American counterpart and it lacked the religious undercurrent. In terms of the two central features of Klein's paranoid schizoid position, preoccupation with threat and persecution, and preoccupation with splitting, American anti-communism seemed more preoccupied with the elaboration of the threat than Australian anti-communism, which was more concerned with the maintenance of society's boundaries. In Australian anti-communist rhetoric, communists were presented as foreign or alien far more often than evil; as threats to the social order rather than purveyors of sin. Our anti-communism had a parochialism compared with America's cosmic battles. Where the paranoid politics of American anti-communism was shaped by the dark symbolism of a Manichaean religious world view, in Australia it was shaped by the society's continuing preoccupation with the maintenance of its borders against outsiders and foreign influences.

In their attempt to rid society of conflict and disorder by ridding it of communists, anti-communists were re-enacting the ancient ritual of the scapegoat, in which collective beliefs and social cohesion are affirmed above the principles of social division.[49] Just as the psychological mechanism of projection rids the self of its disturbing, hostile, unwanted parts, so the ritual of the scapegoat banishes from society those who come to symbolise society's irreconcilable conflicts and insoluble problems. The paranoid style described by Hofstadter is a style for the construction of a scapegoat, that is for the construction of a group which can be seen as the categorical cause of social disorder. Members of such a group are marked with Original Sin and so branded before they act. Once singled out they can be treated as strangers and enemies, driven out of the normal privileges and comforts of social membership, in extreme cases tortured and killed. They are denied their complexity and humanity and in a division of the world between good and bad are all bad. Communists' belief in a fundamental conflict at the heart of capitalist society made them particularly appropriate as symbols of conflict and disorder and their argument that society is irreconcilably divided between capital and labour was met by banishing them.

A FRAUDULENT DOCUMENT

FACED WITH the apparent contradiction between Menzies' anti-communism and his belief in civil liberties, left-wing historians have generally seen the anti-communist Menzies as the real Menzies and the expounder of civil liberties as a hypocrite, or at least a cynical political opportunist. Such confident moral judgements assume a unified political actor; but people are more contradictory and much less unified than moral discourse, with its concepts of integrity, honesty and consistency, urges us to be. This contradictoriness is a fundamental tenet of psychoanalysis, which sees the human subject as divided. In a different way it is also fundamental to much of the recent work on ideology and culture which sees ideologies as providing people with positions from which to speak, and which draws attention to the way people will say, think and feel different things in different positions.

We can look at the language of a politician in two ways. We can see it in terms of ideology – of the available public forms of discourse for talking about the distribution of social and political power, for justifying certain distributions of power and arguing against others. That is, we can look at the language of a politician in terms of the public ideology or discourse in which it is an event. So we can look at things like the history of the ideological tradition on which the language draws, the history of particular images and arguments; and we can look at the underlying structures of discourse which shape the way this history is patterned. The other way we can look at a politician's language is as the language of this particular politician. Every speaker will distinctively shape the images and arguments of the language they are using. It is as if different elements of a particular ideological position light up for different speakers and are in turn lit up by them for their audience. Certain elements in the ideology resonate with their own social and psychological preoccupations more than others, and in the particular cast they give it we see individuals shaping the public forms according to their own personal significance. In his brilliant essay on ideology, the anthropologist Clifford Geertz asks how ideology transforms private sentiment and experience into public forms.[50] Looked at from the perspective of the individual, this question becomes: how do individuals invest private meanings and significances into the publicly available ideologies of their society? Of particular politicians we can ask, how are they able to make the ideologies of their time real enough for themselves to make them real for others? How are they able to care enough about them to be able to operate them effectively? What are the particular arguments and images that hook them in? And why these rather than others?

A politician's language can be thought of as facing two ways: outwards to the audience to be wooed through the skilful manipulation of shared ideological forms; inwards to the politician's own private emotional and psychological experience. Much of the recent work on ideology as a form of representation has increased our understanding of the public face of this language, showing the way politicians' language is shaped by the general public discourses in which they participate, how once a person takes up a position in a particular ideological formation certain feelings, ideas and ways of seeing seem to follow naturally. But when we look closely at particular speakers, we see that what follows naturally varies, however slightly, from one political subject to the next. In this interplay between cultural forms and the individuals who use and remake them, cultural forms displace individuals as sources of cultural meaning, even as individuals strive to make meaningful if temporary unities out of their experience of themselves and their world.

Menzies took longer to be convinced of the need to ban the Communist Party than many of his colleagues. Once convinced, however, he was quickly able to reorient his arguments towards the urgent need to rid society of 'this alien and foreign pest'.[51] He drew, as did his colleagues, on the anti-communist ideology already established in Australia. This ideology shared in the general preoccupation of pre-war Australia with keeping foreign, impure and corrupting influences out of the country, whether they were the darker skinned people of Asia, dangerous foreign pests and diseases, seditious literature or communist agitators. The anti-communist discourse which Menzies took up after his decision to ban the Communist Party was a public discourse shaped to maintain social harmony and order by isolating and expelling threats to the social order. In taking it up, however, Menzies gave it a distinctive shape. Exploring this we are drawn deep into Menzies' own view of social order and the sorts of threats he most needed to keep at bay.

Anti-communist ideology ascribed a number of characteristics to communists: they were powerful, wicked, cunning, conspiratorial, atheistic, materialist, destructive, full of hate, bitter, envious; and all these characteristics accorded with some aspects of communists' behaviour and beliefs. The ideology offered a choice to its users as to the particular characteristics they might take up and elaborate in their campaign against the communists; different aspects of the ideology could light up for different people. For fellow Liberal minister Percy Spender, for example, speaking in the Second Reading Debate, it was the communists' tightly organised conspiracy, a conspiracy which became quite fantastic in his elaboration. Spender rejected Chifley's argument that there were already sufficient powers on the statute book to deal with treasonable acts:

> Is that so? If the right honourable gentleman has any understanding of the nature of the Communist

conspiracy he knows very well that the Communists carefully avoid criminal acts by individual Communists. Each Communist carefully fits into the Communist mosaic. Each of them can commit an act with which he or she cannot be criminally charged, but in combination all such acts constitute a conspiracy by the Communists to carry out, by whatever means they have at their disposal, the final Communist objective of gaining control of this country by non-parliamentary, revolutionary or fraudulent means.[52]

In his autobiography Spender makes almost no mention of the campaign against the communists after the 1949 election when he was a member of Cabinet; the fight against communism was not something that invited comment when he looked back on his political career.[53] Yet the vividness of his image of the mosaic conspiracy suggests that he was passionate at the time. For the Roman Catholic Labor members, it was the communists' atheism and their attack on religion which drew them in.

For me, reading Menzies' Second Reading speech for what is distinctive in his anti-communism, the theme that stands out is the communists' duplicity. While he alludes to the destructive intentions of communists, far less imaginative effort goes into elaborating this destructiveness than into elaborating the cunning fraudulent methods the communists use to pursue their aims. It is the means more than the end which seem to capture Menzies' imagination in this speech – the way destructive designs are cunningly hidden behind a respectable facade and the problems this raises for those trying to combat them.[54]

If ever there has been a fraudulent document, he says, it is the constitution of the Communist Party of Australia.

It is, on the face of it, fraudulent, because it piously claims that the party is a firm supporter of the United Nations, that it believes in world peace, and that it does not aim at establishing a totalitarian State. It even professes to adopt the democratic method, because it talks about the necessity for winning a majority of the Australian people. Such a fraudulent affair I have rarely looked at. It is a case of 'look like the innocent flower but be the serpent under it'. If we look for the serpent under it, we shall find it at once. The whole thing is so inconsistent with the beliefs of Russian communism that I felt rather thankful to find that the Australian Communist, forgetting for the moment this air of respectability, put himself, to use his own words, 'into line with the great teachings of Marx, Engels, Lenin and Stalin'.[55]

Menzies then develops his case against the Australian communists by discussing Stalin's *The Foundations of Leninism* at some length, citing Stalin's advocacy of a revolutionary vanguard and the need for the revolution in one country to be supported by revolutions in other countries, and stressing his commitment to violent revolution. 'Let no one be woolly-minded about this matter. When Stalin talks about revolutionary power based on violence, he means exactly what he says.'[56] In these lectures, says Menzies, Stalin gives us a sidelight on fraud. He has stated:

'The revolutionary will accept a reform in order to use it as a means wherewith to link legal work with illegal work, in order to use it as a screen behind which his illegal activities for the revolutionary preparation of the masses for the overthrow of the bourgeoisie may be intensified.'

> Does that not ring a bell in the minds of Australians? Have they not seen, time after time, the Australian Communist with all this wicked scheming in his mind, getting alongside people, and claiming the merit for some reform, and the credit for some wage increase or some advance, because, as his leader has said, it is necessary to link the legal with the illegal so that the fraud may be all the more successful. Such quotations as I have given may be multiplied.[57]

Similarly, Menzies sees the duplicity of the communists displayed in the way they are able to draw innocent people into serving their ends:

> The real and active Communists in Australia present us with our immediate problem – not the woolly headed dupes, not the people who are pushed to the front in order to present a respectable appearance, but the real and active Communists... Nothing nauseates me more than to discover the skill with which these Communists can put into their vanguard some deluded Minister of the Christian religion.[58]

The union movement is a favoured site for such deception:

> Surely it must be clear to all honourable members that the more skilfully the Communist in a trade union, carrying out the Communist tactics to which I have just referred, plays his cards for office and power, the more likely he is to delude many of his fellow trade unionists into voting for him. Indeed, that kind of delusion is his business.[59]

The picture of the Australian working class which emerges from Menzies' depiction of the cunning communist is not flattering; although maintaining their innocence, it sees them as easily led and easily deceived by masters of clever words. Menzies quotes from a pamphlet by Lance Sharkey, a prominent communist who was jailed by the Chifley government in 1949 for sedition. The Communist Party was attempting to wrest the control of the union movement from the ALP and Sharkey was urging members to struggle against reformism in the union movement; in this the shop committee's role was to prepare and mobilise the workers for strike action: 'In a revolutionary situation,' writes Sharkey, 'the Shop Committee would be one of the chief instruments for drawing the whole of the working class into the fight, into the street, and the general revolutionary struggle.' Of this Menzies says:

> he refers to that apparently innocent body, the shop committee. Again he is uncommonly frank, so frank indeed that it is a pity that some of the fools who are deluded by these people should not know what they really stand for. He sees the shop committee as a weapon for dastardly Communist designs... Let us understand that all those things, so good in their fashion, so capable of being well-used, are seized upon by the Communist, if he is in the right position, to use them as a means of engineering his own ends.[60]

One final quote to illustrate Menzies' preoccupation with the theme of the communists' duplicity and fraudulent methods. Replying to the argument that to ban the Communist Party will merely drive it underground, Menzies says:

> In the light of what we know of the international and domestic activities of communism, that argument is not to be taken seriously. Some of the deeds of the Communists see the daylight, but their planning is done by stealth and in secrecy. In short, they are underground already. One thing that we can be certain about, and that I am grateful for, is that once the taint of illegality is placed on this organisation of conspiracy its capacity to delude well-meaning people into providing it with a respectable 'front' will be sensibly diminished.[61]

It is the communists' fraudulent and cunning methods which justify the extraordinary legislative measures taken against them, such as the legislation's retrospectivity. Otherwise, when the Bill is passed, 'there will be no party members or officers to be affected by it', and the government would look a fool.

I began my work on this speech of Menzies with the record in the *Commonwealth Parliamentary Debates*. The theme that stood out in the speech as recorded there was the communists' skilful duplicity, their fraudulent masking of their wicked designs behind respectable façades. To my reading this seemed to be the theme which carried the personal significance with which Menzies invested anti-communism. I found confirmation of this in Menzies' papers at the National Library. These papers include Menzies' draft for the speech as well as the copy from which he actually spoke, marked 'Reading Notes' and set out in tabular form, with capitals, underlining and the red ribbon on the typewriter all used to guide pause and emphasis in delivery.[62] This was an important speech for Menzies and he had put a great deal of work into the preparation for it.

Comparing the report in the *CPD* with the draft, the theme of duplicity is much less marked in the draft than in the speech Menzies actually made. For example, in the draft the Constitution of the CPA is dismissed with one sentence – 'It is on the face of it a fraudulent document.' The elaboration of the substance of the fraud and the quotation from Lady Macbeth – 'look like the innocent flower, but be the serpent under it' – have been added during delivery; so has the description of the Australian communist getting alongside people to claim merit for some reform or wage increase in order to link the legal with the illegal, the comment about the deluded minster of religion, and a couple of the other references to the communists as duplicitous.

Although the theme of the communists' fraudulence is present in the draft, it is far stronger in the speech Menzies actually delivered. Menzies preferred not to read his speeches, but to deliver them to his audience, bringing the themes and arguments to life at the time of speaking. The copy labelled 'Reading Notes', which he used in the House, has pencilled notes at the points where some of the most significant divergences occur between the draft and the speech delivered – 'look like the innocent flower, but be the serpent under it' is pencilled in beside the paragraph on the constitution of the CPA, and 'Christianity is the greatest minority in history, but it recognises the State – "render to Caesar"' at the point at which he invokes the deluded minister of the Christian religion. These reading notes seemed to confirm my initial interpretation – that the theme of communist duplicity was indeed of particular significance for Menzies. When he came to deliver his speech before the House, this was the theme which he worked up to give it urgency and conviction. Here, in the communists' duplicity, was the hook which drew Menzies into anti-communist ideology; here was the kernel of personal resonance which he used to reorient his argument from a firm commitment to civil liberties to a determination to ban the Communist Party.

Why should this theme resonate for Menzies? An obvious interpretation will immediately present itself to those schooled in the cynical view of Menzies as himself a skilful manipulator of words, who was able to fool a gullible Australian public into believing in him, and who had little real respect for ordinary Australians. The communists, also clever with words and skilful manipulators, would thus carry for him an uncomfortable reminder of his own political chicanery. More subtly, it can be argued that the communists' duplicity was perhaps an uncomfortable reminder to Menzies of the inherent duplicity in all political language in the mouth of an ambitious politician who furthers his own career by appearing to be other than he really is – an ordinary person who understands other ordinary people, 'a singularly plain Australian' as Menzies once described himself, when, in the scope of his ambitions, he was anything but ordinary and plain.[63]

JOHN STUART MILL AND LADY MACBETH

JOHN STUART Mill and Lady Macbeth can be taken to represent the two poles of Menzies' political imagination: the one a founder of liberal thought to which he claimed to be an heir; the other a woman who urged her husband on to a murderous assault on the social order. Exploring these two poles illuminates the ambivalent commitment to civil liberties revealed in Menzies' anti-communism, as well as his understanding of legitimate and illegitimate social conflict.

In the same series as 'The Forgotten People', Menzies made a number of broadcasts on President Roosevelt's Four

Freedoms – freedom of speech and expression, freedom of worship, freedom from want, and freedom from fear. The first two broadcasts, on freedom of speech and expression, contain an elaboration of his understanding of civil liberties in which he makes copious use of John Stuart Mill while systematically distorting his central arguments.[64]

Menzies begins by stressing the unnaturalness of civil liberties: 'the whole essence of freedom is that it is freedom for others as well as for ourselves'; 'most of us have no instinct at all to preserve the right of the other fellow to think what he likes about our beliefs and say what he likes about our opinions'. Still smarting from the public criticism which preceded his resignation as Prime Minister in 1941, Menzies recalls his own experience:

> As you probably know, I am one who has in recent years had a severe battering from many newspapers, but I am still shocked to think that intelligent men, in what they believe to be a free country, can deny to the newspapers or to critics of any degree the right to batter at people or policies which they dislike or of whom they disapprove.

Metaphors of physical combat run through the broadcast: '... if truth is to emerge and in the long run be triumphant, the process of free debate – the untrammelled clash of opinion – must go on.' Menzies does not represent freedom of speech as freedom to say what one thinks, but as freedom to attack and batter the views of others and to defend one's own.

From John Stuart Mill's *Essay on Liberty* Menzies quotes passages which deploy quite different imagery in their defence of personal liberty.

> There is a limit to the legitimate interference of collective opinion with individual independence:

> and to find that limit, and maintain it against encroachment, is as indispensable to a good condition of human affairs as protection against political despotism.

and,

> As the tendency of all changes taking place in the world is to strengthen society and diminish the power of the individual, this encroachment is not one of the evils which tend spontaneously to disappear, but, on the contrary, to grow more and more formidable.

Mill's imagery in these passages is of a private space which must be protected, of boundaries which must be maintained against encroachment. For Mill, freedom is not freedom to attack but freedom to be left alone. Even when their positions seem closest, when Mill is arguing for the importance of freedom of speech to the establishment of truth, Menzies transforms Mill's argument, that only if every opinion is open to refutation can we assume its truth, into an argument for the necessity of conflict if the truth is to emerge. He quotes Mill:

> 'Complete liberty of contradicting and disproving our opinion is the very condition which justifies us in assuming its truth for purposes of action; and on no other terms can a being with human faculties have any rational assurance of being right.'
>
> In other words [says Menzies], it is a poorly founded and weakly held belief that cannot resist the onset of another man's critical mind.

The image of the self which underlies these passages from Mill is quite different from that which underlies Menzies' arguments. For Menzies, the self is a well-formed fortress, its boundaries strong enough to be battered. The freedom Menzies wants is the freedom for such confident little battlers to compete, to test their strength against each other in the public arena, and to win or lose. Menzies is not interested in the processes by which either opinions or selves are formed in the first place, only in their fate in battle and in the appropriate ways of dealing with defeat. For him opinions are already formed attributes of the self, part of what gives the self its public character, to be wielded as weapons in the establishment and defence of that position and character. In Menzies, too, the self's attention is always outwards, from its boundaries, never inwards, to the processes of the inner world.

In Mill, the self is more tenuous – a space rather than a fortress; it fears being taken over by others and wants the freedom just to be in its own way. Mill's arguments for civil liberties are predicated on his argument for the sovereignty of individuals against the despotism of both the state and custom, so that they may pursue their own mental, moral, aesthetic and spiritual development in their own way: 'There is no reason that all human existence should be constructed on some one or some small number of patterns. If a person possesses any tolerable amount of common sense and experience, his own mode of laying out his existance is the best, not because it is the best in itself, but because it is his own mode.'[65] Mill is interested in individuals' cultivation of themselves, the process whereby the self, or the individual, develops towards its potential. The self is not seen as already formed, but in a process of becoming, still open to differences, ambiguity and contradiction, and with little or no interest in testing itself and its certainties through public conflict. These certainties are not attributes of the public self, of use only in so far as they establish the public character, but are related to deeper and more private quests. Freedom of speech and thought can allow people to think different things; opposing views don't have to fight it out; people can remain confused, uncertain as to the answers, still searching and exploring.

The contrasting imagery of self underlying Mill's and Menzies' defence of freedom of expression reveals the intrinsic limitation of Menzies' commitment to civil liberties. Menzies justifies civil liberties not in terms of the benefits they bring to individuals but in terms of the benefits they bring to the social whole. Civil liberties are thus not intrinsic to his conception of the self as they are for Mill, but are more like the rules governing dealings between already well-formed individuals, who are conceived of as mainly intent on competition with each other and, more primitively, as preoccupied with externalising conflict and warding off threat. When the threat becomes too great, only a short step is needed to argue for the suspension of the rules, or for the source of the threat to be ejected from the game. That is, only a short step is needed to the preoccupation with the distinction between them and us and to the authoritarian paranoid mode. This is much harder to reach from Mill's view of civil liberties. Not only is the self far less invested in competition, and so not already on battle alert, but civil liberties, some area of freedom, is necessary for the very formation of the self; without it the self will suffocate and die.

In this broadcast Menzies justifies difference and social conflict as serving the common good. This is the basic argument bourgeois liberalism used to justify the social benefits of both market capitalism and liberal democracy. Certain types of aggression are seen as creative rather than destructive and thus are socially sanctioned. But aggression is still aggression, and its destructive potential is never far away. Towards the end of the broadcast Menzies alludes to a different form of aggression, and to the temptation of public men to silence their opponents.

> I speak as one with some practical – and occasionally painful – experience, when I say that the arrow of the critic is never pleasant and is sometimes poisoned. Much criticism is acutely partisan or actually unjust. But every man engaged in public affairs must sustain it with a good courage and a cheerful heart. He may, if he can, confute his critic, but he must not suppress him. Power is apt to produce a kind of drunkenness, and it needs the cold douche of the critic to correct it.

Menzies was not always so supportive of critics' freedoms. In 1937 he threw Parliament into an uproar by arguing against parliamentary privilege for remarks about other members of Parliament. Parliamentarians should not be free to insult each other publicly and so 'snatch people's reputations away from them', he said.[66] The reputation snatched away and the critic's poisoned arrow suggest a different sort of public conflict from fortress-like selves giving each other as good as they get. In the course of the broadcast the focus of Menzies' discussion of freedom of speech shifts from the clash of opinions to the much narrower problem of critics' attacks on public men. This is a long way from Mill's argument that a received truth must not be protected from refutation if we are to be confident in believing it. The essay ends on a note of resolution as Menzies invokes an idealised England risen above the temptations with which lesser mortals must still struggle. 'Of all the countries I have visited, England is the one where freedom of thought and expression is best understood. And that fact has given to the English people a wide tolerance of opinion and a quiet wisdom of understanding which we have yet to achieve.'

The shift from the critic's battering to his poisoned arrow hints at two different forms of attack and two different forms of conflict – one open and legitimate, the other sinister, covert and unfair. It also hints at selves who are far more vulnerable than is suggested by Menzies' confident claim to be shocked by those who would deny the newspapers their right to criticise. The difference between these two forms of aggression is made much more explicit in a later broadcast from the same series, 'Hatred as an Instrument of War Policy', in which Menzies discusses the emotions one should feel towards a war-time enemy.[67] There is manly, full-blooded aggression which is appropriate in war, and there is hatred: 'It is conceded the world over that the Australian soldier is a good fighter. But I have never heard it suggested that he was a good or persistent hater.'

The broadcast was prompted by anti-Japanese propaganda which incited Australians to despise the Japanese. Apart from the foolishness of despising, and hence underestimating, such a skilful and resourceful enemy, Menzies rejects the belief 'that the cultivation of the spirit of hatred among our own people is a proper instrument of war policy'. Hatred, he argues, must not become a 'chronic state of mind'. 'I think it was Napoleon who was credited with saying that "hatred is the mark of a small man". And if that epigram referred to the continuous and settled hatred, not of the evil in human beings, but of human beings themselves, then it was unquestionably true.'

As in the earlier broadcast Menzies looks to England for guidance and recounts a conversation with Winston Churchill in which Churchill said, 'In war, fury; in defeat, defiance; in victory, magnanimity; and in peace, good will'. Menzies comments:

> Don't you think that is a fine doctrine? And note the language. He didn't say, 'In war, cold and calculated and cultivated hatred'; he said, 'in war, fury'. There is nothing artificial about fury, and least of all about the honest fury of an outraged citizen who is determined to defend himself and his home and his beliefs from barbarian attacks.

Menzies variously describes hatred as 'deepseated and enduring', 'chronic' and 'persistent'; it is 'cold, evil and repulsive', compared with 'honest and brave indignation'. He concludes, we 'should refuse to take the honest and natural and passing passions of the human heart and degrade them into bitter and sinister policy'. The quality which most distinguishes hatred from anger for Menzies is hatred's persistence; where anger is rash and impulsive, an emotion that sweeps over one and gives strength, courage and the capacity to risk one's life and to kill, hatred is a fixed characteristic of the person, a disposition rather than an emotion.

The hating person does not act on sudden impulse but on a deeply nursed sense of grievance. The Chicago psychoanalyst James Alexander argues that it is bitterness that turns anger to hatred: 'As a mordant fixes a dye in the fabric of the textile, so does bitterness fix hostile aggression'.[68] In modern, open societies bitterness is a powerful political emotion, associated particularly with the pain inflicted on people by unequal distributions of power, status, wealth and life chances, and motivating people to challenge prevailing social and economic arrangements. It is given a particular force in capitalist liberal democracies by the tensions between the ideals of legal and political equality and of equality of economic opportunity, and the realities of many people's life experiences. Bitterness is associated with a burning sense of unfairness or injustice; a response to the narcissistic wounds of inequality, it refuses to accept those wounds as inevitable characteristics of the self but blames external circumstances. The defenders of inequality want, instead, to see the cause of inequality in the inherent defects of the less successful: they are too lazy, too unintelligent, or too dependent to have prospered by their own efforts. As a final resort they are blamed for bearing the disfiguring emotions caused by their social circumstances and accused of being motivated by envy, spite and malice. This is the familiar ideological ploy of blaming the victim, in which attention is deflected from the injustices of society to the defects of those who talk about and suffer from them. As well as serving obvious ideological purposes, this attribution of illegitimate aggression to those who challenge the status quo can serve psychological purposes for those who compete in the main arenas of power.

These broadcasts on freedom of speech and expression and on the role of hatred in war give us a picture of the way Menzies distinguished between legitimate and illegitimate social conflict. In legitimate social conflict well-formed selves compete within a well-understood and accepted framework of rules and conventions. They give their all during the contest but shake hands when the winner is clear and retire to fight another day, licking some surface wounds perhaps, but bearing no deep hurts and nursing no desire for revenge. In illegitimate conflict people filled with chronic and bitter hatred attack their enemies furtively, with poisoned arrows and malicious, cowardly attacks from behind.

Menzies' view of legitimate conflict and the proper way to handle aggression and defeat is deeply embedded in Australia's British-derived political and legal institutions.

Both Parliament and the courtroom are set up as arenas of ritualised conflict between male protagonists who fight it out verbally within complex systems of rules, conventions and procedures, framed by the bourgeois ideals of legal and political equality. (Reminiscing about the Bar in his autobiography *Afternoon Light*, Menzies describes it as 'the fierce but bloodless battle between "learned friends"'.[69]) Such ritualised conflict between men is seen as the appropriate way of both expressing and resolving social and political conflict. Competitive sport similarly enshrines this idealised pattern of conflict. As participants or supporters, people learn and reflect on the emotional strategies necessary for releasing aggression's creative energy, while ensuring it does not get out of bounds and damage either the self or the other players. In sport, though, the playing field is generally level.

Menzies was deeply committed to this way of experiencing and resolving public conflict. Parliament and the Bar were his chosen areas of work, and watching cricket was his chief and most public form of relaxation. Menzies valorised the manly virtues – ambition, competitiveness, assertiveness, independence – but only when they were expressed and contained in ritual conflict. What happens when the structures containing aggressive, competitive, ambitious men break down? What happens when the rage and fury do not pass at the end of the day but stay on, and turn to hatred? And what of the feelings of those outside the ring, of those without the money, the qualifications, the opportunities or the right to fight for their interests? For despite the bourgeois ideals of political and legal equality, economic, racial and gender inequalities distort the playing field and interests do not get an equal chance. As well as having to bear the disfiguring emotions caused by their own social circumstances, those outside can easily become the repositories of the illegitimate emotions of those inside the ring.

The manly aggression of competition throws its own shadow in the temptation to succumb to the more destructive forms of aggression – the cold passions of envy, bitterness, malice, vindictiveness and revenge. Much of the fascination of politics as moral drama lies in watching competing men negotiate the line between legitimate and illegitimate aggression, in watching how they deal with the humiliating public defeats of political life, the feints and subterfuges they use to maintain the appropriate demeanour of sportsmanlike behaviour and the inevitable slippings of the mask. For the cold passions must be kept at bay, their harms and their claims denied and, if possible, projected onto others.

The shadow of illegitimate aggression cast by the codes governing the public behaviour of competing men can easily be laid over a map in which the cold passions have particular social locations. Of interest here is the social emotional map of those who hold power, rather than a map which accurately charts the social distribution of emotional propensities. The socially powerful attribute the cold passions to those excluded from the central arenas, along with the cunning, deceitful ploys of those unable to express their aggression in the legitimate arenas of open conflict. Here we see a link between Menzies' stress on the communists' duplicity and his more general orientation to aggression. Bearing the bitter, envious emotions of the excluded, the communists express their aggression duplicitously, hiding it behind soft words of peace and innocent-seeming actions.

When Menzies described the communists as underground already, operating by stealth and in secrecy, he seemed dimly to have recognised their role as bearers of repressed and denied aspects of both contemporary social existence and individual psychological reality: to have recognised them as scapegoats for the social divisions and injustices which the official ideology denied, and to recognise them as bearers of forbidden and denied desires. It is as if Menzies saw that communism was shaped by the exclusions of particular forms of social and psychological order, and so, like the unconscious itself, must use cunning and subterfuge to slip past the censor, masking its unpleasant truths behind apparently innocent façades.

Outside the arenas of legitimate male conflict will be the denied and disowned bitterness, envy and malice of the competitors – the under-side of their legitimate manly aggression, the hurts and resentments in defeat which do not pass at the end of the day but which must, nevertheless, be disowned. Outside, too, will be those unable or not allowed to compete – the poor and dispossessed and the communists who are their strident, militant voice, non-whites and women. Whether or not those outside are themselves subject to the cold passions, their powerlessness makes them easy conscripts in the internal psychological dramas of the powerful. And as in the darkness of the unconscious, there is a promiscuous intermingling in the outer darkness. Those peering from the well-lit and orderly arenas out at the spiteful, malicious, cunning faces of the excluded can easily mistake one for another; in defending the boundaries, one intruder can seem as threatening as another. Both racism and anti-communism are discourses of social cohesion in which the sharp division is between who is in and who is out, and the differences among those outside are of little interest. So, Tommy White, the Minister for Trade and Customs in the Lyons government, could slide between aliens, non-whites, criminals and communists without noticing the difference. And from the point of view of those denying the emotional consequences of social, economic and political inequality, there is little difference. Envy, bitterness, deceptiveness and cunning can be railed against as well in one bearer as in another.

While communists, women and non-whites are all excluded from legitimate public conflict, they all have different histories, and are excluded on different bases. Middle-class white men are middle class, white and men, and the dynamics of the oppositions middle and working class, white and non-white, male and female, are not the same. They are, however, all oppositions, and it is possible for experiences or emotions attached to one to slide very easily to the other. So the working class, the non-white and women can all be seen as passive or dependent in comparison with an assertive male independence; and they can all be seen as bearers of furtive, illegitimate aggression in comparison with the open conflict of powerful, male contestants. All are excluded from the circle of light, and so all may at times resort to cunning, subterfuge and illegal means. And all are likely to be damaged by social relations which exclude them from power and so to succumb to the bitterness and hatred which so often accompanies such damage. It does not matter for the purpose of this argument which is the generating opposition; the point is that whenever one of the oppositions comes into play it is very easy for it to draw energy and meaning from the other. So Menzies' anti-communism could draw energy both from the racism of white Australia and from the misogyny of the dominant culture.

Menzies was a successful member of a society in which power was unevenly distributed between men and women, and in which justifications of this unequal distribution of power, and denial of many of its consequences, were embedded in its dominant forms of thought. Menzies was able to recognise the strengths of women when they remained in their traditional social roles of wives and mothers, and it was one of his political achievements to recognise the political demands of women in the home; however, when women impinged on the public world of competing men, they threatened its precarious stability. It is hard to get at this aspect of Menzies' political imagination, but his responses to two of Shakespeare's women provide powerful clues.

The quotation from Lady Macbeth with which Menzies described the fraudulence of the Communist Party's constitution, 'look like the innocent flower, but be the serpent under it', is Lady Macbeth's advice to her husband as they prepare to welcome Duncan to their castle; their genial hospitality must cover their murderous intent. Menzies also quotes from *Macbeth* in the broadcast on freedom from want. Sounding his familiar warning against the debilitating effects of government paternalism, he reminds his audience, 'for we all know security is mortals' chiefest enemy'.[70] This very slight misquotation of Hecate's advice to the witches, as they prepare to meet Macbeth for the second time to make the prophecies which will lure him to his doom, indicates that he was quoting from memory. Again the theme is deception.

In 1935 on his first trip to England, as the ship steamed across the Great Australian Bight to Perth where Lyons and his wife were to join the party, Menzies recorded in his diary that he was reading *Macbeth*.[71] It was fitting reading for a man who was bridling his ambition before the obviously lesser talents of his Prime Minister. Curious, I wondered if the copy Menzies was reading then was in the library he left to Melbourne University. As well as numerous collected editions of Shakespeare, all published after 1935, the library contains some pocket editions, including a copy of *Macbeth* published by Dent in 1935. This may or may not have been the one he was reading on the ship, but it had been read and marked lightly in pencil, as was Menzies' habit with his reading. When I found the copy had been marked, I expected the marked passages to deal with the dangers of ambition; but I found otherwise. The wonderful insult, 'the devil damn thee black thou cream fac'd loon, where gottest thou that goose look' is underlined, as well as part of Macbeth's lament on hearing news of his wife's death, 'Life's but a walking shadow...' Nearly all the other marked passages refer to the treachery of language in the mouths of women.

In the scene where Banquo and Macbeth first meet the witches, Macbeth's 'Stay you imperfect speakers, tell me more', and Banquo's 'What, can the devil speak true?' are marked, together with Banquo's presentiment of doom hidden in the witches' words:

> And often times to win us to our harm,
> The instruments of darkness tell us truths,
> Win us with honest trifles, to betray's
> In deepest consequence.

Just like the duplicitous communists, the witches hide their dark intentions behind apparently innocent façades. Further on Lady Macbeth's exhortation to Macbeth to get on with the terrible deed is marked:

> ...yet I do fear thy nature.
> It is too full of the milk of human kindness
> To catch the nearest way...

as well as,

> Letting I dare not wait upon I would
> Like the poor cat in th' adage.

Also underlined is Hecate's advice to the witches on their further delusion of Macbeth, which Menzies uses in his lecture on freedom from want: 'And you all know security is mortal's chiefest enemy', and Macbeth's greetings to the witches, 'How now, you secret, black, and midnight hags.'

With its Scottish setting *Macbeth* was a play likely to appeal to Menzies, and its theme of ambition resonated with one of the major themes in his life. Picked out in Menzies' markings is a case for the defence of Macbeth. Ambition gives purpose and energy to a man's life, but unchecked it can lead to the sort of violence against the social order which Macbeth commits when he murders Duncan. It is women, first the witches and then Lady Macbeth, who excite and goad Macbeth's ambition beyond its proper bounds; it is they who lure him to deny his fundamental social and political obligations and so to become an enemy of his own society; it is they, playing on the very qualities in which his strength lies, who destroy him. The case for the defence is of a man deceived, duped by the false words of women and tempted beyond endurance.

Lady Macbeth seems to have had a prominent place in Menzies' imagination. Percy Spender's wife, Jean Spender, recounts the following experience from the early 1940s when Menzies' stocks as leader of the United Australia Party were low. Percy Spender was one of the cabinet members Menzies suspected of plotting against his leadership. Changing trains at Albury, Jean and Percy Spender found themselves queuing for coffee behind the Menzies. She recalls, 'the great man turned to me, looked down what seemed like the two feet or so between our heights, beetled his heavy eyebrows and declaimed, not too pleasantly, Give me the dagger, Lady Macbeth.'[72] When rivalry and treachery were in the air, it was to Lady Macbeth, rather than her husband, that his mind turned. Women were linked in Menzies' imagination with the illegitimate, covert forms of aggression he attributed to the communists. Praising Frank Packer, he wrote: 'I have heard him charged with being too tough or too rough in his treatment of people. My answer has always been, and still is, that all his faults are masculine; that he hits his opponents with a straight left; he does not stab them in the back... If he wounds he wounds from the front.'[73] (A related comment on Nehru, 'He uses words to conceal the direction of the blow', suggests that Asians too were linked to covert, deceitful aggression in Menzies' imagination.[74])

Discussing another of Shakespeare's women in the late 1920s at a lunch-time talk on *The Merchant of Venice,* Menzies made crystal clear the link between women and deception. He was a much-sought-after speaker at the time, and the talk is witty and light, with sufficient erudition to flatter the audience. He argued, against the received interpretation, that Portia's behaviour in the famous trial scene was far from admirable. Portia, he said, is characteristically regarded as representing the three things which we all expect from a woman – beauty, wisdom and wit; but we must add one more – dishonesty; when we combine wisdom, wit, beauty and dishonesty, then we invariably have a most attractive woman. In the trial scene, Menzies argued, Portia resorts to measures which do not come within the limits of truth and accuracy, to measures which are outside the rule of law. Portia, a female intruder into the male world of the courtroom, does not understand its rules and so threatens social order, deceptively masking the threat with her wit and beauty.[75]

Anti-communism is a rhetoric for the defence of social order. The values being defended are assumed and all the psychological energy goes into various means of warding off threat. The homes of the middle class, the island continent of Australia, the competitive public selves of legitimate political conflict, all are bounded units as much concerned to exclude as to include, nurture and create, their security depending to a large extent on the success with which their boundaries keep at bay both social and psychological threats. The danger is that when all the energy is in the defensive boundaries the protected centres will atrophy.

Menzies' ambivalent commitment to civil liberties has its origins in his understanding of the self. For Menzies the self was primarily public, invested in its competitively established public position rather than in the processes and satisfactions of the inner world. The dangers to freedom of thought and expression posed by his campaign against the Communist Party failed to move him because Menzies already knew what he thought. His opinions were attributes of his public self, fixed and subject to possible defeat in the public arena, but not themselves part of a continuing dialogue with either himself or others. The deeper, more rigorous individualism of John Stuart Mill remained a closed book to him as he justified individualism in terms of its social benefits rather than its intrinsic ends. This reflected the imaginative investment of his own self in the public rather than the private world.

II
PRIVATE LANGUAGE

ENGLAND

AN IMAGINED PLACE

To Wordsworth

Great Master, let us sit and learn of thee!
    Give us the sense of glory that was thine!
Show us the visions that we do not see,
    Of Nature's wonders, and of things Divine!
We hear the thunder rattling through the skies
    We see the lightning's fitful fancies play;
We hear the wild waves and their echoing cries,
    And we are thrilled, yet know not what they say!

But, thou, blest Spirit, in the storm didst see
    A visionary power, strong and clear;
And, while the black heavens shrieked aloud with glee,
    A call to dedication thou didst hear!
The very grass to thee had voice to speak,
    The humblest flower had strength to move thy heart!
Then teach us, guide us ere our faith grow weak,
    Show us the sunset ere its hues depart!
            R.G. Menzies, 1913[1]

AT THE end of 1910, when he was almost sixteen, Robert Menzies received, for the Ewen Memorial Prize for Bible Knowledge, Senior Division, at the Cairns Memorial Church, East Melbourne, a leather-bound copy of *The Poetical Works of Wordsworth*. This copy is in his library which he donated to his alma mater, the University of Melbourne. Displayed much as it was arranged in his home, his collection of English literature is headed by several presentation copies of the works of English poets. Such books were standard prizes and gifts to successful young people to take with them from their school years into the life ahead. The inscription in a second volume of Wordsworth, presented to Menzies in 1913, wishes him 'a successful career'.

The volume he received in 1910 has been read and many passages marked: well-known ones like the poem which begins 'My heart leaps up when I behold/ a rainbow in the sky', and 'Composed upon Westminster Bridge'; several passages suffused with longing to be one with a feminised nature; and two passages celebrating the poet's love of England.

> *I travelled among unknown men,*
>   *In lands beyond the sea;*
> *Nor England! did I know till then*
>   *What love I bore to thee.*

and

> *We must be free or die, who speak the tongue*
>   *That Shakespeare spake; the faith and morals hold*
> *Which Milton held. – In every thing we are sprung*
>   *Of Earth's first blood, have titles manifold.*

These markings are not surprising ones for an ambitious youth of sixteen, dutifully reading the books presented to him as guides to life and mastering the language that will be the instrument of his success.

Sixty years later, when he was Chancellor of the University of Melbourne, Menzies surprised members of an English Chair Committee by saying, 'I suppose no one reads Wordsworth these days', and launching into a recitation from the opening passage of Book One of the *Prelude*. He made two slight slips, but he kept the rhythm and the line pauses.[2] This was not the smattering of Wordsworth one would expect from a man of his age and education, the sort of poems marked in his schoolboy prize, but bespoke an interest in poetry beyond acquiring the standard furnishings of the mind of his time. Indeed, in a short essay in *Melbourne University Magazine* published in 1914 Menzies is dismissive of those who pride themselves in having at home an expensively bound copy of their Wordsworth or Tennyson, yet ignore the attempts of student poets 'to express thoughts a little higher than the everyday'.[3]

Menzies' poem 'To Wordsworth' was written when he was almost nineteen. It expresses a sense of exclusion from a source of knowledge and wisdom.

> *Great Master, let us sit and learn of thee!*
> *Give us the sense of glory that was thine!*
> *Show us the visions that we do not see,*
> *Of Nature's wonders and of things Divine!*

Nature does not speak to the poet as it once did to Wordsworth, and the poet pleads with Wordsworth to be an intermediary – to 'show us the visions that we do not see'.

> *We hear the thunder rattling through the skies*
> *We see the lightning's fitful fancies play;*
> *We hear the wild waves and their echoing cries,*
> *And we are thrilled, yet know not what they say!*

Nature here is a vehicle for emotions, the meaning of which remains unclear – we are thrilled by the thunder and the wild waves, yet we know not what they say. That Wordsworth, too, was striving after a world from which significance seemed to have departed is not noticed; he is deemed to be one with the world, 'a blest Spirit to whom the very grass had voice to speak'. Of the poems Menzies published in *Melbourne University Magazine*, 'To Wordsworth' is one of the better ones, its diction slightly less cliched and its rhythm slightly more convincing than most of the others. It manifests, however, the problem of which it speaks, of experience unconnected with a language able to render that experience convincingly. 'Wild waves', 'the very grass', 'the humblest flower', 'black heavens' – these are all vague, unspecific words, referring not to any real experience, but to the idea of an experience, not to any real landscape, but to an abstract, unexperienced Nature.

In the essay in which the young Menzies defends the efforts of student poets who 'strive a little higher than the everyday', he also pleads for Australian poetry and praises the poetry of Henry Kendall. Kendall's 'To a Mountain' he holds to be the 'most Wordsworthian of our local poetry exhibits, and Kendall our greatest poet', because 'he has trodden in solitude the wonderful places of our land, has trembled before the wild majesty of the hills'. He quotes some particularly portentous lines of Kendall about the awesomeness of a mountain, and ends the essay by extolling the virtues of being alone with Nature, 'inscrutable of yore but telling wondrous tales to those who will listen to her' and respond to 'the rolling ocean', 'the music of wind and wave', 'the foaming torrent and sweeping tide'. These cliched images of romantic nature betray not only Menzies' lack of poetic talent but the absence of any integrated experience of the Australian land, or sea for that matter. The flat land around Jeparit, where Menzies grew up, was a long way from majestic hills, rolling oceans and foaming torrents. Not it but an idealised romantic landscape mediated through English literature, poetry in particular, was nature to Menzies, and it was this imagined landscape which was imbued with those thoughts, 'a little higher than the everyday', which were poetry's proper object.

The structures here are familiar: they repeat in different ways both the sense of loss and exclusion which is at the heart of Romantic poetry, and the preoccupations of an adolescent on the edge of the adult life. They also repeat the familiar theme in Australia's colonial experience of the sense of exclusion from the metropolitan centre. The debilitating effect on Australian culture of the conviction that the source of meaning and authority lies elsewhere has been written about before, most eloquently by Arthur Phillips. Phillips discusses not just the psychological effects in his famous essay 'The Cultural Cringe', but also the difficulties for writers who must use a language which has been shaped by those who see not what their eyes see – 'the writer cannot be free who speaks the tongue that Shakespeare spoke', he says.[4] Australians' estrangement from the land has also been written about. Less pondered upon, however, have been the benefits the disconnection of language from experience may offer to those who embrace it. The history of Australia's relationship with Britain has made the creation of an independent Australian culture seem more problematic than Australia's continuing deference to Britain. The latter has seemed a natural continuity, easily explained by Australia's continuing economic and political dependence. I do not want to dispute such explanations but rather to raise the question of the psychological dynamics of this deference in people for whom Britain was an imaginary, not an experienced place.

Menzies' love of England is part of his public myth: his admirers have granted to him a particular affinity with the British people, while his critics have mocked him for what they see as an anachronistic, sentimental attachment. Unlike his contemporary, Richard Casey, Menzies did not visit England during his childhood nor receive part of his education there. He was forty when he first saw the white cliffs of Dover as a member of the Australian delegation to King George V's Silver Jubilee. In his formative years and the first part of his adult life his relationship with Britain was entirely imaginary. Reflecting in 1950 on what the British Commonwealth meant to him, Menzies begins with, 'To me it means... a cottage in the wheat lands of the North-West of the State of Victoria, with the Bible and Henry Drummond and Jerome K. Jerome and *The Scottish Chiefs* and Burns on the shelves.' The associations then immediately jump thirty years to glimpses of landscapes and people from his first trips to Britain: '... the cool green waters of the Coln as they glide past the church at Fairford; the long sweep of the Wye valley above Tintern, with a Wordsworth in my pocket... King George and Queen Mary coming to their Jubilee in Westminster Hall', and so on.[5] His first association with Britain was through books, creating an imagined relationship so strong that it could transform the weatherboard house in the small Mallee country town in which he spent his childhood into 'a cottage in the wheat lands'.

Menzies was uplifted rather than intimidated by this imaginary place; his relationship with Britain fits neither the cringe nor the strut, the two types of colonial personality Phillips described so well – the one deferentially self-deprecating, the other aggressively self-assertive. Nor is it the confident, erect passage which is Phillips's ideal; Britain matters too much to Menzies for this relationship of courteous equality to be an apt description. To understand what Britain, her people, her history, her landscape, her culture, and her language meant to Menzies is one of the tasks I have set myself in writing this book. Neither those who take it at face value as a deeply felt love for a real place, nor those who see it cynically as pompous posturing, seem to me to grasp the paradoxical nature of Menzies' relationship with Britain: the fulsome emptiness of his deep love for an imagined place, and the aggression and envy this deep love helps keep in place. Menzies' England thrills him, like the wild waves and their echoing cries in 'To Wordsworth', yet he knows not what it says. Thus he can, to some extent, deploy it for his own psychological needs and make it say what he pleases.

Menzies' England is early associated with 'the strivings to reach a little higher than the everyday'. This phrase neatly condenses two meanings which are closely connected for Menzies: the striving after spiritual meaning which is the young Menzies' intended referent of the phrase; and the striving of an ambitious young man to reach the centre of power. The everyday is both the petty causes and worries of material existence and the mundanity of life in the provinces. England, the centre of power and significance, can redeem them both.

Menzies kept a diary of his first trip to England in 1935. On the voyage he reflected on the superior qualities of the British race, comforting himself during boat drill with the observation that he was on a disciplined British ship, observing at various colonial ports the benefits of British civilisation as British colonial officers 'calmly go on their way giving to these people what obviously they could never give to themselves'.[6] Such reflections were rehearsals for the praise Menzies lavished on the political institutions, architecture, wisdom and landscape of England after his arrival. The sighting of the white cliffs of Dover set the tone:

> At last we are in England. Our journey to Mecca has ended, and our minds abandoned to those reflections which can so strangely (unless you remember our traditions and upbringing) move the

souls of those who go 'home' to a land they have never seen.[7]

But they had read about it. Menzies' diary of this first trip is remarkable for the rapturous sense of identification he felt as he visited the places lived in by the men whose books he had studied and whose lives he had read about. Three days after arriving he visited the Houses of Parliament.

> Enter the great hall of William Rufus, and find on the floor a brass plate marking where Warren Hastings stood his trial nearly 150 years ago. Stand beside it recapturing the great description by Macaulay and listening for echo of ringing tones of Burke's great denunciation. For the moment, almost imagine I am Hastings (*mens aequa a arduis*) until I remember that 'his person was small and emaciated' and realise I am not cast for the part.[8]

Three weeks later, after a day in Buckinghamshire he wrote:

> What a day! I have literally been in the presence of the Great Charter among the barons assembled at Runnymede; I have seen the very handwriting of the man whose sword and character and mind made England a free country; I have stood where stood many times the great John Hampden and have sat a while in the invisible presence of the greatest poet of liberty. How could any Englishman tear down the temple built by these great hands? The survival of a free Parliament in this land is not to be marvelled at. One realises that a Parliament for England is no mere result or adoption of a political theory (as it was on the Continent) but something grown from the very roots of the English life.[9]

Menzies felt no distance between the England he first visited and his earlier idealisations, no distance between himself and the great John Hampden, no awkwardness in Milton's presence, no sense of himself as different, other, strange, Australian, or even as a man from the mid-twentieth century. All was continuity of experience and easy identification.

For Menzies, England was a literary and historical landscape and he recognised immediately the ideal of a humanised landscape he had learned from English literature.

> Away we go (how I love these names) through Frampton Manseel and Sapperton back to Cirencester. There is nothing wild about the landscape, which indeed possesses a sort of 'civilised' beauty which is nevertheless a wonderful stimulant to the mind and spirit.[10]

His diary includes numerous poetic references. He quoted Wordsworth in his entry on King's College, Cambridge, and his pulse raced when he saw the sign 'To Granchester, to Coton'. 'So half a mile along the road we go "To Granchester, to Granchester" and enter the churchyard where, alas, the Church clock no longer stands at ten to three.'[11] Opposite this entry he has written several lines of Rupert Brooke's poem, concluding with 'Until the centuries blur and blur/ In Granchester, in Granchester'. Written in Berlin as Brooke remembered his childhood home, the poem yearningly recreates an absent place. Its easy blending of past and present fits well Menzies' straining after the sounds and sights and men long gone. Menzies' England was peopled with the men of the past and they had an almost palpable presence for him – Robert Walpole looked down on him from the wall of the Cabinet Room at 10 Downing Street,[12] he almost imagined he was Warren Hastings, he seemed to see John Hampden's disappearing plume, he wondered if the rafters of Westminster Hall still rang with the voices of Cromwell and Burke. At Gray's Inn Hall 'the great line of Benchers from Bacon to Birkenhead' looked down from the walls.[13]

Menzies drew on these early weeks in England in an address he made in July to the delegates to the Empire Parliamentary Association assembled in Westminster Hall. Charged with the duty of replying to Prime Minister Stanley Baldwin's welcome to the delegates, he had for once written out his speech so that he 'shall not collapse in the presence of the shades of Edmund Burke and Fox and Sheridan'.[14]

> No son of the race can stand, as I have had the privilege of standing, on the fields of Runnymede, on the drive of Great Hampden House, in Westminster Hall, whose rafters still ring (if sound be indestructible as the scientists tell us) with the voices of Cromwell, of Edmund Burke, of Stanley Baldwin, of the great lawyers whose courts for centuries opened out of this room, without realising with dramatic force that the growth of Parliament is in truth the growth of the British people; that self government is here no academic theory, but the dynamic power moving through 800 years of national history.[15]

The dominant metaphor informing Menzies' descriptions of English social and political institutions was Edmund Burke's image of the tree growing slowly from roots set deep in the stable, unchanging yet nurturing earth. Somewhat over-extended, it symbolises the strength and continuity of British parliamentary institutions.

> ... its roots were deeply set in the history and character of the British people. In those countries

where it had fallen a parliament was adopted as the embodiment of an attractive theory. As a fully grown tree it was carefully transplanted and watered and cared for. And at the first real blast of the storm it fell. It was not really rooted in the soil.[16]

Under firmer control, the same metaphor underlies reflections on the strength of English poetry.

I am today learning to understand, as I never understood before, the secret springs of English poetry and English thought and the getting of that wisdom which infuses the slow English character. The green and tranquil countryside sends forth from her soil the love of peace and of good humour and of contentment.[17]

In the diaries of this trip, as in the later discussions of England which draw on them, Menzies regularly used the metaphor of the tree to describe the relationship between the English past and present, from the strength of Parliament, to the 'quaint old customs' of the London vintners which survive because 'they have their roots in history',[18] to the villages of Gloucestershire which 'appear, like trees, to have grown out of the soil'.[19] As a central symbol of conservatism's representation of social and political change, the tree not only carries the idea that contemporary social and political arrangements are natural and therefore inevitable, but that they have evolved without conflict. An organic image, it makes almost impossible the depiction of struggle, defeat, injustice, oppression or radical social change, all of which require an image of society as made up of parts whose interests do not automatically coincide. It is also essentially a rural image, tied to an idealisation of the social relations of the English countryside.

Menzies' pleasure in the English countryside has been shared by generations of Australians seeing for the first time the green and pleasant land for which their education and reading had prepared them. Striking in Menzies, though, is his almost instant movement from the pleasures of recognition to the confident, knowledgeable voice of long acquaintance, and the absence of any sense of irredeemable difference which assails so many Australians on first visiting England. In early June, after he had been in England for two months, he visited a stately home in the North Riding of Yorkshire where a church spire had been erected to celebrate its owner's winning of the Derby. His diary records an authoritative disquisition on the harmonious 'compounding of the sacred and the secular' in the domestic life of the English country families, and on their notion of a good man, all written as if based on a lifetime of experience and observation.[20] There was nothing he saw which surprised or puzzled him, from which he felt excluded, or of which he disapproved, not even this erecting of a church steeple for a horse, with which not every simple Presbyterian would have been comfortable. There were, however, a few moments of disappointment: the cold mechanical tone of Anglican services, the Free Churches' intemperate embrace of politics;[21] and the smell of poverty in the streets of Edinburgh.[22] He did not dwell on this poverty, or reflect on its causes. To do so would have required the employment of ideas about British social and political history that could not be encompassed by the metaphor of the tree.

The political uses of this metaphor were integral to British conservative ideology of the day, with its attempt to construct the image of a unified nation in the face of labour's language of class conflict.[23] In this, Stanley Baldwin, who welcomed the parliamentary delegates to Westminster Hall, was a crucial figure. It is worth discussing Baldwin a little, because there are many similarities between his rhetoric and Menzies', as well as differences, which help illuminate the role Englishness played in Menzies' imagination.

Baldwin was Conservative Prime Minister of Britain in 1923, 1924-29 and 1935-37; he was also a powerful figure in Ramsay MacDonald's National Government of 1931-35. These were times of intense political unrest in Britain. Near universal suffrage had been introduced in 1918 and the Conservatives viewed the newly enfranchised masses with trepidation; they also feared the growing power and radical ideas in the labour movement. Would it be possible to hold back labour within the constitution? Baldwin reworked Conservative Party ideology to deal with labour as its main but legitimate foe. In this period Baldwin developed a new cultural identity for conservatism around commitment to constitutionalism and social harmony, and the idea that the Conservative Party was representative not of a class but of the whole people. And he presented his ideas in a popular idiom – something unprecedented for a Conservative prime minister. The central task was to develop the image of the Conservative Party as a party of nation not of class, and he did this through the idea of England. Baldwin presented the English constitution as the product of slow, organic growth which demonstrated the innate common sense and good nature of English people; ruptures in the evolution of parliamentary democracy and representative government were generally smoothed over. More convincing than his representation of English history were his detailed representations of rural England, in which Englishness and continuity were condensed in an invocation of the temporal rhythms of the natural world. England was the English countryside and its timeless ways, lifted out of history by the continuity of race.

Menzies' England had much in common with Baldwin's, and from the perspective of Australians for whom much of

English history is a romanticised blur, it can seem identical. But Menzies' England was even more harmonious than Baldwin's. Not even Baldwin could smooth over the social and political collapse of the 1640s, and he presented Cromwell as alien to English traditions. Menzies could be as excited by Cromwell 'whose sword and character and mind made England free' as by the ringing tones of Edmund Burke. There was an unreality about Menzies' construction of English history, and a corresponding thinness in his descriptions of the English landscape, which show up clearly when his prose is compared with Baldwin's. Shortly after his first trip to England, Menzies wrote a short portrait of Baldwin, which he later published in *Afternoon Light*.[24] He wrote of Baldwin's 'deep love of England', and his 'sympathetic understanding of the people and the countryside which has nurtured them'. Whenever possible, he wrote, Baldwin escaped from the cares of politics 'to the country with its beech and oak and elm, and the song of the lark at heaven's gate, and the slow smoke of wood fire mounting to the sky'. Menzies' evocation of England is general and conventional when compared with those of the man he is praising.

> The sounds of England, the tinkle of the hammer on the anvil in the country smithy, the corncrake on a dewy morning, the sound of the scythe against the whetstone, and the sight of a plough team coming over the brow of a hill... and above all, most subtle, most penetrating, most moving, the smell of wood smoke coming up in an autumn evening, or the smell of scutch fires.[25]

Menzies had little real experience of the English countryside on which to draw and none of the childhood experience which gives freshness and conviction to descriptions of the natural world. Lark, beech, elm and oak – perhaps Menzies could have identified them, perhaps not. These words stand less for real natural species than for a generalised idea of a nature which is loved and from which, like the nature evoked in the early poems, he feels excluded.

In 'The Forgotten People' Menzies, like Baldwin, was combating labour's language of class conflict with consensual symbols. As an Empire man, nationalism was unavailable to him and he relied, instead, on the symbol of the home which, while its national location remained unspecified, drew its meanings from the original Home, as England was still called by the Australian middle class. Most had never seen Home, and they were ready to credit Menzies with the deep knowledge and understanding of it he claimed. The unreality of Menzies' England was also theirs, as was the longing for 'something a little higher than the everyday' in which all conflict and all striving could be transcended.

CENTRE AND PERIPHERY

ENGLAND WAS the centre of Menzies' world, the source of all that was good and valuable. Menzies expressed his attachment to English history, literature, traditions and institutions many times during his long life, and always with the complete and utter conviction of a true believer.[26] In an extraordinary speech he made in 1940 on the occasion of the Centenary Thanksgiving Meeting of the British and Foreign Bible Society of Victoria, it is almost as if God's word only had an English form. Menzies gave three reasons why one should be interested in the Bible: 'this English Bible of ours' is the greatest storehouse of enthusiasm one can discover; 'it has given to us... the language that we speak; and it has influenced the imagination, speech and character of our race'.[27] The speech not only lacks any discernible religious sentiment, but fails to acknowledge, to an organisation which has devoted itself to translating the Bible, that it exists in any language other than English. No doubt war-time enmities contributed to this failure, but the speech reveals the extent to which England served essentially religious functions in Menzies' life, providing a realm of values which imbued not only everyday reality with significance, but a book considered by many to be sacred already.

Menzies' deep attachment to England is not remarkable in a person of his age and background; what is remarkable though is the publicness of its display and the tenacity with which he clung to it in the face of changing political realities. Born when the British Empire seemed supreme and when Australia was securely part of it, Menzies grew up in a society filled with the rhetoric and imagery of Empire.[28] Ballarat, the city of his parents' birth and young adulthood and of his own late primary and early secondary education, was a fiercely loyal imperial city, whose considerable achievements were regarded by its inhabitants as evidence of the greatness of the British race.[29] One of his first memories was of the death of Queen Victoria, and one of his favourite boyhood books *Deeds that Won the Empire*.

Melbourne, to which the family moved in 1909, was also a city whose pride and confidence depended on its imperial connections. Gold had given it the money to create cultural institutions comparable to those of the metropolitan centre and so to develop an image of itself as the Empire's southern metropolis. The headmaster of the school he went to, Wesley, aimed to re-create Dr Arnold's Rugby in the Antipodes,[30] and the University of Melbourne where he studied law was modelled on English ideas of education, though tempered with the more utilitarian emphasis of the colonies.[31] The law he studied and later practised was derived from British law, and the Privy Council remained at the apex of the Australian legal system – the highest court of appeal; the section of Little Collins Street where barristers had their chambers was even known as Chancery Lane. Similarly, when Menzies entered politics he became a member of a legislature modelled on the Westminster traditions, with conventions and symbols derived from British parliamentary practice.

All the central public institutions of Menzies' formative years were modelled on British institutions and derived their legitimacy from their British connections. Britain was the source of all that was valuable in Australia, and Australia's achievements, in turn, were essentially British achievements, confirming the greatness of the centre and adding to its glory. Throughout his life Menzies stressed not only the worth of all things British, but the essential Britishness of Australia and her achievements. Australians were Britons in another part of the world, their achievements confirming the essential greatness of the British race.

In his writings about the British Empire, and later the Commonwealth, Menzies always pitted the language of family, kinship and community, in which relationships are based on mutual assumptions and implicit understandings, against more abstract, legal ways of understanding Britain's ties with her former colonies. The most extended statement of this is in a manuscript he wrote during the voyage to England on his first post-war trip in 1948, in which the strength of the Empire's familial bonds is contrasted with the contractual relationships of the United Nations.[32] Entitled after Tennyson's 'Ulysses', 'Not to Yield', it is an odd, rather frantic piece of writing, as if exhortations, eloquent pleading and cogent argument could change the political realities of the post-war world. It was never published, though parts of it appeared in later writings.[33]

Urging Britain to consider the help her former colonies could give her with the post-war economic problems,

Menzies argued for a redistribution of 'Empire population': 'a migrant from Britain to Australia is not lost to Britain; he merely serves the true interest of Britain in another part of the British Empire'; those who see migration to the dominions as a loss to Britain fail to see 'the indissoluble unity of the British people everywhere'. Such people, he wrote:

> appear never to have absorbed even a hint of the stimulating truth that the boundaries of Great Britain are not on the Kentish coast but at Cape York and Invercargill. If our great Empire is only a thing of fragments, then we must discuss migration quite differently. If it is in reality a living and breathing and everlasting unity, then we will no more question the movement of people from England to Australia than we would question a movement of people from Yorkshire to Somerset or from Melbourne to Perth.

Here a metaphor of organic unity expresses the indissoluble bonds between Britain and her dominions; at other times he appealed to the strength of the emotions and instincts on which it is based. When King George VI died he wrote for the *Sunday Times*:

> The death of the King has once more reminded us that our great Commonwealth is united, not by legal bonds, not by the Crown as an abstract notion, not by fine-spun constitutional theories, but by a common and all-powerful human emotion which discards form and penetrates instantly to the substantial truth.

Australia's unity with Britain is thus not a matter of statutes and formal agreements, nor even of friendship as is its relationship with the United States, but 'a warm and inarticulate instinct'.[34]

For Menzies, ties of blood, race, language, history and kinship linked British people everywhere, independent of the political and economic realities of the relations between the nation states in which they lived. This unity was most powerfully expressed in their common allegiance to the Crown, a theme on which Menzies dwelt at length on the occasions of the coronation of Queen Elizabeth II and her subsequent visit to Australia. For the members of the Commonwealth:

> the person of the Queen still embodies a sense of common history, common experience, common understanding, common interest. She is the symbol of spiritual ideals which transcend the doctrine of specific religious faiths. She stands for service. She gives service. She inspires service. And with all this, she is the symbol of the complete freedom and independence of all the nations which acknowledge her as their Head. She is the unity in their diversities.[35]

Shared allegiance to the Queen was the basis of Australia's national unity and the coronation was a great act of national communion.

> It is a basic truth that for our Queen we have within us, sometimes unrealised until the moment of expression, the most profound and passionate feelings of loyalty and of devotion. It does not require much imagination to realise that when 8 million people spontaneously pour out this feeling they are engaging in a great act of common allegiance and common joy which brings them closer together and is one of the most powerful elements converting them from a mass of individuals to a great cohesive

> nation. In brief, the common devotion to the Throne is part of the very cement of the whole social structure.[36]

Intriguingly, the conservative social theorist Edward Shils interpreted the meaning of the coronation in almost exactly the same terms as Menzies.[37] Shils's Durkheimian framework stressed the integrative functions of ritual, and his analysis helps bring out the image of society as a centred unity which informs the way Menzies imagined the relationship between Australia and Britain. In the essays in his book *Center and Periphery*, and particularly in the title essay, Shils reflects on the mechanisms of social consensus.[38] He is interested in how people feel themselves to be members of a social whole, and he argues that society has a centre which is both the centre of power and authority and the centre of the order of governing symbols, values and beliefs. This centre, he argues, because it is the source of great power over the lives of people, partakes of the nature of the sacred.

> The existence of a central value system rests, in a fundamental way, on the need which human beings have for incorporation into something which transcends and transfigures their concrete individual existence. They have a need to be in contact with symbols of an order which is larger in its dimensions than their own bodies and more central in the 'ultimate' structure of things than their routine everyday life.[39]

People have a need, as Menzies so often said, to reach out to things a little higher than the everyday.

The image of society as a centred unity which can include all within its circumference is a profoundly ideological one, aggressively confronting the Marxist image of a society divided against itself in its interests, values and allegiances. From the Marxist perspective, ceremonies such as the coronation are blatant attempts by ruling elites to consolidate their ideological dominance, distracting attention with the glitter of pageantry from the conflicts that divide. Menzies was well aware of this effect of royal pageantry. Watching the trooping of the colours for the King's Birthday on his first trip to England he noted in his diary, 'These are poor days in England for the reds!'[40]

Ceremonies of unity also help contain the divisions and conflict at the heart of the liberal view of society. The image of society as made up of competitive individuals presents problems for social cohesion. Because individuals are seen as being naturally in competitive conflict with each other, rather than naturally bound together through bonds of affection and the need to co-operate, social order and cohesion become a problem. How are independent, self-reliant, competitive individuals to be welded together into a social whole? The rule of law and the conventions controlling competition prevent conflict between individuals from becoming too destructive, but they do not establish society. One of the solutions is the stress on duty and obligation to others and responsibility to society. Another is the allegiance to common, transcendent symbols which lift people out of their walled-in, individual, separate selves to participate in the joys of social attachment and solidarity.[41]

England for Menzies was not just the source of all that was valuable in Australia, but the place where all the divisions and conflicts of human experience were transcended: man and nature in her humanised landscape; past and present in her slowly evolving political and social institutions; imperial centre and dominions in the family of race; the competitive conflict of aggressive individuals in their common allegiance to the crown. Whenever England appeared in Menzies' speeches, and it did often, it was as both an exemplar of the high and selfless standards of which humanity is capable, and as a resolution to whatever conflict or problem was being discussed. 'Harmony,' Menzies told the assembled parliamentary delegates in Westminster Hall, 'is the essence of the best things which England has given to the world.'[42] At the centre, wisdom, power, beauty are already achieved and all striving can cease.

'MY ENGLAND'

To see England as Menzies' Mecca, the source of all value and the place where all conflicts and divisions are resolved, is to see only one side of Menzies' relationship with England. The diaries of Menzies' first trip are for the most part hymns of praise, filled with rapturous excitement at seeing England at last and connecting the place imagined over four decades with a real place; but another, more anxious voice runs through the diaries. Menzies' diaries record not only his recognition of the places and qualities he had long imagined, but his competitive measuring of himself against the men of the centre and his anxiety that they will recognise him as one of them.

Menzies' main means of making his mark in England was through his many public speaking engagements, and he records his own assessment of his various performances and their reception. He was delighted with the response to his speech to the delegates to the Empire Parliamentary Association when he spoke with Baldwin in Westminster Hall, 'the first Dominion Minister ever to speak in this historic spot'. His ability to hold his own at the centre was overwhelmingly confirmed: 'A magnificent audience gives me an ovation at the finish and I am deluged with congratulations. Tonight at the Imperial Institute I am excited to find my speech, so to speak, the talk of the town.' It was reported verbatim in *The Times* and scores of people spoke to him about it.[43] Menzies' skills as a legal advocate were similarly confirmed in the highest court. He had come to England with a private brief to appear before the Privy Council in a patents case. He won the case and one fellow lawyer told him, 'that is the best reply in a patents case I have ever heard'.[44] On being invited to become an Honorary Master of the Bench at Gray's Inn he wrote, 'an Honour usually reserved for Prime Ministers!!!'[45]

Menzies closely observed the language skills of the English public men he met; many of the thumb-nail sketches in his diary include comments on voice, conversational style or oratorical ability; and he remarked on the quality of the various speeches he heard. At an Empire Society Banquet the speeches were bad and he longed to make one.[46] A month later he wrote of a dinner at Claridge's, 'I become more and more gloomy – where are the after dinner speeches?'[47] He observed the British politicians in Parliament – Ramsay MacDonald was superb, but the idol, Winston Churchill, had feet of clay: 'His language is good, but his expression hesitating, and he practically reads what he has to say.'[48] Skill at public-speaking was one of Menzies' most valuable political assets. Casting a competitive eye over English politicians, by his own standards he measured up pretty well. The point of interest here is not so much Menzies' success, but his concern with his performance and how it rated. Here we see what was missing in the rapturous identification with landscape and history – Menzies' awareness of the gap between himself and England.

A speech he made at Chatham House shortly after his arrival reveals a tension in Menzies' relationship with England that can easily be missed, and indicates his awareness that perhaps not everyone in England sees Australia in a way reciprocal to his view of England. He was determined to keep England up to the mark, and reminds the assembled members of the English ruling class of their familial obligations to their former colonies.

> ... we are usually very concerned to know what the outlying portions of the Empire are thinking about the centre, but I want to reverse the process and invite you to consider what the centre of the Empire is thinking about the outlying portions...
> ... surely nobody who understands the integral relationship between the British Isles and Australia can imagine that our common destiny is to be assessed in terms of the pounds, shillings and pence that one may have invested in the other.[49]

That he could even ask such questions shows the doubts sown by the Englishmen he had met in his talks on trade who disapproved of Australia developing her own industry and who did not seem so much to have the good of Australia at heart as the use Australia could be to them.[50] Protesting Australia's loyalty, he also protested his own claims to England. Referring to his visit shortly after his arrival to the Great Hall of William Rufus he said:

> I would ask people in Great Britain to try to realise the feelings that pass through the mind of an Australian of British birth who stands in a hall like that and who recaptures this sense of the past. It is no use saying to him as if he were a stranger, 'We will be perfectly friendly with you'. His retort will be, 'Friendship is not enough. I have stood in this Hall and I know that I have thought of *my* Hastings, not merely yours; of *my* Empire, not merely yours; of *my England*, not merely yours.[51]

Here the colonial man from the periphery was staking his claim to the centre, and demanding that the centre stay true to his ideal of it.

Menzies was determined to hold England to her position as the centre of the Empire. This was a common theme in his speeches in England throughout his life and an important part of his public reputation there. During his war-time trip of 1941 he toured London and provincial cities, praising the English for their courage and fortitude during the blitz and reminding them of the support of the Dominions.[52] He came into conflict with Churchill over the latter's strategy of defending England first and what Menzies saw as his insufficient involvement of the Dominions in the direction of the war.[53] In 1948, returning to Britain for the first time since the war, Menzies was distressed at the want of 'empire imagination' he found.[54] In 'Not to Yield' he argued for the need for a reinvigorated, reintegrated Empire and reaffirmed his faith in the unity of the British Empire and the mutual dependence of its members on each other. Britain's post-war crisis was an Empire, not just a British problem, and the outer portions of the British Empire, under imaginative leadership and inspiration, were just as capable of coming to each other's help in the problems of peaceful reconstruction as in the military and manufacturing activities of war.[55]

Menzies had a great need for Britain to stay strong, and took it upon himself to help her to do so. Arriving in Britain with his manuscript of 'Not to Yield' complete, he made speeches to the English about his ideal England – strong, good, tolerant, just, the centre of a great, powerful and harmonious Empire, and told them that this England could still be real, if only they believed enough and acted on those beliefs. Not surprisingly, Menzies struck a chord in England with this theme. When, twenty years later, *Afternoon Light* was published, Menzies gave a highly successful BBC interview in which these themes were sounded again. *Afternoon Light* became a bestseller in Britain, lukewarm reviews notwithstanding. His editor at Cassells, writing to Menzies to encourage a sequel, said that British people saw him as the last of the great Churchillian figures, and responded to him from the 'deepseated yearning that still remains in this country after the glory that has departed'.[56] Perhaps Menzies, the man from the outer empire, could represent that yearning most powerfully because for him the glory of England had always been an object of yearning.

Two discourses of power are present in Menzies' writing: the imperial discourse of centre and periphery; and the liberal discourse of society as composed of aggressive, competitive individuals in conflict for scarce resources, such as money, prestige, truth and high office. These two discourses are related, both in non-labour ideology and for Menzies himself. The political relationship is relatively easy to see. From the Marxist perspective, the imperial imagery of unity distracts from the irreconcilable conflicts of society, and from the liberal functionalist it provides a realm of unifying symbols to contain the conflict of competing individuals. In both arguments the appeal to unity helps contain and control social conflict, although there are radically different understandings of the causes and the value of this conflict.

The psychological relationship between the two discourses for Menzies is perhaps less easy to see. His relationship with England most obviously fits the centre-and-periphery model; it is this model, in fact, which I have used to explicate it. However, the competitive, critical, demanding voice of the other discourse at times breaks through the hymns of praise to demand recognition. The political psychologist Alan Davies has suggested that when looking at highly mobile, ambitious people, the desire to be central may be as important in understanding their motivation as the will to power, and that drawing closer to the centre may more nearly fit the way such people experience their own progress through life than, for example, climbing a ladder.[57] It may particularly fit the way they *prefer* to imagine their progress and success. The contrast between nearer and further away is far less pushy and competitive than that between the higher and lower rungs of a ladder, with its suggestion that one may have climbed to power over the backs of others. The discourse of centre and periphery allows political ambition to present itself more benignly than the discourse of competitive individualism, and so can keep at bay doubts about its cost, to both oneself and others, by presenting advancement as the natural attraction of like to like. Later, Menzies' psychological geography will be mapped more fully to reveal the way his frequently expressed love for England and praise for the unifying dream of Empire held in check both his own competitiveness and his deep-seated ambivalence about England.

INLAND BORN

JEPARIT

POLITICAL HISTORIAN Cameron Hazlehurst has noted how often Menzies reminisced about his childhood, how he remembered the first car or the first telephone, or commented on the contrast between the material circumstances of his childhood and the comfort and technical achievements of today: 'the urbane big city politician of the 1930s had memories of a frontier boyhood'.[1] Talking to the Institution of Engineers in 1939, he said that although he could now reach his birthplace, Jeparit, in five hours driving over a first-class road, he did not, neither did he go to other interesting places in Australia, simply because he had never accustomed himself to thinking of places a hundred miles or so away as being easily and comfortably reached in two or three hours.[2]

One might expect a politician from such a background to be committed to the interests of rural people, to fighting to overcome the deprivations consequent on distance from the city. Menzies, however, did not become the supreme political representative of rural Australia but of the comfortable urban middle class, and he was frequently out of sympathy with the Country Party which did represent the sort of people among whom he grew up. What meaning did this 'frontier boyhood' have to the man who spoke so eloquently to the pride and anxiety of the Australian urban middle class? Was it just the place he left behind? Returning again to 'The Forgotten People' I will argue, on the contrary, that far from being left behind Menzies' 'frontier boyhood' was crucial in shaping his political imagination.

As public political language 'The Forgotten People' is part of the struggle between labour and non-labour in Australia over the way people identify themselves and their political interests; it draws on the historic struggle between socialism and liberal individualism and their competing views of both the possible and the preferred relationships among people. But the speech has an inner face. In any political speech the match between the inner and outer faces of the language will vary, although there will always be some point of connection through which the speaker's personal meanings can enter into and animate the public forms of political discourse. The argument of 'The Forgotten People' is embodied in image and anecdote rich with allusion to Menzies' own childhood and family experience.

'The Forgotten People' is Menzies' most creative speech. To appreciate its rhetorical and literary qualities, the vividness and economy with which it argues, one only needs to compare it with the following passage written some years earlier which similarly sets out to convince its audience of the 'supreme importance of the individual'.

> There was a time (or so I imagine) when misfortunes tended to drive a man inwards, on to his own resources; a process which developed fortitude and ingenuity, the two great qualities which go to make up the pioneering spirit. But today, faced with the same kind of misfortune, we are all too inclined to turn outwards to the resources of others; a process of mind which breeds neither fortitude nor ingenuity, unless perhaps it is the misplaced ingenuity of the safe-breaker. When I say this, I do

> not mean to say that all virtue has gone from us. I am merely pointing out that our present fashion is a bad one; that the pioneering qualities which are latent in all of us need to be appealed to; that we are listening to too many false prophets. The old hatred of dependence is temporarily at a discount. And the danger of all this is not merely that it weakens the backbone, but that it also saps the spirit.[3]

Here Menzies is heavy, moralising and wordy compared with 'The Forgotten People' where the pithy claim 'Leaners grow flabby, lifters grow muscle' conveys the same point. The power and richness of 'The Forgotten People' are evidence of the deep personal experiences on which Menzies was drawing in this speech. Faced with misfortune in the early 1940s he responded, as he had earlier exhorted others to, by turning inwards, to his own resources; and there he found the idealised image of his childhood home. The weatherboard house behind the shop in Jeparit is the prototype of the home in 'The Forgotten People', his parents of its independent, hard-working inhabitants.

'I was the son of people of fierce independence, and learned early the importance of standing on my own feet', Menzies writes in *Afternoon Light*.[4] Elsewhere he comments on his parents being well-read and well-spoken despite their meagre formal education, achievements he explains by the Scottish tradition of self-improvement elaborated with the very same example he uses in 'The Forgotten People' – the Scots ploughman wanting his son to go to a better school, and he in turn wanting his son to go to university.[5] Robbie Burns's poem, 'The Cotter's Saturday Night', with which Menzies illustrates the spiritual dimension of the middle-class home, was one of his father's favourite poems.[6]

Menzies' childhood, however, provided far more than vivid examples of middle-class virtue and anecdotes and details with which to elaborate them; it was the source of the general strategies for dealing with difference, with adversity, and with the misfortune of colonial birth which structured his political outlook. The home as Menzies elaborates it in 'The Forgotten People' is the foundation of all that is valuable in both society and the individual. But the stress on the independent virtues associated with the home, in contrast to the virtues of community and social interdependence, has a defensive side. The home can be a rich and secure site of meaning and experience; but it can also be a retreat from experience and from an outside world that is different, alien, hostile. The house in Jeparit was as much a refuge from experience in an alien world as it was a secure source of value and meaning.

Menzies was born in 1894 in the seven-year-old town of Jeparit on the Wimmera River, the fourth child of James and Kate Menzies, both children of British immigrants who had settled in Ballarat. James's family was Scottish, Kate's Cornish. The Menzies and their three young children had recently moved to Jeparit to open a general store. They gave their fourth child the second name of Gordon, after General Charles Gordon, a hero of Empire who had been killed defending Khartoum.[7] Jeparit is the site of 'the cottage in the wheat lands of the North-West of the State of Victoria with the Bible and Henry Drummond and Jerome K. Jerome and *The Scottish Chiefs* and Burns on the shelves' with which Menzies began his 1950 account of what the Commonwealth meant to him.[8] The repeated definite article, the solid confident nouns – cottage, wheat lands – the capital letters, the careful listing of the books on the shelves, spaced out with repeated 'ands', all indicate Menzies' attempt to locate this cottage firmly in time and space. But there is a tension between this confident naming and the tenuousness of Jeparit's existence during Menzies' childhood.

The Wimmera–Mallee region of northern Victoria is part of the lower Murray Basin. The Wimmera River, starting on the higher land of the Grampians, runs through this low country in a series of lakes, towards but never reaching the Murray, dissipating in the sands of the Wirrengren Plain.[9] To the Koori tribes of the area, the Wotjoballuk, the Wimmera River was a northward path, a trade route to the Wirrengren Plains, the meeting place and corroboree grounds of Wimmera and Murray River Kooris.[10] The riverbed was made by Purra, the Kangaroo, in flight from Doan the Glider Possum. His strong, purposeful leaps gouged a deep path and the place where he stopped to graze became Lake Hindmarsh. He went on slowly, feeding on sour quandongs at the place that became Lake Albacutya, and wended his way through sandhill country till his tracks became indiscernible.[11] The Kooris' first contact with the European invaders was probably with Major Mitchell in 1836, and in 1843 the first white settlers arrived to take up runs. By the 1850s whole groups of the Wotjoballuk were extinct and by the 1870s those surviving were largely dependent on the whites.[12]

The Wimmera was opened up for settlement from the 1870s to the 1890s. In 1885 the longest wire-netting fence in the world was built from the South Australian border along the 36th parallel, nearly to Birchip, in a vain attempt to keep the rabbits infesting the land around the Murray from moving down into the Wimmera. It ran some miles north of the site for Jeparit which was marked out on the Pine Hills Station. Jeparit, which took its name from the Wotjoballuk name for the area, was established in 1889 and by 1891 had twelve buildings and a population of fifty-five. With the construction of the railway from Dimboola three years later to transport the new settlers' wheat, the town expanded. The Menzies family arrived as part of this expansion to set up a general store to sell goods to the settlers who were busily clearing the land of its natural vegetation.[13] This was predominantly several species of dwarf Eucalyptus trees known as mallee, which Menzies describes as 'the stunted Mallee scrub', although redgums and yellow-box grew along the river and around the lake. In *Afternoon Light* Menzies remembers the heat and the dust:

> As clearing went on, the scrub being rolled and burned, the hot winds of summer would blow the sand into hillocks and drifts. There were tremendous dust-storms which darkened the skies. The summer heat was intense and dry. One of my childhood memories is of one week in which the shade temperature rose by steady degrees to 120°F.[14]

Jeparit was on the edge of settlement when the Menzies family moved there, and it still is. The land has not stood up well to farming. Some twenty miles the other side of Lake Hindmarsh the Big Desert begins. Looking north and north-west one looks towards what seemed to the settlers to be Australia's barren centre. The area has irregular rainfall and a fragile topsoil which has been badly damaged during its hundred years of cultivation. Menzies remembers the time at Jeparit as one of hardship for the family. Nature at Jeparit was hostile and unpredictable. When Kate and James Menzies arrived the Wimmera River was in flood; less than ten years later there was a drought in which the river receded to a series of stagnant pools and the lake dried up; then 'an astonishing thing happened. Up from the bed of the lake there came a green tuberous growth, fibrous but succulent'.[15]

Menzies' childhood memories repeat the familiar experiences of Australian settlers in the harsh and alien new land. An anecdote from the biography by Ronald Seth, with the ostensible theme of young Robert's precocious erudition, carries the image, enshrined in Lawson's 'The Drover's Wife', of a woman alone in the house protecting her children against a threatening natural world. Young Robert was evidently much taken with the story of the siege of Badajoz, an incident in the Duke of Wellington's campaign against Napoleon's Frenchmen in Spain. Shortly after he had been reading about it, 'a wind of hurricane force hit Jeparit in the middle of the night'.

> The houses of the little town were built of boards, and Mrs Menzies, who was alone in the house with the children – James Menzies was away attending to political business – feared that the great wind would blow in the sides of the store. So, calling the boys to help her, she flung herself against the wall, hoping that her strength on the inside would be equal to the hurricane's pressure on the outside.
> Robert – 'as usual', says Frank – was the last one out of bed. As he ran to help his mother, he called out to her: 'It's all right, Mother! It's nothing to the siege of Badajoz!'[16]

The anecdote displays, as well, a central characteristic of the young Menzies – the evasion of actual experience through comparison with some more intense, imagined reality.

His parents both worked hard, his mother frequently serving in the shop, but the new settlers often had little money and had to rely on credit. 'Life for my parents was, in a financial sense, difficult and even grim.'[17] Menzies' parents occupied the classic position of the petit bourgeoisie – small shopkeepers juggling debtors and creditors, forced to practise self-denial through thrift and hard work in order to survive. But the denials of their class position were increased by their geographical location. For a pioneer family on the edges of Empire and of settlement, the costs and renunciations of a settler's life in the New World amplified the petit bourgeois ideology of the Old. Not only had these pioneering families to struggle for their financial security, they had to struggle for it in an alien and often hostile nature far from their world's centre.

And who would witness their struggle? One obvious association to 'forgotten' in the Menzies family's experience was the sense of being on the edges of Empire. The books the family read all referred to a land which none of them had experienced. Menzies' parents were Australians not through choice but because of their parents' decision to emigrate. Here, in this distant outpost, were they forgotten, despite their virtuous upholding of the moral and cultural traditions they ascribed to the centre and their careful learning of the King's English? And would the centre recognise them if they ever got there? To address the Australian middle class as forgotten was to evoke fears of neglect that went beyond their apprehension at the growing power of socialism to the core of their unease and insecurity about their place on the globe.

In this hostile, distant, alien place, the home became both a refuge and the major source of cultural meaning. Menzies refers often to the closeness and security of his childhood home. His most frequent picture is of the family gathered around to listen to one of the members reading from the books he lists so carefully in his speech in 1950. These books appear minus the Bible, in *Afternoon Light*, and in the biographies, for which Menzies, his brother Frank and sister Isabel were major sources.[18] Speaking in 1967 at the unveiling of the spire built in Jeparit to commemorate his achievements,

Menzies said of Jeparit, 'It was a great place in which a family might grow up... we lived at home, we became fond of reading, and reading for each other, and discussing matters with each other. This produced a very well knit family atmosphere and had encouraged me, in particular, to be a student'. Growing up in that circle 'we got to learn something about the things that mattered in the world... we acquired some moral and spiritual standards'. Looking back on his life, Menzies liked to recall that:

> it was here at home in this little town, much smaller then than it is now, in this little town that I had the great privilege of learning for the first time something about the meaning of duty, something about the rights that other people had... something about books, something about the whole art and science of reading and of study. Honourable standards of conduct from which, I hope, not consciously to have departed. These were a great inheritance.[19]

The picture is of a family drawn in on itself, reading in a small weatherboard house beneath a vast night sky of people and places far away, reading in a flat, dry landscape of the mists and glens of Scotland and the River Thames, reading to establish the standards of conduct which will last a lifetime, no matter what experience might have to teach. The Menzies family had only a few fragments of European culture to hold against the surrounding darkness, but the lesson was invaluable for their fourth child. It taught him 'something about books, something about the whole art and science of reading and study'. He found more books in the local Mechanics Institute Library, books about the Napoleonic Wars and the deeds that won the Empire, more books in Ballarat, and more still when he arrived on a scholarship at Wesley where he was awestruck by the size of the library.[20] Here in these libraries he discovered the great writers of English literature and his knowledge of them, particularly of Shakespeare, became one of his public emblems.

GERMANS AND ABORIGINES

JEPARIT IN Menzies' childhood was not only peopled with British settlers like the Menzies, but with German Lutherans and with the demoralised remnants of the Wotjoballuk tribes. Many of the early settlers in the Wimmera came in on the road from Adelaide and among them were Lutheran families from the German settlements in the Barossa, travelling in old-style covered German wagons, who formed parishes at Horsham, Rainbow, Jeparit and Nhil.[21] Menzies remembers being sent by his parents to the consecration of the Jeparit Lutheran church, which still stands next to the Methodist church the Menzies family attended. The service was conducted in German and took two and a half hours.[22] On the Honour Roll of the Jeparit State School which Menzies attended are German names – Hamdorf, Reicheldt, Schultze, Domaschenz. Menzies' first biographer, Allan Dawes, describes the German settlers with their earth-floored houses as 'the backbone of the community'. These hardworking, self-reliant, religious families displayed all the petit bourgeois virtues Menzies praised in 'The Forgotten People', but they displayed them in a foreign idiom, and so were all but invisible to a discourse which located these virtues in the historical experience of the British race.

Cameron Hazlehurst raised the question of the relationship between Menzies' 'frontier boyhood' and the urbane big-city politician of the 1930s. As Bernard Smith reminds us in his immensely wise Boyer Lectures, *The Spectre of Truganini*, 'frontiers are not places, except in Antarctica, where men meet nature, but where they confront other cultures and systems of law conflict'.[23] Menzies spoke to urban dwellers, the comfortable burghers of Camberwell and Rose Bay, many of whom would rarely have seen let alone spoken with an Aborigine, yet whose prosperity depended on their dispossession. When they thought about them at all, it would have been within the self-justifying racist stereotypes of the day. Menzies' experience of Australia's first inhabitants was more immediate and added another layer to the defensive wall with which he encircled the petit bourgeois home.

Menzies spent his childhood in a landscape in which signs of prior occupation were obvious. Trees by the river where he swam bore the shapes of cut-away bark canoes and food carriers; and there were the remains of campsites around Lake Hindmarsh and along the Wimmera River. The Menzies children often played by the river and walked in the bush, which was rich with native birds, animals and flowers.[24] Descendants of the Wotjoballuk tribe still lived in the area in Menzies' childhood. Ten miles south of Jeparit at Antwerp on the road to Dimboola were the remnants of the Ebenezer mission. Established by Moravian missionaries in 1859 on a site that had been an important camping ground for the Wotjoballuk tribe, it existed with varying prosperity till 1903 when its land, apart from the church block, was resumed by the government and the few remaining inhabitants sent to Lake Tyers. Its limestone church, now roofless, and some other buildings still stand, surrounded by the scattered graves of Moravian missionaries and members of the Wotjoballuk tribe. Aboriginal families who were not living at the mission remained in the district until the 1920s when most were forcibly removed to Lake Tyers.[25]

In the late 1960s, Menzies was asked if he had any memories of Aborigines in Ballarat. He replied that while he had no memories of them in Ballarat he did have 'vivid memories of them up in the country'. 'There was a settlement of them at Antwerp and they're not easily to be forgotten, because – er – they had a natural gift for football.' He recounts an anecdote about an Aboriginal champion, 'as tough as they come', playing barefoot and displaying an instinct for the game. After this praise his tone becomes more dismissive.

> But apart from that the Aboriginals were even then rather on the fringe; they lived in a rather primitive way, they weren't a significant element in the community – er – I don't think there was any prejudice against them. I think it's not always understood that the Aboriginals, like most of us, like to live together and be themselves and by themselves; they didn't have any particular ambition to be anything else. They'd go into one of the towns, Dimboola or even Jeparit, from time to time, but they were rather an idle community, and at that time of course, it hadn't occurred to anyone to try to do something about them. But they were not numerous.[26]

'Not numerous', 'idle', 'on the fringe', 'living in a rather primitive way', all these undermine the image of confident, aggressive energy with which Menzies' reply began, as well as betraying, in the elaboration of disclaimers of their importance, a certain discomfort with the subject and irritation with those who regard it as interesting or important. Such responses are part of white Australia's standard view of the Aborigines who survived the violence of the frontier period to become a problem which would not conveniently die and so necessitated the invaders keeping their hearts hard against the knowledge of the oppression, injustice and human misery their presence continued to cause.

Menzies formed his views on Aborigines at the turn of the century, when Australian thinking about race relations was dominated by Social Darwinism, an application of Darwin's theories of evolution and the survival of the fittest to human societies to justify one society's conquest and dispossession of another.[27] Describing the Aborigines in the late 1960s, he appeals to Social Darwinism's hierarchy of races: they are 'the not very numerous survivors of a race of people whose recorded history is scanty. They are not, it is generally thought, comparable with the Maoris of New Zealand, though they have produced a number of people of talent and achievement, and will produce more in the future'.[28] In the draft of an encyclopedia entry written about the same time, Menzies refers to the arrival at some unknown time of 'aboriginal natives' who began 'their wandering existence'. He mentions the early conflict between Aborigines and settlers, but does not dwell on it.

> In the early days of white settlement, there were many disastrous conflicts between the settlers and the aborigines... today – out of a total population of over 13 million, the aboriginal population has been established as about 80,000, 60,000 of whom live in the North and West, in the sub-tropical and tropical areas. It will thus be seen that, numerically, the indigenous racial problem is of no great magnitude, though it does give rise to a good deal of debate, and, of course, constant demands to improve the status and treatment of the native people. But there is no internal racial problem either quantitative or qualitative, in the sense that there is in the United States or in South Africa or to a substantial extent recently in England.

The moral problem hinted at by the admission of conflict is reduced to a matter of numbers. He goes on to discuss White Australia, and to defend Australia's national immigration policy as not based on the idea that 'in their very nature the white people are superior to the black or brown or yellow people', but 'upon a recognition that they are in many respects fundamentally different, and that to ignore that fact would be to permit the coming into existence of acute divisions in society'.[29]

The sentiments Menzies is expressing here are not unusual for people of his generation, although they are guarded, avoiding extreme racist views. A younger Menzies was not so careful. A comment in an essay on Australian poetry written in 1917 shows him participating in Australian racism at its crudest and most vicious. Discussing the poetry of James Brunton Stephens, he cites with hearty approval his poem 'To a Black Gin', written in the 1870s. It is an appalling poem, typical of much of the popular racist verse of the time in which Aborigines were depicted as clowns, the butts of comedy and cruel displays of wit.[30] Its dominant emotion is disgust at Aboriginal sexuality, female sexuality in particular. Menzies wrote:

> His humour, if one allows for a somewhat extravagant indulgence in punning, is excellent. Some of the phraseology of 'To a Black Gin' is wonderfully pleasing:
>
> *'Thy nose appeareth but a tranverse section;*
> *Thy mouth hath no particular direction –*
> *A flabby-rimmed abyss of imperfection.'*
>
> His punning, often good, is shown in the verse –
>
> *'Thy dress is somewhat scant for proper feeling,*
> *As is thy flesh, too – scarce thy bones concealing;*
> *Thy calves unquestionably want revealing.'*[31]

Menzies also praised 'the strong vein of humour' in the companion poem 'A Piccaninny' in which the poet laments over the fate which awaits the 'dusky fondling' in growing into a filthy and disgusting dam like her mother.[32] From his early racism to the dismissive comments in the late 1960s and the *Encyclopedia Britannica* entry, Menzies failed to extend any imaginative human sympathy to the Aborigines; he continued to think of them within the Social Darwinist terms of the turn of the century, both seeing them as the lowest rung on the ladder of human races and blaming them for the destitution to which the white invasion had reduced them.

Faced with misfortune, Menzies had earlier argued, one should turn inwards, a process which will develop fortitude and ingenuity, 'the two great qualities that make up the pioneering spirit'. It is not a process, however, which will develop sympathy or compassion for others. Pioneers at the frontier fought nature and denied their knowledge of the inhuman treatment of the Aborigines on which their chance at landed independence depended. Not only did the forgotten people harden their hearts against the labouring classes who ate, drank and made merry and so squandered their resources to become potential claimants on the resources of others; they also hardened their hearts against the land's original inhabitants, infuriatingly at home in this alien land but reduced by the white invasion to claimants on charity and unwanted irritants to white consciences.[33]

Reading together in the small weatherboard house on the edge of the Wimmera River, the Menzies family turned inwards, away from the uncomprehended Australian bush and away from the knowledge of the fate of the Wotjoballuk tribe, whose name they probably did not even know, to an imaginary world of Scottish chiefs and men boating on the Thames. The position of dependence to which the white invasion had reduced Aborigines made them an obvious target of an ideology centred on the virtues of independence; the implication of the settlers' treatment of the dispossessed tribes in Australian petit bourgeois ideology, however, is more general than this, and explains much of both its anxious, arid defensiveness and its derivativeness.

The Australian settlers' continuing dependence on British culture has most often been interpreted in terms of nostalgia. In his Boyer lectures, Bernard Smith presents an alternative explanation, arguing that the settlers' rejection of the Australian bush and nostalgia for England masked their guilty knowledge of the brutality with which the land had been cleared for settlement. After the frightful atrocities of the pastoral occupation of Australia, a blanket of forgetfulness settled over white Australians' thinking about the Aborigines. They repressed their guilty knowledge of the massacres, and surviving Aborigines were rounded up onto reservations with the hope that out of sight they would stay out of mind and the Australian landscape could be transformed to remove their traces.[34] The continuing repression of this guilty knowledge, argues Smith, opened up a morality gap between black and white Australians, between the settlers and the place they lived in, which has had profound implications for the development of Australian culture, divorcing it from its historical experience and dooming it to aridity and dependence. While this gap remained, Australian culture was not in a position to speak about the human condition in this part of the world, but only about the private hopes and fears of the victorious white component of our society.[35] Australian culture took two paths – the arid path of mateship most associated with the labour movement, and the displaced Europeanism of those who aspired to something higher. Writes Smith, 'at times it would seem as if all the culture of old Europe were being brought to bear upon our writers and artists in order to blot from their memories the crimes perpetrated upon Australia's original inhabitants'.[36] Such Europeanism, 'sedulously cultivated in our universities, has been narrowing... trivialising cultural experience into a kind of emblem of the educated'.[37]

Denial rather than nostalgia is at the root of Australia's continued dependence on overseas culture, argues Smith. In the last essay I will argue that denial is also at the root of Menzies' personality, and that again England is used to fill the gap when knowledge and experience are shunned. This homology of structure between Menzies' personality and the culture for which he spoke perhaps explains why he spoke for it with such conviction.

The family of Menzies' childhood was the prototype for the petit bourgeois family – frugal, hardworking and home-centred – whom he praised in 'The Forgotten People'. They were also a pioneer settler-family, a family who endured much of the hardship of life in the new settlements being established in the Australian bush, and who could not help but know of the misery which the white invasion had brought to the Aborigines. The emotional pattern appealed to in 'The Forgotten People', in particular the defensive drawing tight of the boundaries of the home and the self, and the harshness towards others and the determined self-reliance which this implies, also fit the particularly Australian aspects of their experience. That none of this experience is explicit in the political symbols with which Menzies works in 'The Forgotten People' is, paradoxically, one of its strengths. The relevance of such experience to life here is denied; and in its steadfast reliance on the images and tropes of English petit bourgeois ideology the speech reinforces the conviction that English experience is the best possible guide to

Australian experience. And, in so far as the historical specificity of English experience is repressed in the operation of the symbol of England in Australia, it suggests that the values being argued for are universally and self-evidently true.

Jeparit in Menzies' childhood contained all the elements against which Australian petit bourgeois ideology defined itself and from which it anxiously withdrew into a defensive assertion of its virtues: the hostile and unreliable land, the dispossessed Aborigines, and foreigners. Although Menzies replaced the land of the lowan in which he was born with an imaginary English landscape, and consigned both the remnants of the Wotjoballuk tribe and the pious German-speaking settlers to the world outside the charmed circle of the British race in which he showed almost no interest, he did not leave his experience of Jeparit behind when he moved to the city; rather it gave urgency and conviction to his espousal of the cause of Australia's forgotten people for he knew, perhaps better than many of them, what the walls of their homes were attempting to keep out.

KNOWLEDGE, CULTURE, EXPERIENCE

AN INSTINCTIVE CONSERVATIVE

MENZIES BECAME the supreme representative of imperial Australia, of those whose geographical, cultural and political imaginations were essentially imperial and whose sense of personal significance depended on being part of a political and moral order whose centre was London. Participation in the imagined community of the British Empire aided the denial of the reality of Australian experience, in particular the moral reality of the Australian settlers' appalling treatment of the Aborigines, which created the need for an idealised England risen high above the slaughter and squalid inhumanity of the frontier. The settlers' homes became fortresses of Empire inside which the values and culture shaped by a different historical experience and landscape were taught to their children. Evasion of experience was also a characteristic of Menzies' public political style; there was thus a homology between the homes of the forgotten people, constructed to protect their inhabitants from unwanted knowledge and experience, and Menzies' political self.

Donald Horne's description of Menzies as a 'frozen Edwardian' captures well the way Menzies carried throughout his life the attitudes he formed in his childhood and youth at the turn of the century. These attitudes, particularly those about the place of Britain in the world, were an increasing political burden to him as he aged, making him slow to respond to the changing balances of global power, in particular to the decline in Britain's power, and to the break up of the British Empire. This aspect of Menzies' political views has been well documented and Menzies himself has written of the regret he felt at the transformation of the British Empire into the British Commonwealth.[1] Menzies' imperviousness to experience, however, is not just to be seen in his commitment to the ideal of the British Empire; it was in fact the hallmark of his general public political style, pervading all public expressions of his political ideals and commitments and establishing the position of confident certainty from which he wrote and spoke.

Here is Menzies writing in *Melbourne University Magazine* in 1915 when he was twenty years old, appealing to his fellow students to open their eyes to the beauty of the university grounds:

> The years will pass. We will go forth as men to the wider study of the world's great school, and we will look back, often with tear dimmed eyes, to the days passed in joyous sunshine and the shadow of the great hall. When that day comes, we will think, not of small vicissitudes or petty defects, but of the enshrining glory of it all! Time will have wrought many changes, but one scene will remain year after year – the vision of sunny lake and lawn, none the less clear because the dust of years has thrown its veil between![2]

Menzies assumes a posture from which he can write with utter confidence of how he and his fellow students will feel in the future. The pompous sentimental tone is more appropriate for a man of eighty than a man of twenty and was so regarded by his student contemporaries. One, Clem Lazarus, responded to another essay, in which Menzies instructed his fellow students on their duty, with a satirical poem:

> *On the Empire pour your gush,*
>   *Throw the Shop a platitude;*
> *Shower on Mister Hughes some mush,*
>   *Strike a* Loyal *attitude.*[3]

The attributes that aggravated students forty years later – the gush, the platitude, the Loyal attitude – were already in place in the twenty-year-old Menzies' public persona and were already seen, by some at least, as pompous, stagey and inappropriate.

Cameron Hazlehurst observes, 'from the time we begin to have any public expression of young Robert Menzies' opinions and values to the time, half a century later, when he had become a conservative icon, there is an unmistakable unity and consistency in the style and content of what he had to say'.[4] The same quotations, anecdotes and arguments appear again and again throughout the published speeches. When he published *Speech is of Time* in 1958, Menzies included the essay 'Freedom in Modern Society' written more than twenty years earlier, adding in a footnote that although he has mislaid the record of to whom he delivered the speech, years ago, he would not seek to amend it.[5] Twenty years or more, which include a world war and substantial experience as prime minister, is a long time to hold to one's views unamended.

Menzies was a person singularly lacking in curiosity about other people, other cultures, other ways of life; the German-speaking Lutherans in Jeparit awoke no such interests. Nor was it sparked when he finally left Australia: calling at ports in Asia and the Middle East, Menzies betrayed no excitement at the astonishing variety of human experience, no curiosity or puzzlement about the way people in other cultures see the world. Rather, everything he saw merely confirmed his belief in the superiority of the English. Sailing past the coast of Africa he reflects on 'the persistent Englishness of the English' and concludes 'the more I see of such people the more satisfied I am that while doctrinaires and theorists speculate about self government for natives, the British calmly go on their way giving to these people what obviously they could never give to themselves'.[6] After talking with German Jews on board ship he records, 'The more one sees and hears about other political systems, the more one realises that the English notion of freedom as the object or end of government is the best.'[7] Twenty years later during the Suez crisis Menzies' complete lack of curiosity about the Egyptians was striking to observers.[8] Casey's attempts to advise Menzies on the way the Egyptians saw the situation were to no avail. When Menzies visited India in 1959, he did not, according to Australian High Commissioner Walter Crocker, 'ask a single question about India... He wanted to see none of the sights and he had no curiosity about and no interest in India or Indians.'[9] Nor did Menzies' curiosity ever extend to contintental Europe. Alexander Downing notes with surprise that Menzies travelled hardly at all in Europe and showed no interest in European languages. 'I fail to understand,' he wrote, 'how he could have deprived himself of these fountains of our civilisation.'[10]

Menzies was uninterested in testing and expanding his views and knowledge through experience of the world, a trait which fitted well the image of the relationship between the self and its opinions which was implicit in Menzies' ambivalent record on civil liberties. For Menzies, a person's beliefs and opinions were attributes of the self, whose chief value was in establishing the public identity of the self in competition with others; the self was thus not a self in process, changing in response to new experiences, testing views and opinions against reality, shaping and reshaping them in a quest for understanding and meaning, but a self already formed whose chief preoccupation was the struggle for public advantage.

Menzies donned the opinions which were to be the public attributes of his self very young. They are there in his early writings in *Melbourne University Magazine*, but Menzies saw them as beginning even earlier, in his boyhood arguments with his grandfather, John Sampson, a staunch supporter of the labour movement, who would debate the leading article of the *Sydney Worker* with him. 'Even then,' writes Menzies, 'I suppose I was an instinctive Conservative, and I usually disagreed with it, I would say so politely and give my reasons.'[11] Later, I will suggest reasons for Menzies' precocious commitment, reasons why, at so young an age, he suspended questioning, doubt and puzzlement and assumed such a confident and knowing pose. For the remainder of this essay I want to develop my characterisation of Menzies' public political self as a defence against knowledge and experience through a discussion of Menzies' cultural interests.

Interviewing Menzies in 1968, Barry Jones commented that *Afternoon Light* reveals little of Menzies' inner life and proceeded to ask him about his tastes in reading, music, art and architecture, the implication being that these tastes will reveal the inner man. Menzies' answers are predictable and his musical tastes required a deal of prompting from Jones.[12] Like Jones, I also take Menzies' cultural interests as a clue to his inner life, but will argue that rather than revealing a hidden, private plenitude, they reveal an emptiness which is the inevitable result of the way Menzies constructed himself and his relationship with others. Culture's potential as a realm of tough, rich and demanding experience remained unrealised for Menzies, and he has become for many Australian artists and intellectuals one of the chief representatives of Australian philistinism.[13] There is pathos in Menzies' occupancy of this position, however, for he valued his cultural interests and knowledge, and, in his youth at least, had some literary aspirations.

THE SORRY TALE OF THE ROYAL ACADEMY OF AUSTRALIAN ART

MENZIES' REPUTATION as a philistine began with his notorious attempt to found an Australian academy of art in the 1930s when he was Attorney-General. This began with the laudable aim of committing the Commonwealth government to patronage of the arts, but quickly became embroiled in a public controversy over modern art which revealed how little Menzies understood the way many artists viewed their activity.[14]

The controversy began when, shortly before the academy's launch, Menzies opened the 1937 autumn exhibition of the Victorian Artists' Society to which a number of modernist painters had been invited to contribute. Standing in front of the pictures, with many of the painters present, Menzies was deliberately provocative. Describing himself as 'the prime mover' of the proposal to form an academy of art in Australia,[15] he elaborated its virtues.

> The Federal Attorney General (Mr Menzies) in supporting his project said the best argument in its favour was that in all the great artistic centres of the world academies had been in existence for many years. Academies, said Mr Menzies, served not only to set standards for the work, but also to raise the

standards of public taste by directing attention to good work. Every academy had its critics. If there were no people suspected of being conservative there would be no fun in being a revolutionary. The establishment of any standard or any body which might be accused of being conservative gave rise to criticism which helped to keep the world moving. He had been told there was no room in the exhibition of the London Academy summer exhibition for the moderns, but if anything could be more modern than some of the work he had seen in Burlington House then he would like to be informed what modern work was. It seemed that some forms of modernity consisted of doing all things that Rembrandt would not have done, and to be really original the artist had to paint a face in the form of a cabbage and vice versa.

Mr Menzies added that an academy would encourage people in every form of artistic experiment. Neither painters nor any other class which was content to stand still and merely copy what someone else did would ever accomplish much. In all experiments certain principles applied. They represented part of the whole tradition of art or any other matter which involved the artistic sensibility of the community. In visits to the leading galleries of the Continent last year he had learned two things – that the greatest art spoke in a language that every intelligent man could understand, and that if artists such as Rembrandt really could paint then some of the people who called themselves modernists spoke an entirely different language.[16]

This speech exemplifies Menzies' public self. There is the untroubled adoption of a pose of confident and authoritative certainty, based on a relatively small amount of knowledge. While Menzies was putting forward views held by many established figures in the art world, they were not views he had come to himself after long and careful study of art. He may have made a few visits to European and English galleries and viewed the work of some great masters, but he would already have known his opinion of what he saw; his visits would merely have confirmed the views associated with the conservative political and cultural views with which he already identified. The speech displays, too, Menzies' characteristic construction of social and political activity in terms of competition: 'If there were no people suspected of being conservative there would be no fun in being a revolutionary.' This jocular remark is revealing of Menzies' lack of interest in the substance of cultural activity, as distinct from the public fate of already formed opinions and ideas. His automatic identification with the conservative position leaves no room for consideration of the merits of the radicals' cause, and in fact suggests that Menzies does not even recognise that such causes may have substantive merits and be motivated by more than the desire to establish oneself as a rebel.

If competitive struggle for public recognition is at the core of one's understanding of cultural activity, then one is very likely to think some organisation is necessary to 'set the standards', and judge the outcomes. And if, like Menzies, one has early and 'instinctively' identified with a conservative political position, then one will need guidance as to appropriate conservative judgements; one's attention will require direction to the good work, the appropriate opinions and tastes for a conservative. To find that this is an easily assimilable representational art where the boundaries between cabbages and faces are firmly maintained will simply confirm one's sense of having chosen wisely in one's initial social and political identifications. There is nothing in the experience of art which will challenge the adopted certainties. If, on the other hand, some painters are engaged with substantive intellectual, emotional and aesthetic problems in their work, then the establishment of such standards will at best be irrelevant to and at worst destructive of the real object of their work.

The lack of connection between Menzies' view of artistic activity and that of many practising artists was obvious in the outraged responses to his speech. Adrian Lawlor's wittily polemical *Arquebus*, published later that year, documents the ensuing controversy during which Menzies was drawn into elaborating his position and defending his layman's right to hold opinions about art.[17] Responding to Norman Macgeorge, a lecturer in art, who asked whether Mr Menzies thought that art should be non-progressive and that we should be forever content with representational art, Menzies replied:

> It is true, however, as Mr Macgeorge claims, that I find nothing but absurdity in much so-called 'modern art', with its evasion of real problems and its cross-eyed drawing. It is equally true that I think that in art beauty is the condition of immortality – a conclusion strengthened by an examination of the works of the great European masters – and that the language of beauty ought to be capable of being understood by reasonably cultivated people who are not themselves artists.[18]

Adrian Lawlor describes these remarks as 'drastically silly', and lampoons Menzies' claim that his aesthetic judgements have been based on 'an examination of the works of the great European masters': 'For how many months, pray, was he in Europe? What sort of "examination" could this have been? And an examination of what?'[19] Although backed by a substantial body of opinion among the older generation of artists, Menzies was clearly out of his depth. 'Just as it would be ludicrous for an artist to argue a knotty problem of law, so it is ludicrous for Mr Menzies to lay down what is good drawing and good art', wrote Melbourne painter George Bell.[20] Not only was Menzies' aesthetic judgement questioned, but so was his knowledge of art history. Didn't Menzies know that great artists had often been scorned and misunderstood in their own time? El Greco, Whistler and Van Gogh were all cited against him. More tellingly, some participants in the debate questioned the seriousness of Menzies' interest in art. What, asked Basil Burdett, 'has liking or disliking to do with art? Artists today no longer design their work purely to give us pleasure... If likes and dislikes are to be our criterion, we shall not get far with modern art.'[21]

Menzies defended himself against such criticisms with a mixture of bravado and threat.

> If artists believed that laymen were not fitted to criticise art then, said Mr Menzies today, he would like to know this: – Why do they exhibit paintings, and offer them for sale to laymen?
>
> Do artists offer their work for sale because they think that the bad taste of laymen will induce them to become purchasers? Or is it because they think there is something in their art which is capable of being appreciated by men who are incapable of drawing anything more complicated than a cheque?...
>
> I am sorry that Mr Bell should have been so angry as to forget his customary good manners. No

> doubt he is quite correct when he says that I am not myself a painter. He might be right when he says that I have a pedestrian mind. But in spite of these disabilities the fact remains that I am a typical person of moderate education, I hope reasonably good taste, and a lifelong interest in the fine arts.
>
> In other words, with all my individual defects, I represent a class of people which will, in the next 100 years, determine the permanent place to be occupied in the world of art by those painting today.[22]

In his 'final word' on the subject one can detect an element of strain, perhaps even of pathos.

> My last word in this controversy is that I deny Mr Bell's underlying assumption that only a painter can criticise a painting, only a composer can criticise a song, only an architect can determine the beauty of a building, only a botanist can assess the glories of a garden, only a dramatist can critically appreciate Shakespeare, and that unless you happen to be a poet yourself you must never dare to offer an opinion whether Shelley was a greater poet than William Watson. – Well, I'm sorry, but I don't want to be excluded from all the pleasures of life, so I must disagree.[23]

Notice here that what Menzies is defending is not his right to learn from and enjoy great art, but his right to judge it, to determine who is the better poet, which the best song, and so on. This is not all that the pleasure of art means to Menzies, but it is an important part, and shows the gulf between his attitude to art and that of those who take it seriously as a mode of thought and expression. It also shows the dangers inherent in his attitude to art from the point of view of a serious artist. An academy in which art lovers such as Menzies were influential would be likely quickly to become a disciplining, credentialling institution. This potential was all too apparent at the opening dinner of the academy which dismayed Sydney Ure Smith, who had been a supporter. Menzies, he said, was 'too influenced by the pomp and ceremony, by the outward appearance, by "names" and "labels" as such'.[24]

A love of art disconnected from the intellectual and emotional work of art becomes a love of mere outward appearance, part of an emblematic culture in which participation in cultural pursuits becomes a marker of social status. Menzies' concern to judge and to establish hierarchy in part shows his characteristic construction of all social and cultural action as competitive struggle, and his interest in the outward fate of the public self rather than in the inner world expressed in the painter's work. It also shows the insecurity of a self-made man who needs a well-marked-out and authoritative hierarchy to guide his cultural aspirations. It is here that the note of pathos enters Menzies' determination not to be excluded from all the pleasures of life. Five years later, in 'The Forgotten People', Menzies spoke less defensively about the pleasures of art. One of the virtues of the middle class is that it provides 'the intellectual life which marks us off from the beast: the life which finds room for literature, for the arts, for science, for medicine and law'.

> The artist, if he is to live, must have a buyer; the writer an audience. He finds them among frugal people to whom the margin above bare living means a chance to reach out a little towards that heaven which is just beyond our grasp. It has always seemed to me, for example, that an artist is better

> helped by the man who sacrifices something to buy the picture he loves than by a rich patron who follows fashion.[25]

What is this heaven which is just beyond the grasp of these frugal people, the realm of the pleasures of life from which Menzies is determined not to be excluded?

It is, to begin with, a reward for hard work, for pleasures foregone. The contradiction between the bourgeoisie's pleasures and the artist's work is endemic to the role of the artist under capitalism. In the debate over the academy, Menzies continually stressed that the artist was, in the end, dependent on the cheque books of his buyers, and that the possession of these cheque books gave them the right to have and to air their laymen's opinions on cultural matters. However, there is something more to Menzies' representation of the forgotten people's interest in culture than this. Reaching out to something higher, they are both reaching out to the cultural knowledge and power which marks those socially above them, and they are reaching out towards things of intrinsic value. For artists and intellectuals who have suffered from the cultural presumptions of the bourgeoisie, it is difficult to concede that inextricably intermingled with upwardly mobile social pretensions are genuine aspirations to participate in cultural activity. But without the time or the commitment to take such activity seriously – it remains a reward after serious work – cultural aspirations are easily perverted into markers of social status. Such was the path taken by Menzies' own cultural aspirations. One can see in the sorry tale of the academy the perversion of what was at one level at least a serious intent to promote cultural activity. The path is more clearly seen in the fate of his literary aspirations.

LITERARY ASPIRATIONS

MENZIES' LOVE of literature was a well-established feature of his public self by the time he was at Wesley College. He is reputed to have watched the schoolboy cricketers practising at the nets with a copy of Shakespeare under his arm and to have matched his knowledge of Shakespeare against their cricketing skill. One story has it that while a student who was a very good cricketer practised his bowling and batting, the young Menzies regaled him with Shakespeare.[26] Menzies became an enthusiastic schoolboy poet during his time at Wesley. The headmaster, ex-Rugby scholar L.A. Adamson, instilled a spirit of fierce competition into his 'boys' and for a short time before World War I verse writing was a highly regarded intellectual pursuit, almost as glamorous as the sporting achievements the school enjoyed at this time.[27] Menzies regularly won the Shakespeare Society prize in which contestants had to learn many hundreds of lines of a set play.[28] One of the leather-bound volumes in Menzies' library was won at the Melbourne Shakespeare Society Exhibition in 1911. Knowledge of literature was not just a characteristic of Menzies' public self, however; it was a means to his success. In the Senior Public Examinations of 1912, Menzies came first in the state in English Language and Literature, and on the strength of this achievement won a scholarship which enabled him to attend Melbourne University to study law.

The playful competitiveness in Menzies' early love of literature carried into his later life. John Bunting suggests that one of the reasons for Menzies' success in the early 1950s in borrowing 150 million pounds from the International Bank was the special rapport he had with the chairman of the bank, Eugene Black. This rapport, says Bunting, was based on their shared love of literature, Shakespeare in particular.

'They conversed as if at a literary occasion, revelling in each other's interest and knowledge, swapping quotations, each totally in the other's grasp.' Paul Hasluck comments on Menzies' liking for 'the conversation of well-read men in which a passing allusion to any of the great writers could be picked up readily and could convey a whole chapter of meaning in a passing phrase'.[29] These anecdotes show something of the way Menzies deployed his knowledge of literature: to define his public persona, to state an allegiance to certain traditional values, to participate in playful oral competitions with other men.

Menzies' writing about literature while he was at university, however, reveals a more private and serious engagement which, although it faded as he got older and more publicly successful, indicates a core of genuine conviction at the heart of his cultural activities. At this period of his life, poetry mattered to Menzies; he read it, and in the poetry he wrote he tried 'to express thoughts a little higher than the everyday'. Imitative as this poetry is, it does display a certain seriousness of purpose, even if this is for the most part the earnest expression of wistful melancholy characteristic of so much youthful poetry. He also wrote about poetry, urging his fellow students to take it more seriously and expressing the hope that one day 'Australian literature will take a very high place among the treasures of all time'.[30]

In 1917 he wrote a three-part essay on Australian poetry for *Melbourne University Magazine* which draws on a remarkably wide knowledge of Australian poetry for a twenty-three-year-old at that time.[31] Marvelling at 'the number of writers of undoubted merit produced by Australia during its brief history', he surveys this history from Kendall and Harpur to the Bulletin School, and beyond to some brief references to contemporary poets such as Bernard O'Dowd; he does not mention the poet of his childhood landscape,

John Shaw Neilson. The poetry of Harpur and Kendall appeals more than the galloping rhythms of Adam Lindsay Gordon or the Bulletin School; in it, and particularly in Kendall, he finds the qualities he values in poetry: 'poet-like, his mind goes out to the songs he cannot sing – vain gropings towards the impalpable world of imagination always just ready to flower into song'.

Whatever one may think of Menzies' judgements in this essay, they are judgements based on knowledge and thought and, most importantly, they are his own. He is not relying on the guidance of already established conservative thought, which in this period would have rejected all Australian poetry in favour of the English masters, but venturing into an area where standards of judgement have not yet been laid down. This alone makes it remarkable among Menzies' published writing. Also remarkable is the absence of combativeness in its tone and of competitive imagery in its representation of cultural activity. Although Menzies assesses and judges the poets he discusses, his tone is reflective; he does not pit them against each other as participants in a competition, but backs his judgement with relatively detailed discussion of their work. This essay is evidence that Menzies was capable of engaging with the substance of high cultural pursuits and not just with their form, but it is a capacity which lies dormant once he embarks on his successful legal and political career. His papers contain a few poems written in his later life, but although they display a certain facility with versifying, there is scant evidence in them of that 'striving to reach a little higher than the everyday' which he had praised in his youth. Perhaps once the worldly meaning of that aspiration had been achieved, its more spiritual meaning lost its interest.

A parody he wrote in 1926 for the Savage Club, where professional Melbourne men gathered to lunch and dine, gives a picture of the confident, jocular masculinity which by then set the tone of much of Menzies' recreational cultural activity. Called 'Club Fever' and with due apologies to John Masefield, here are the first and the last verses.

> *You must come down to the Club again, to the place where the Savages are,*
> *Where all we ask is a tall glass on the top of a gleaming bar,*
> *And a good friend and a loud song, and a firm hand shaking,*
> *And a bob in and the last round when the grey dawn's breaking.*
>
> *You must come down to our Club again, to our Club with the vagrant life,*
> *Where the world stops at the front door and goes back home to his wife;*
> *Where all we ask is a merry yarn from a laughing fellow rover,*
> *And an hour's sleep and a fair head when the long night's over.*

Menzies was a keen club man all his life, not the clubs of serious business and connection like the Melbourne Club, but the descendants of the Bohemian dining clubs like the Savage Club, where 'members would hang their dignity in the cloak room' to engage in 'showing off' and 'the giving and receiving of disrespect'. He was also an enthusiastic member of the West Brighton Dining Club, where there was a regular choral dinner, and of the K.K. Club.[32] These clubs offered Menzies a chance for off-duty fun where he could display his wit and literary erudition; the more serious, reflective interest in literature evident in his writing in *Melbourne University Magazine* would have been out of place, not to say an invitation for ridicule.

From 1936 to 1963 Menzies was a member of the Parliamentary Committee which made the final decisions on the disbursement of money from the Commonwealth Literary Fund on the advice of a board composed in part of practising writers.[33] While Prime Mininster, Menzies administered the CLF in a highly personal way, seeing himself in the role of patron, dispensing not just money, but also advice and even checking the occasional manuscript for grammar and punctuation.[34] Vance Palmer (Chairman of the Advisory Board from 1939 to 1953) praised Menzies' interest in literature. 'Menzies, brought up in a humanist atmosphere, prides himself on his fondness for poetry. He has definite literary tastes, conservative but sound. Sceptical about most things, he is quite convinced of the importance of literature.'[35]

Palmer's generous judgement is half-right, Menzies undoubtedly was 'fond of poetry', but this did not stop his literary judgements being overtaken by the same confidently opinionated reactionariness which characterised his stance on Australian painting. In his portrait of Chifley in *Afternoon Light* he describes their shared literary tastes.

> I shall never forget one meeting at which some new poet, of the school which substituted words for meaning and elusive incoherence for rhythm, was highly commended. One of his poems was read out. I turned to Chifley with an interrogative eye-brow. He looked across the table at the distinguished Australian authoress and said, 'Miss..., I hope you will forgive me. But I think it is all bloody nonsense.' I was grateful to him, for I thought him dead right.[36]

There is nothing here of the modest pluralism Menzies displayed in his 1917 piece on Australian poetry. The anecdote betrays a disengagement from serious literary interest which allowed Menzies' literary judgements in the early

1950s to be easily drawn into the black-and-white discourse of anti-communism.

During 1952 the CLF was attacked in Parliament by two anti-communist members of the ALP and by W.C. Wentworth of the Liberal Party for favouring communist writers such as John Morrison and Judah Waten.[37] Menzies defended the Fund; he had little choice as he was its chairman, and besides he had no love for the perpetrators of the attack. In contradiction to Menzies' trenchant defence of the integrity of the Fund in Parliament, political historian Richard Hall has discovered in the Australian Archives a departmental memo which shows that Menzies' defence was misleading. Earlier in the year he had appended a note to the bottom of a departmental minute informing him that Judah Waten, a recipient of a CLF fellowship, had been a member of the Communist Party and 'was still regarded as a Communist at heart', and which read, 'In future all names put forward should be investigated by security. This case is scandalous and embarrassing, and does not add to my somewhat meagre confidence in the Advisory Council. (21/2/52).'[38] Security checks stayed in place until John Gorton's prime ministership, and during that period there is a noticeable absence of grants to writers with clear associations with the Communist Party. As well, the literary magazines *Overland* and *Meanjin* had to tread carefully to avoid jeopardising the assistance they received during this period.[39]

The book for which Waten received the fellowship, *Alien Son*, was a story of a Jewish immigrant childhood well within the bourgeois narrative tradition and would have posed no challenge to Menzies' literary taste. His response to Waten's fellowship is solely and simply a matter of Waten's being 'a Communist at heart'. The term communist was a label which sharply divided its bearers from other members of society, denying them the possibility of any moral or cultural worth as it attempted to deny them their civil liberties. Menzies' interest in and knowledge of literature was not enough to make him pause before the simplifications of anti-communist discourse applied to literature, but foundered in the same shallows as his defence of civil liberties: a personality turned away from the complexities and ambiguities of the inner life to the competitive struggle of public selves.

Reputedly Menzies once said, 'I'd like my epitaph to be, "He had many faults but he loved poetry".'[40] He seems to have kept alive some literary ambitions throughout his life: Kevin Perkins reports that on his retirement he told some of his intimate friends that, 'All I want is three years of sanity and health to do some writing, the one thing I've always wanted to do.'[41] To retire to one's books was a fitting end to a public life. In 1939, speaking of the place of the university in the modern community, he had said:

> I pity the man on whom a real darkness descends when the bright lights go out. Rather would I be the man who, when the tumult and shouting dies, enters into the company of his books and his thoughts and the conversation of his friends. The world does not lack examples of those who, called to great practical responsibilities, fated to incur the wear and tear of life to the full, have found in what we call the higher learning the essential means of stability and wisdom.

Among other things, such cultural activity provides a refuge from the narcissistic wounds of political life. He goes on:

> The great Asquith's letters bear witness, as do many of his speeches, to that love of pure learning which had much to do with his loftiness of outlook, his imperturbability in the face of the slanderous attacks of little minds and venomous tongues, the measured beauty and power of his eloquence... Balfour and his philosophy, Churchill and his history, Deakin among his books: the story of our own race abounds in examples of witnesses to the grace and power of pure learning.[42]

Menzies was granted his three years, but the writing he did must have sorely disappointed his youthful literary aspirations, let alone his more mature ambition to be a man of letters. He published a volume of lectures, *Central Power in the Commonwealth* and two volumes of memoirs, *Afternoon Light* in 1967 and *The Measure of the Years* in 1970. The memoirs are fragmentary and disappointing, with no inside stories to illuminate the motivation of himself or others, no admissions of past mistakes or misjudgements, no penetrating analyses of people or events. They are anecdotal and self-justifying, with a determinedly light touch and frequent moments of sentimentality.

Afternoon Light has more substance than *The Measure of the Years*, though both recycle ideas and anecdotes that can be found in Menzies' speeches over the years. In the early 1960s Menzies had put off a would-be biographer with the excuse that as he intended to write an autobiography himself he didn't want his anecdotes over-exposed.[43] This indicates a limited store, with little confidence that new experiences will replenish it, bringing to light new memories or new perspectives on old ones. And he was right. *The Measure of the Years* includes three pieces on cricket, two on legal memories and an anecdote about meeting J.M. Barrie in the

Cotswolds in the 1930s. There is a little unused memoir material among his papers but it is of the same ilk – vignettes of people he had known and more reminiscence about the Bar.[44] The material is thin and even if he had been spared the ill-health which began shortly after he retired, it is unlikely he would have been able to produce much more.

The authorial posture of Menzies' memoirs is that of the after-dinner speaker delivering an entertaining and perhaps informative address to like-minded people. His tone is light, anecdotal, humorously self-deprecating – 'in any case, history or the historians will be more interested in many of the people of whom I write than, I profoundly suspect, they will be interested in me'.[45] It is a literary mode honed to display the public man to a public audience, but it is ill-suited for the more intimate, reflective dialogue of books. Fifty years of public speaking separate Menzies' essay on Australian poetry from the publication of *Afternoon Light*; after fifty years public speaking is all he can write.

A HOLLOW MAN?

PONDERING WILLIAM Dobell's portrait of Menzies, Manning Clark saw him as a hollow man.

> I remember standing in front of it for well over an hour one afternoon in Canberra, chewing over the simple question: what is it about? None of the obvious explanations seemed to fit: it was not about an arrogant man, or one absolutely corrupted by absolute power, or a lonely man... or an innocent boy from Jeparit who had gone to Melbourne and fallen among thieves who had stripped him of his apparel and beaten him and the wounds had never healed. I was just about to give up in despair and

admit defeat when I noticed that one of the hands was resting on the monogram of empire. So I looked again greedily at the face and suddenly realised that what Dobell wanted people to see was that there was nothing behind the facade or mask Menzies presented to the world: that Menzies, as a representative leader of our public men, had become a hollow man.[46]

Clark's image of Menzies as a hollow man is of a man without an inner life, a man who has become so identified with the public projections of his self that there is nothing left behind the public face. Before pronouncing Menzies hollow, Manning Clark deploys the theatrical image of the façade or the mask. Contemporaries of Menzies more sympathetic than Clark also use theatrical images to describe Menzies, although they give Menzies the benefit of the doubt and assume that behind the public man they know there is a real person to whom they do not have access. Paul Hasluck, a perceptive and sympathetic observer of Menzies, writes:

> Many commentators referred to him as a showman or as an actor. As I studied him, I saw behind the façade a very shy man, a man who was loth to expose himself and slow to give away even to those close to him his inmost feelings. He acted a role not because of a wish to parade himself but because of unwillingness to expose to public view his most deeply personal self. In that sense I think he was a very shy man.
>
> He seemed to be an actor on the political stage, for professionally he was a politician and he chose what political part he would play so as to preserve both his dignity and his privacy while establishing a claim to be trusted with the nation's affairs. He

> seldom dropped out of his public role when he was on public view... In keeping with his shyness Menzies did not give himself away easily. He guarded his private self. This is one of the reasons I suggest why men in different walks of life, only seeing the view given in public, have varied accounts of him.

When Hasluck tries to elaborate on the existence of the inner man, though, he can give it little substance; the inner man just seems to be the man off-guard.

> The nearest I myself came to seeing the private man, apart from the occasional glimpses of him in the family circle – and I will not intrude into that sacred zone – was when at the end of a heavy day he relaxed in a small company and yarned about something that had little to do with politics.[47]

Percy Spender also invokes shyness to explain the difficulty of penetrating Menzies' public self. He argues that the outwardly composed, suave, urbane and self-possessed Menzies concealed considerable shyness. 'It was this shyness which explains, I think, the detached and somewhat cold figure he presented to his parliamentary associates, most of whom stood in secret awe of him.'[48] Here the shyness is explained as simply defensive, although with unfortunate consequences, but Spender goes on to give a more destructive edge to the shyness than Hasluck, linking Menzies' skills in public performance to a detachment from and insensitivity to the feelings of others.[49] Howard Beale makes a similar link: 'Because Menzies was not a man to wear his heart on his sleeve, it was not always easy to discern his real feelings, but he did often seem to lack sympathy, and the ability or inclination to project himself into the minds of others and thus to understand and feel with them.'[50]

I have not so far found a contemporary who claims to have known Menzies intimately. John Bunting, of whom Alexander Downer says, 'I am sure of all the people in Menzies' life, he regarded Bunting as one of his closest friends',[51] clearly did not so regard himself. He writes that Menzies had no 'universal friendships, by which I mean friendships for all purposes'.

> They were in separate compartments: political, the law, business, clubs, cricket and so on. Here and there they would overlap, but mainly they did not. There was, so far as I know, no one, again family apart, on whom he was dependent, and with whom he might share confidences or troubles.[52]

Revealed in these biographical reflections from Menzies' contemporaries is a disappointment that they have failed to reach the *real* Menzies, and the feeling that there is a degree of incompleteness in their grasp of the man. The conventional biographer, too, may well feel frustrated by the paucity of personal material in Menzies' voluminous papers. How can one reach the private Menzies behind the public performance? But if the task proves so hard, perhaps it is because it is misguided? Perhaps one is looking in the wrong place and the solution is, like the purloined letter, right in front of one's nose: the public man *is* the real man and the task is to read his life and his character where we find it – in the shape of the public life.

FATHERS

AMBITIONS AND IDEALS

MENZIES REGARDED politics as 'the greatest and most responsible' of all the civil vocations[1] and saw the essence of the political vocation in relation to public affairs as the provision of 'exposition, persuasion, and inspiration' to the public. The politician, he wrote, should 'temper the frequently absurd asperities of political conflict by seeking to stir up only noble and humane emotions'.[2] Politics, on this view, is all about the furtherance of ideals and the rendering of service; it is about devotion and selfless duty, and Menzies frequently reminded his audiences of the hard work and long hours of those with political responsibilities.[3] His claim, 'I have worked hard all my life, much harder, I feel sure, than many of my critics', is repeated many times during his political career.[4] But politics is also about power, fame and glory, and competing with others for the chance to enjoy them. The pursuit of power can always be rationalised as being in the service of ideals – one only wants power to protect and further the values one holds most dear – but such denials of the pleasures and gratifications of power are rarely convincing. Menzies pursued power, gained it, lost it and gained it again, and while there is little explicit discussion of power in his speeches and writings, he was not immune to its pleasures.

The polarised representations of Robert Menzies' place in Australian politics include polarised assessments of his personality. Where his admirers praise his ideals and see him as a man of great talent and high principle, who brought to the service of the nation exceptional gifts and a strong sense of duty,[5] his detractors focus on his pursuit of power and see him as vain, ambitious and self-centred, a man who tacked and turned with the prevailing winds and put his undoubted skills at the service of the rich and powerful.[6] Neither view is totally convincing. The admirers must gloss over too much, and have little to say about Menzies in the first two decades of his public life, except that he learned his lesson well in 1941; the detractors, adopting the rhetoric of hard-boiled realism as they unmask the sordid and self-seeking behind high-sounding talk, take no account of how Menzies saw himself and ascribe to him a scarcely credible degree of conscious hypocrisy.

In the 1940s, before Menzies' later political success had polarised responses to him, his personality was seen by close observers as bewildering and contradictory. The parliamentary journalist Warren Denning described him as 'the Mona Lisa of Australian politics' and concluded that 'the essential difficulty in interpreting Mr Menzies as a personality, is that there were several natures within the one man, natures which were contradictory and sometimes mutually-cancelling. Out of this came the lack of a continuity of purpose, or even of thought, which contributed much to his Prime Ministerial difficulties'.[7] Alan Reid uses the same image of several men within the one to describe his life as a whole: 'as I watched Menzies over nearly thirty years I sometimes wondered whether four different people shared the name'.[8]

To bring some order to this apparent multiplicity of personalities is one of the challenges faced by anyone trying to understand Menzies. My order focuses on the tension between Menzies' ambitions and his ideals: his ambition to be a famous, powerful man, and his desire to live a life of noble service to institutions and people he valued.[9] This tension is at the heart not only of Menzies' personality but of his place in the culture, in particular the meaning of his relationship with England which was both the source of his ideals, and, it will be argued, the ultimate but unacknowledged goal of his ambition. On the one hand, Menzies can be seen as driven by ambition as he pursues fame and recognition in high political office; on the other, he can be seen as led by ideals as he aspires to values higher than the everyday. I will trace the tension and the shifting balance between these two poles of Menzies' personality at key points in his life – his childhood, his early political career, his first prime ministership, his fall in 1941 and the rebuilding of his political career during the 1940s.

JAMES AND KATE MENZIES

WHAT WERE the dynamics of family life in the cottage on the wheatfields? What sort of people were Kate and James Menzies? How did they relate to their fourth child and how did he relate to them? Such questions are difficult to answer for any family and my answers are speculative: they fit the evidence available to me of Menzies' childhood and they give a plausible account of aspects of the later public life. Writing about Menzies' childhood is made extra difficult by the scarcity of material. There are no surviving family papers – nothing to compare with the letters between the young Casey and his father, say – to give insight into the dynamics of Menzies' early family life. There are, however, numerous anecdotes of his childhood recorded after he became a significant national figure. Some of these come from Menzies himself, some from his older brother Frank Menzies, some from his sister Isabel Green, and some from people who knew the family. These are all shaped by the knowledge of Menzies' later career, but there is a remarkable consistency in the story they tell of a precocious, ambitious boy close to his mother and somewhat at odds with his demanding father.[10] As well, there is Menzies' own portrait of his parents in *Afternoon Light*, in which we see Menzies' parents as he wanted to remember them; through his emphases and omissions can be discerned the traces of childhood strategies.

Menzies presents his mother as cheerful, warm and loving, with 'remarkable talents': 'Everybody loved her'; 'Like the sundial she numbered only the sunny hours.' According to Dorothy Blair who knew the family when it first moved to Melbourne, Bob was his mother's favourite: 'Mrs Menzies ... doted on Bob. He was the centre of her universe & could do no wrong; nobody else really mattered!'[11] Menzies' closeness to his mother extended to her family with whom he felt a special affinity – he was regarded by both himself and the family as a Sampson.[12] Kate Menzies' father, John Sampson, was a Cornish miner who had been first president of the Creswick Miners' Union and was a lifelong unionist and labourist.[13] It was while reading to him from the *Sydney Worker* that Menzies discovered he was an instinctive conservative. The old man was delighted when he disagreed with the newspaper's views: 'He used to say to my mother – who was a great favourite of his – "Kitty, I see a great deal of myself in the boy Robert".'[14] Bob believed he was his grandfather's favourite grandson.[15]

Alongside his grandfather, Menzies claims his mother's brother, Sydney Sampson, as another important early political influence. 'He was a wise and widely-read man. When I was no more than twelve or thirteen years old, he would talk to me, as if I were years older, about such matters as the American Constitution! Needless to say he soon had me ransacking the meagre resources of the local "Mechanics' Institute" Library. Then and later he had a great influence on my mind.'[16] Perhaps the fact that Sydney Sampson had rebelled against his own father's political views to join an anti-labour party endeared him to the young Menzies. Sampson represented the Wimmera in Federal Parliament for thirteen years, until 1919 when his refusal to accept the endorsement of the Farmers' Union on the Burkean grounds that he must be a free agent led to his defeat by the endorsed candidate.[17]

Menzies told one of his biographers that the three people who influenced his life more than any others were his mother, his uncle Sidney Sampson, and his wife.[18] His father is conspicuously absent from this list, which is surprising, for he had an active political career. James Menzies' regular attendances at the meetings of the shire council in Dimboola were Menzies' first introduction to the idea of government: 'And I am bound to say that the Old Man was as emphatic about the politics of Dimboola as ever I have been myself about that of the nation.'[19] Later he was a member of the Victorian Parliament for ten years. A deep ambivalence comes through Menzies' description of his father. He stresses the complementarity of his parents' marriage, but his mother's calm reasonableness only highlights his father's difficult personality.

> Where he was explosively intolerant, she was calm, human and understanding and in the end, with patience, would secure a victory for sweet reasonableness. Father was a great one for getting things done. In this he was completely unselfish, for all his great crusades were for others. But in the battle he could inflict wounds. My mother healed them. She had a calm and, I think, beautiful face.

Similarly, the political lessons he attributes to his father are mainly negative.

> When my father went into the State Parliament, he was a mass of nervous energy. The nerves took charge when he made his maiden speech. After a few sentences he paused, and collapsed. He made a good recovery, but it was an inauspicious beginning. He did not become a Minister, but he was listened to. Even as a youngster, I thought he had some disabilities. He was eloquent, but over-emotional. He had no originating humour, and so took everything in the House too much *au grand serieux*. The first 'disability', as I have called it, had a curiously contrary effect upon me. Temperamentally linked as I was with my mother, and although I have always had a lot of emotion in me, I learned to distrust its public expression. When my father was in full spate at some meeting, and drew the tears from his audience, I am ashamed to say that I used to shrink in my seat and say to myself, 'I wish Father wouldn't do that!'

After such a strong repudiation of his father's example, Menzies does attempt to excuse his father, claiming that because 'He had not been through the disciplined experiences of the Law' the things that were deepest in his heart were nearer to the surface in expression; and that despite the sore need in the world for objectivity, 'there is a great place in life for beliefs so strongly held that they must find utterance and sway the hearts of men'.[20] Patronisingly, he gives his father a role to play, but it is not one with which he identifies, and the differences between them are no longer just a matter of temperament, but also of training: Menzies' education in the law has helped him leave his father's unschooled emotionalism far behind.

James Menzies was a passionate, strong-minded man. He was, says Isabel, 'always the head of the house, very much the head of the house'; and he backed his authority with passionately administered physical punishment.[21] Menzies remembers it clearly in *Afternoon Light*:

> The nervous tension which he had tended to make him both dogmatic and intolerant; in a very modified sense, a 'Barrett of Wimpole Street'. His temper was quick. We, his sons, got to know that 'whom the Lord loveth, he chasteneth'. We were not a little frightened of him, and found our regular refuge in the embracing arms of our mother who afforded us the comfort of her own understanding, balance, and exquisite humour.[22]

In an interview in 1969, he says, unprompted, 'I've known a few irascible men. My own father was a most irascible man. "Whom the Lord loveth he chasteneth".'[23]

Two anecdotes indicate something of James Menzies' attitude towards his fourth child. Dorothy Blair recalled how Mrs Menzies doted on Bob also remembered that he 'was quite a worry to his Father, who seemed incapable of understanding his roughshod methods of overruling everything & everybody'. She described an incident she witnessed at the family dinner table in January 1914, when Bob was a young university student. He became involved in a heated discussion which, she said, sounded like 'Bob Menzies against the Rest!' It became so noisy that Mrs Menzies suggested that those who had finished their meal adjourn outside to finish the argument. As they left, Mr Menzies turned to one of the guests 'and apologised for his "bumptious son Bob's precocity"'. The point of her story is that the man then said,

'Never mind, James, there goes one of our future Prime Ministers', but what is of interest here is James's obvious impatience with his son.[24] According to Isabel Green, when Bob first went to the Bar, his father would tell him how to conduct his cases, notwithstanding the fact that he had no knowledge of the law.[25]

The second anecdote tells of James finally recognising Menzies' talents. Menzies invited his parents to hear him present his first case to the High Court. He performed extremely well and the judge, Mr Justice Gavan Duffy, took the unusual step of complimenting him from the Bench on his performance. His parents too complimented him, his father, according to one of Menzies' biographers, 'a little shyly, because, strangely, it seems, he had not realised the full scope of Robert's talent'. Later, his mother told Robert that on the way home his father had said to her, 'It seems that I've underestimated Bob.' This anecdote appears almost word for word in both Dawes' manuscript and Seth's biography. Talking to his biographers many years later, Menzies still relishes the triumph.[26]

Each child in a family has a distinctive relationship with their parents — sometimes it is almost as if different children have different parents — and we can compare Menzies' accounts of his parents with those of his siblings. In particular, Frank Menzies, the second-eldest child, had a very different view of James Menzies from his younger brother's. He disagreed strongly with the account of his father in the Seth biography, which Seth claimed had come from Bob. 'It was not my estimate,' Frank later told Perkins; 'But Bob had his own estimate, so I let it stand.' He felt Bob never really appreciated the old man's character and he was at pains, in both interviews to which I have listened, to bring out his father's admirable qualities.[27] He describes his father as a wonderful man — warm, religious, intemperately generous, going any distance to do a good turn, and very emotional. He suggests that a lot of Bob's characteristics were formed in reaction to his father, and that 'if he had had more of Father in him' he would have been a warmer personality.[28] Frank also queries his brother's account of the family's hardship during their childhood. While life was hard there was not, Frank stresses, any real deprivation; they were a middle-class family and never lacked anything. He suggests that in denigrating his beginnings Bob is really denigrating his father, and that because he was so close to his mother he may have resented her being kept in the country.[29] The implication here is that Bob felt his mother deserved a better life than her husband had given her. Isabel Green shares Frank's high regard for their father and questions the role Menzies gives to John and Sidney Sampson in his early political education. The family were, she says, brought up on a diet of politics and on the legislation passing through State Parliament; Menzies didn't have any contact with John Sampson until he went to Ballarat, and then it was not much as he was working very hard.[30]

The testimony of two of James's other children, combined with the facts of his political career, suggest that we should approach Menzies' evaluation of his father with scepticism. James Menzies was a powerful, passionate, energetic man who was effective in his social world and who achieved considerable success in his life. He was, after all, a Member of Parliament for ten years, a not inconsiderable achievement for a man of little education and no social connections. More to the point, when Menzies was young his father was a big man in the small world in which the family lived. He was not a father who could be easily dismissed by his son, no matter how talented that son, nor how favoured by his mother. Biographer Allan Dawes comments on the tone in Menzies' voice when he talked to him of 'the Old Man', 'you can hear the capital letters in his voice', and he cites a family friend who says, 'I am sure Menzies would never in his father's lifetime have dared to do any act which he could not have declared without shame to his father, and that has been the key to his approach to the conventions of public and private morality throughout his life.'[31] A photograph of Menzies with his parents when he became Prime Minister in 1939 shows James as a compelling personality still. Later in his life Menzies was very ready to concede his father's superiority in Jeparit. At the unveiling of the memorial spire which the people of Jeparit erected to celebrate their most famous son, Menzies said he felt rather like the jackdaw in borrowed plumes, for what he had done for Jeparit was insignificant compared with what his parents had done.[32] There was some evidence of tension – his sister Isabel reported that she had never seen him so nervous[33] – but by then, of course, Menzies had moved far beyond Jeparit.

The picture that emerges of Menzies' relationship with his parents is not unusual: of a boy closer to his mother than his father, of a father whom the son regards as stern, difficult, irrational even, not appreciating his son and not doing as well by the mother as the son thinks she deserves. His discomfort with his father's passion and emotionalism hints as well perhaps at discomfort with his parents' sexuality. It is one of the common variations on the Oedipal triangle in which the boy is for a time locked in rivalrous combat with his father for his mother's love. Two very different evaluations of the young Menzies emerge from the evidence: the admired, highly valued self reflected in his mother's doting gaze; and the bumptious upstart who needed his father's firm hand. Menzies' early scholarly success and his determined ambition seemed designed to prove his mother's valuation right and his father's wrong.

Menzies' ambition originated, according to his own account, with the visit by a phrenologist to the local school.

> He said I would be a barrister and public speaker. I knew what a public speaker was, for my father was, in a sense, the local politician and a speaker of renown. But what was a barrister? I went home and was told. From that day on, my course was charted and my mind clear, provided that I could win enough free passages, that is, scholarships and exhibitions, to bring me to port.[34]

A more elaborate version of the same incident appears in Seth's biography in which his mother is the first recipient and interpreter of the phrenologist's reading. She tells him that to be a lawyer 'you have to study hard, go to good schools and the university and all that costs a lot of money, far more than we have'. 'I'll work hard and win scholarships', is young Robert's reply.[35] It is unlikely, of course, that the ambition originated with the phrenologist's prediction; far more likely that the prediction gave it a focus as the young boy determined to go beyond his father's role as a local public speaker. Once focused, it soared: Frank recalled that he had great ambition very early on – while still in Jeparit he aimed to be not just a barrister but the Chief Justice of Victoria.[36]

Young Menzies worked hard to fulfil his ambition, and was well rewarded. From the Ballarat East State School, which he attended while boarding with his grandmother, he won a state scholarship which enabled him to continue his secondary education. He topped the state, and Seth's account, drawing on both Menzies' and his brother Frank's memories, captures something of the excitement this caused in the family and in young Robert. He then went to Grenville College, a small private school where he studied for the Junior School Examination. Seth reports Menzies' description of his study regimen: 'Every evening, regular as clockwork, I got up from the table at quarter past six, and went up to my room. Every evening, regular as clockwork, at twenty past six, I sat down to my homework, and I worked solidly every evening until twenty minutes past midnight. I did six hours prep every night, except Sundays, of that first year.'[37] Because of his obvious scholarly aptitude, the headmaster of Grenville College, with an eye to the school's academic reputation, pushed him to sit for the Senior School Examination well in advance of the normal age. He worked extremely hard for it but failed, the only examination in his life he did not pass first time.[38] James Menzies was disappointed and 'gave him the rounds of the kitchen', stressing to him that there was no hope of university unless he won a scholarship. Shortly after this the family moved to Melbourne. James wanted Robert to continue his education at the Presbyterian Scotch College, but as some of his friends from Grenville were at Wesley, Menzies called on the headmaster, Dr L.A. Adamson. He told Dawes that, 'The Old Man was not very pleased about it, but there you are.'[39] Once at Wesley, Menzies continued to work hard, shunning sport and social life for his books; having failed once, he could not afford to fail again.[40] And he did not. He won a Government Exhibition to attend the University of Melbourne where, in accordance with the phrenologist's prediction, he enrolled in law.[41] At university there was no relaxing of the pattern of work already established, and Menzies continued to work far into the night with no time for sport or social life.[42]

In his first year at university Menzies published a short piece on the theme of ambition in *Melbourne University Magazine*, called 'Confessio Somniantis' (Confessions of a Dreamer). The dreamer stands in 'a land of death', filled with the sounds of 'sad remembrance' and 'angered bitterness'. Past him goes a procession 'white-clad, ghastly in the uncertain light. With eyes downcast they marched, and in their sunken cheeks, their dull stare, I saw no sign of hope'. Asking 'What men are these? What land is this?' he is told 'This is the land of the Past; and these shuffling forms – these are the Ghosts of Ambitions Unrealised!'[43] 'Confessio Somniantis' is a confused, portentous piece, but its psychological message is clear – without ambition and striving, life is dead and empty. At university and at the Bar Menzies continued to work prodigiously to ensure that he would never find himself in the land of ambitions unrealised. He took out a first-class law degree, quickly established himself as a leading barrister and took silk at an unusually young age. In 1928 in his early thirties he entered Victorian state politics where he stood out among his mediocre colleagues; and when he moved across to federal politics in 1933 he immediately became Attorney-General. After Joseph Lyons' sudden death in 1939 he became Prime Minister.

Again the story is conventional – an ambitious boy of humble background rises to prominence by dint of his own hard work and superior qualities. It is the classic myth of a socially open, competitive, individualist society. In 1966 the people of Jeparit where this rise began erected a spire to honour Sir Robert, as he was by then. The spire, a tall, thin obelisk topped with a thistle, rises from the flat landscape, its height matched only by the wheat silos across the way and some old red gums. The inscription on the base reads:

> The spire symbolises the rise to world recognition of a boy who was born in Jeparit and who rose by his own efforts to become Australian Prime Minister and a statesman recognised and honoured throughout the world.

For Jeparit there is a little reflected glory; for Sir Robert the spire is a symbol of origins surpassed, perhaps even of origins made irrelevant. For the more humble the origins, the more remarkable the individual, and the more the superior qualities manifested in the rise to eminence seem to cast doubt back on the origins. As Menzies' brother so perceptively pointed out, Menzies' stress on his humble beginnings implied a denigration of his father.

A FAMILY ROMANCE

A FEW years after the young Menzies' skull was revealing his potential to the phrenologist's fingers, Freud wrote a short essay called 'Family Romances',[44] in which he described the common childhood phantasy of replacing one's real parents with ones deemed to be more worthy. With this phantasy, Freud argued, the child attempts to reconcile his first exalted view of his parents, when they were the measure of his world and to be big like them his most intense desire, with his dawning awareness of their limitations. 'He gets to know other parents and compares them with his own, and so acquires the right to doubt the incomparable and unique qualities which he had attributed to them.'[45] He gets to know, too, the wider social world and to discover, by degrees, the category to which his parents belong. The child's response to the discrepancy between his real and imagined parents is to decide that his parents are not, in fact, his real parents, and to devise stories to explain this. Fairy tales and myths are full of royal children brought up in humble circumstances, while today's children speculate about adoption and mix-ups in the hospital. As well as allowing the child to retain his earlier idealisations of his parents, such stories allow the child to retain an exalted sense of himself: the offspring of divine parents can only be an infant god, hence the idealised parents of early infancy mirror the infant's grandiose sense of his own power and worth. Freud stressed that these imaginative romances are not rejections of the parents at all, but are based on 'the child's longing for the happy, vanished days when his father seemed to him the noblest and strongest of men and his mother the dearest and loveliest of women'. Detailed examination of the commonest of these imaginative romances, in which both parents or the father alone are replaced by grander people, reveals that the new, aristocratic parents 'are equipped with attributes that are entirely derived from real recollections of the actual and humbler ones'.[46]

When the child acquires some sexual knowledge, the parents' different roles in procreation are incorporated into the story and interact with the Oedipal desires to vanquish the father and possess the mother. Henceforth it is only the father whose parental role is denied. Imagining himself to be illegitimate, the child can keep his mother close and familial while replacing his father with a remote, imaginary father whose superior virtues cast a glow on himself. The boy can thus evade his Oedipal struggle and achieve an illusory victory over his father by reorganising the family's emotional space to eliminate the humiliating aspects of his biography – his unimpressive father, a hopelessly limited existence, and brothers and sisters who continually remind him of the intolerable fact that love must be shared.[47]

There is an obvious cost, however, in the boy's family romance, for by evading the Oedipal conflict he denies himself the chance to learn its lessons. In Freud's classic account of the Oedipal crisis, the boy's fear of castration forces him to give up his incestuous desires for his mother and his murderous aggression towards his father. The boy replaces his desire to possess his mother and defeat his father by an identification with his father in which he strives to become like him, to learn from him and to acquire his strengths. The Oedipal conflict is concerned with truth: in it the boy confronts the facts of life. These are not just the facts of his parents' sexual relationship, but the facts of relative size and capacities – the limits of his childish powers compared to his father's and the need to earn his adulthood. In this sense the Oedipal conflict confronts the child's desires and preferred view of himself with reality, and his defeat forces him to admit that there are some things he cannot do for now, some things he does not yet know; but the promise is held out that one day he will be a man like his father, with all a man's capacities and knowledge.

But what of a gifted boy who is his mother's favourite and whose talents seem set to carry him far beyond his parents and his limited origins? He can refuse to be forced into submission, sidestepping the father's strengths and replacing him with one more grand. If, in fact, such a boy does achieve success, his strategy will seem confirmed, for how could such an ordinary, limited father have brought forth such a gifted, successful son? He must belong elsewhere, far from this provincial world, among people of his own kind. Such a romance is an enormous spur to ambition as the boy tries to realise the grandiose self of his dreams, the self he perhaps imagines he sees reflected in his mother's eyes.

The family romance of most adults lies buried in their pasts, but traces can be seen in the stories they tell about themselves and their parents, and in the stories about themselves they try to make come true in their lives. As the soaring spire in Jeparit suggests, Menzies' life story seems one of origins surpassed, a family romance come true in which a poor boy of humble origins, of worthy but uneducated parents, rises higher, ever higher, quickly fulfilling the phrenologist's prediction and surpassing his childhood ambition to be Chief Justice of Victoria, to become Prime

Minister of his country and a familiar of royalty and great men. He moves at his ease among the cultured and powerful at the centre of his society, displaying by this very ease and familiarity that he really was one of them all along.

Freud's account of the family romance and its use in evading the father, however, alerts us to the deeper psychological dynamics of such a life story; in particular it prompts us to look more sceptically at Menzies' denial of his father's influence, and at the precocious formation of his political views. It also helps illuminate the source and direction of his ambition and gives an explanation of why, in the first half of his life at least, the espousal of his ideals so often had a hollow ring.

THE MEN OF ENGLAND

THE FAMILY romance depends on social difference, on children noticing that some other parents are richer, more powerful and more glamorous than their own, and that some other children occupy more significant social positions. It is a defence against the narcissistic injuries inflicted by class and rank on our childhood belief that we and our families are the centre of the world. Marthe Robert, who claims it is the originating plot of the novel, describes it as based on 'our irresistible urge to rise above our station'.[48] It has a particular aptness for the upwardly mobile in a socially open society who use their aggression and competitiveness 'to make something of themselves', who, in 'bettering themselves', inevitably do better than their parents. But as Freud points out, the family romance enshrines a deep irony, for by relegating the actual parents to contingent caregivers, the powerful parent imagos of infancy live on in their transformations – the noble, heroic parents who replace them. Seeking to escape the power of their parents, children only fall more heavily under their spell.

The form taken by a child's family romance and the replacement parents will depend in part on the materials to hand. Freud's subjects lived in the complexly ranked societies of pre-war Europe and had a wide array of social superiors on whom to focus their imaginings. The small social world of Jeparit offered far less scope: there were no large, wealthy landowners, no local squire nor lord of the manor, no glamorous local society. The most notable figure to visit Jeparit during Menzies' childhood was Sir Thomas Bent, the Minister for Railways, to investigate whether the railway line should be extended through Jeparit.[49] There was, however, the wider world mediated through books and through the family's participation in the ideology of the British Empire; here the young Menzies could find plenty of heroes and great men whose achievements could put his father's local and domestic authority well and truly in its place. And he could find in royalty a suitably elevated object for his earlier awe of his parents.

The family romance is designed in part to drive a wedge between the father and mother and it assigns them different roles. My main interest is in the way Menzies' relationship with his father played itself out in his relations with other men during his political career, but I do want to speculate briefly about the likely fate of his childhood feelings for his mother. It is not, I think, too fanciful to suggest that Menzies' feelings for his mother were the basis of his later deep attachments to Queen Elizabeth II and the Queen Mother. When Menzies first met the royal family in 1935, it was the royal women who captivated him rather than the dutiful Prince of Wales,[50] and I think it is significant for his extravagant public devotion to the monarchy during his second prime ministership that the reigning monarch was a woman. With men, no matter how exalted, there was always an edge of competitiveness; Menzies could not help but measure himself against them. Women excited no such demands and provided a refuge from the competitive world of men: when his father 'inflicted wounds' his mother 'healed them'. The Crown similarly stood above conflict. In one of the many pieces he wrote about the Crown and the monarchy, Menzies explains that it is the Crown's absence of legal power (lack of its power to inflict wounds) that is its strength, for lacking legal power it depends on impalpable things such as honour, respect, love and the embodiment of national sentiment and so has authority over the hearts and minds of the people.[51] Lifted above the strife of family or nation, women contain and dissolve conflict between men; they also receive the longing to be free of the need to compete and able to merge with something beyond one's self. Menzies' famous salute to the Queen, 'There is a lady sweet and kind,/ Was never face so pleased my mind;/ I did but see her passing by,/ And yet I love her till I die', echoes his tribute to his mother, 'She had a calm and, I think, beautiful face'; both evoke the child gazing devotedly at his mother's face, the adored mother of early childhood.

At a deeper level, the family romance perhaps also underlies Menzies' association of women with deceit and duplicity. In the later phase of the family romance, when the phantasy of being a foundling is replaced with that of being illegitimate, or at least the child of another father, the elimination of the unimpressive father depends on the mother's duplicity, his ascent on her fall. The mother, who thus epitomises the charm of all women, also displays their characteristic weakness and untrustworthiness; ' "the eternal feminine" and misogyny here reassert their old alliance'.[52] Although, in his facetious remarks on Portia, Menzies presents dishonesty as one of women's charms, it is a charm which disqualifies them from participation in the public world of competing men, and is thus the other side of the coin from their sentimental elevation above it.

Thinly disguised in his later reminiscences of his father is young Menzies' resentment of his father's authority. James Menzies, said his daughter Isabel, was very much the head of the household, and as a child Menzies would have had little choice but to submit. James Menzies' behaviour, however, is only part of the story. What is crucial is how Menzies himself experienced that behaviour. Here the contrast with his brother Frank is instructive. Frank was also subject to his father's authority and to his physical chastisement, but he seems to have responded differently. There is no hint of resentment in his reminiscences, in fact quite the opposite; he was 'really fond of Father'.[53] Frank Menzies is described by one writer as inheriting his father's qualities, particularly his generosity.[54] In Frank we can perhaps see the outline of a quite different resolution to a son's conflict with his father's authority, in which he identifies with the father and takes on his qualities. Bob Menzies' solution was different. He attempted to sidestep his father's power by replacing him in his imagination with one more grand and more suitable to his own estimation of himself. The authority of his actual father was thus the more keenly resented. However, and this is the irony of the family romance, Menzies' solution did not escape his father but only buried him deeper; his childhood awe of his father lived on in his life-long preoccupation with great men.

The young Menzies became a passionate reader and, like many boys, he was drawn to tales of adventure and the heroic achievements of great men. *Deeds that Won the Empire* and Scott's *Ivanhoe* were boyhood favourites, as was W.H. Fitchett's book on the Duke of Wellington's Peninsular Campaign against Napoleon (the source of his knowledge of the Siege of Badajoz with which he compared the storm that shook the Jeparit house). He could recite passages by heart from Jane Porter's *The Scottish Chiefs* and argued with the school inspector about the differences between its version of Scottish history and that in Dickens' *Children's History of England*; in particular, he regarded Dickens' William Wallace as insufficiently heroic.[55] Menzies' fascination with Scottish heroes is a striking example of Freud's argument that the heroes of childhood, on closer examination, carry the attributes of the disclaimed parents; there was no Scottish blood in his mother's family, the Cornish Sampsons.

A poem by Menzies in the 1912 edition of the *Wesley College Chronicle* shows a similar concern with the deeds and valour of past heroes.

> *Ours is the heritage of all that's noble,*
>   *The sacrifice of years that have gone by;*
> *The deeds our fathers did when they were mortal*
>   *Shall guide our steps, like voices from the sky!*
>
> *But whether in the din of some great combat,*
>   *Or in the milder walks of civil life,*
> *The spirit that our yesterdays bequeath us*
>   *Shall watch our beings in their daily strife.*
> *And may we show, to all the world, the presence*
>   *Of that same courage that enriches men;*
> *Forgetting self, we'd hear the commendation:*
>   *'The heroes of the ages live again!'* [56]

It shows, too, a concern with the approval of these heroes. The present generation are watched by the spirits of the past and their gaze both spurs on and validates their lives.

Menzies was at Wesley during the high season of Laurence Adamson's power as headmaster. An upper-class Englishman of private means, Adamson had been educated at Rugby and Oxford and called to the Bar at the Inner Temple. Arriving in Australia in 1886, he was employed as a schoolmaster at Wesley where he threw himself into building up the school's reputation in competitive sport. He became Headmaster in 1902. Adamson believed that a great public school should be the hub of its students' lives, not just a place they attended from 9 a.m. to 4 p.m. on weekdays. He set about developing the atmosphere of masculine solidarity he had known at Rugby, chiefly through sport (which required that boys stay after school and attend on Saturdays), but also through the singing of school songs, many of which he wrote, and through an ambitious building programme to provide a gymnasium and an assembly hall, half the funds for which came from his own pocket. The school community held Adamson in awe; they felt astonished but privileged that this rich, cultivated Englishman had chosen Wesley for his life's work.[57]

A description of Adamson addressing the assembled school shows his style of public speaking to be remarkably similar to the one Menzies was later to develop.

> Point, power of comment, and brevity – the soul of wit – marked Adamson's morning addresses. His wit, if incidental, was always deliciously phrased. He held us completely. We hung on his eyebrow, on his every word. He never talked down to us, or over our heads. To him that would have been a discourtesy – even to us boys. But he had the knack of treating us as men, and men of honour – always, whatever the circumstances.[58]

Here is both a desciption of Menzies' style, down to the use of the eyebrows, and of his ethics of public speaking.

ABOVE: Menzies took a home-movie camera with him on his trip to London in 1941. Here he photographs some war damage. He also photographed members of the royal family and the British political élite.   AUSTRALIAN WAR MEMORIAL

BELOW: Menzies returned to Australia in May 1941 after four months' absence. Flanked by Country Party leader Arthur Fadden and by Billy Hughes, he tells the waiting nation, 'I come back to Australia with just one sick feeling in my heart - that I must come back to my own country and play politics.'   SYDNEY MORNING HERALD

The following four photographs are taken from Menzies' home movies of his 1941 trip to England. NATIONAL FILM & SOUND ARCHIVE
ABOVE: *Strolling at Chequers*.
BELOW: *'Just to prove I met him'* is the caption with which Menzies introduces scenes of Churchill.

ABOVE: *With Lloyd George.*
BELOW: *Winston Churchill.*

Prime Minister again. Shortly after leading the Liberal Party to victory in 1949, Menzies looks relaxed, confident and pleased to be back. SYDNEY MORNING HERALD

ABOVE: *Beginning in his boyhood in Jeparit, Menzies read books to construct for himself an imaginary England in which he could escape the provincial outpost of his birth. On holidays in the late 1950s, he relaxes with the* Pelican Selection of Eighteenth Century Prose. LAUNCESTON EXAMINER
BELOW: *Menzies had an uneasy relationship with the press, distrusting their critical, denigratory aggression. Here he threatens the press with a woomera and spear with which he was presented while visiting the Woomera rocket range in 1953.* HERALD & WEEKLY TIMES

In 1941 on his war-time trip to Britain, Menzies' rise to world eminence came up against the rock of Churchill, and he experienced his first real defeat. In 1969 he unveiled a bronze statue of Churchill presented to Britain by President Tito. UNITED PRESS INTERNATIONAL

Menzies' intense love for the mother of his childhood found one of its transformations in his later devotion to Queen Elizabeth. He greeted the Queen on her 1963 royal tour with the lines, 'I did but see her passing by, and yet I love her till I die.' AGE

ABOVE: In 1965 the people of Jeparit erected a monument to the town's most famous son – a soaring obelisk topped by a thistle. HERALD & WEEKLY TIMES
BELOW: In 1966, Menzies was installed as Lord Warden of the Cinque Ports at Dover Castle, the 'first man from the outer Commonwealth' to occupy this ancient office. ASSOCIATED PRESS

To appeal to his audience's humane passions and to address them courteously as equals were ideals of public-speaking Menzies was later to advocate.[59] Adamson was the first upper-class Englishman to whom Menzies had prolonged exposure and he provided the schoolboy Menzies with a model of public speaking more controlled and dignified than his father's passionate outbursts, and carrying far more cultural power.

Throughout his life Menzies was fascinated by the great men of the past. When he first visited England he saw and heard the shades of great men – John Hampden's disappearing plume, Robert Walpole looking down at him from the wall of the Cabinet room, Edmund Burke's voice ringing in the rafters of Westminster Hall. These were the men with whom he had identified, whom he had striven to become like in his ambitious ascent of the hierarchies of male power, and whose approval he had sought. In Australia Menzies was generally granted his imaginary identifications. In the early 1960s, M.H. Ellis developed an extensive comparison between Menzies and the eighteenth-century Whig politician Charles Fox. 'Menzies,' he wrote, 'is a child of the 18th century... his reading is that of a natural extension of the normal reading of a late 18th-century political intellectual.'[60] This was also how Menzies liked to see himself: a photograph of him on holidays in Tasmania in the late 1950s shows him sitting reading the Pelican selection of eighteenth-century prose. But Australia in the twentieth century was not England in the eighteenth; Menzies was not a child of the eighteenth century but of the twentieth. The question at the core of Menzies' self-identifications was – did he measure up?

When I first began working on Menzies, one of my most striking impressions was of a life lived out before a projected observer. This was partly a sense of a life performed in public before an audience – in the courtrooms and smoke rooms, on the hustings and in Parliament; but it was more than this. It was also the sense that everything Menzies did was offered up for judgement and that the source of this judgement was always external. Menzies sought not just admiration for his achievements, but approval. He was, says his sister, always concerned with the view history was going to take of him, and the judgement of history is evoked often in his speeches and writings, as in the following conversation with Churchill.

> 'You realise,' I said, 'that five years after your death, an event which I hope and believe will be long postponed, clever young men from Oxford and Cambridge or some other seat of learning will be writing books explaining that you were never right about anything!' . . . 'But,' I added, 'not many years later, the clever young men will have been forgotten and your name will be seen clearly at the pinnacle.'[61]

History here seems but a transformation of the watching spirits of his schoolboy poem. To reconcile Churchill to the prospect of criticism he does not appeal to his sense of inner conviction; he does not say, for example, you know in your heart you did what was right, but conjures up the vindicating judgement of history.

The position from which this final judgement will be made is occupied by the father, whom Menzies may have thought he had surpassed in his easy rise to power and fame, but who reappears in the multitude of great men before whom he plays out his life, of whose approval he can never, finally, be certain, and whose position he can never, finally, occupy. This is the cost to the son of maintaining his family romance: avoiding Oedipal defeat by replacing the father with an imaginary and far grander one, he loses the chance to identify with the father and so acquire his strengths; he loses, in a very deep sense, the chance to become a man, like his father, and so no longer dependent on his father's approval because he now carries his father's strength and power within. Instead of becoming a man through the inner conviction which comes with identification, he simply dresses himself up as one, and hence is continually dependent on the gaze of others to validate his claim. The apparent Oedipal victory is hollow, for the father, never confronted face to face, his superior strengths never conceded, continues to hold the boy in his thrall; and the boy, forever evading the Oedipal conflict by maintaining the illusion of his superior gifts, can never move beyond it and himself occupy with equanimity the father's position.[62] He remains a precocious boy, parading in the robes of manhood which he donned too early in an attempt to evade ever having to admit his father's superiority.

The costs to Menzies of his lingering family romance were substantial, manifesting themselves particularly in his striking imperviousness to experience, evident not just in his continuing attachment to the imperial world order of his youth, in his lack of curiosity about other cultures, or in the consistency of his political views over a lifetime, but in his readiness to have opinions on matters of which he had little substantial knowledge – as in his notorious venture into the patronage of the fine arts. His public statements and comments were pronouncements, made with an authoritative certainty which did not seem quite earned. This aura of phoneyness was clearly evident in his student writings which, with the exception of the atypical essay on Australian poetry, have the pompous stageyness of a young man putting on the attitudes and opinions more appropriate to his aspirations than to his current position in life. Inevitably, these attitudes and opinions were conventionally conservative –

the views of the establishment rather than of the creative conservative thinker:[63] if one adopts one's political philosophy at twelve one does not have much option but to take one ready made, even if one later learns to deploy it with ease and conviction. As Menzies grew older he was able to fill out his public persona more convincingly; but some hint of imposture, of duplicity even, remained, and at the end of his life the appearance of achievement seemed greater than the substance.

THE ELEVATED SELF

INFERIORS

Freud's account of the family romance makes clear that it is a story which elevates the self as well as the parents, but it elevates the self prematurely, in defiance of the child's actual status and capacities within the family. Consequently, the child must make great efforts to ward off threats to his assumed status and position, including from his own internal doubts. One of the most frequent adjectives in Menzies' memoirs is 'great'. They are full of descriptions of great leaders, great events, great principles, great human qualities, even great dinners, and he means by this dinners of pomp and circumstance. Something of the weight of history, of momentous deeds and men above the ordinary, moves in the word. The great have the approval of history. Always implied in the judgement is the question of how he himself measures up, both against universal standards of greatness and against other contenders. The deep fear is that he doesn't measure up at all; for a preoccupation with greatness is also a preoccupation with its opposite – with what is little, puny, insignificant, unworthy.

Condensed in the one word 'great' is the tension between the two evaluations of his self which Menzies took from his childhood: the overvalued self grounded in the special relationship he felt he had with his mother and given credibility by his scholastic achievements – the gifted young prince destined to take his rightful place at the centres of power and significance; and the undervalued self all too aware of its limitations as it bridled beneath his father's authority. Much about his relations with others can be understood in terms of the interaction between these two evaluations of the self – one which needed to be maintained, the other to be disproved. The result, as his contemporaries saw it, was a man acutely sensitive to hierarchies of power and to his own position in them. His assumed elevated position had to be kept up, and he was constantly alert to its defence, enacting in his relations with others the competition for public advantage which was central to his political philosophy.

Hierarchies have two directions – up and down. To those below, Menzies was condescending, belittling and occasionally kind, so long as they kept their place. In public he always wore the air of a superior being. This was greatly aided by his height and, as he aged, his bulk. Even as a student he was 'massive and dignified'.[1] Liberal MP Edgar Holt described Menzies' public self in later life:

> To see Menzies put on his public self was an extraordinary spectacle. Towards the end of his term as Prime Minister age was showing in his face and movements. Sitting alone he could look authoritatively like a seventy year old grandfather. He could be stooped shouldered, his thoughts a world away, his hands flat on his knees.
> Suddenly, the bell rings. He stirs himself, he slowly stands up, he issues to himself some mysterious command, the figure seems to grow larger, the face takes on the look of command, and with a paper under his arm, he moves majestically into

the lobby, for the world to see... The performance could not have been achieved by a man physically small. The stature, the massive head, and the sheer bulk were splendid raw material to be used by a master of presentation.[2]

In his younger days, Menzies' sense of public presence was less supported by his public role, and his bearing was widely seen to be aloof, arrogant and cold;[3] at times he even seemed ridiculous, as in the following two anecdotes from his university days in which an awkward country boy, still learning to pass in urban middle-class society, makes a massive effort to maintain his dignity, exposing his superior air as really just front. Dorothy Blair, a friend of his sister, recalled a tennis party at which Bob's exhibition on the court was deplorable. 'He knew the standard of tennis to expect, and should have stayed at home! He tried to "talk" himself out of the situation and shamed us even further.'[4] Brian Lewis, whose sister Phyllis was briefly engaged to Menzies (an event which passes unmentioned in all the biographies), reported a similar incident when Menzies' body let him down. They were fishing in sight of shore when they saw Bob waiting on the pier and pulled up their lines to get him, city clothes and all:

> but it was choppy and Bob felt sick, so we had to pull up the lines again and row back to the pier. We lost a good half hour and a lot of fish. We were embarrassed because Bob was embarrassed. He seemed ashamed that his seemingly formidable figure had been brought down by a petty physical weakness which lesser people did not have.[5]

While his front may have occasionally slipped, mostly it worked, intimidating those around and making them feel small. Dorothy Blair's comment is echoed many times during his life: 'He obviously despised me, as he did all those whose intellectual capacities were less than his.'[6] Menzies deployed his presence in ways which made others feel small. Arthur Fadden observed, 'His own educational attainments and the way he applied them made me conscious of my lack of similar educational qualifications.'[7] Similarly Enid Lyons remembered her first meeting with him. Visibly pregnant at the time she already felt at a disadvantage, but 'the impact of that dominating personality, who quite obviously would never feel at the slightest disadvantage under any circumstances whatsoever, completely overwhelmed me'.[8]

Circumstances conspired to protect Menzies from the blows experienced by other men of his generation in World War I. Despite his profusely expressed patriotism, Menzies did not enlist, something which cost him dear in his later political career. His brother Frank, who made it clear that there were family reasons behind Menzies' decision, also remarked on the effects on his character of missing out on the levelling experience of the army. Bob was, he told Perkins, a 'pretty self-opinionated sort of fellow at University', and 'a few years in the army would have done him a lot of good'.

While he was at the Bar Menzies' air of superiority was a minor disadvantage: it made him less successful with a judge and jury than before a judge alone because he could not always conceal his mental superiority to the witness he was cross-examining which sometimes made the jury sympathetic to the witness.[9] After he entered politics, however, it became a major drawback. While no one questioned his ability and intellectual gifts, many doubted his personality. From the 1930s to the early 1950s, when his electoral victories finally quashed the critics, doubts were continually expressed about his ability to win the support of the Australian people.[10]

The liabilities of Menzies' elevated sense of self were perhaps greatest in his dealings with political colleagues: he was very sensitive to criticism;[11] he surrounded himself with men who were no challenge, the 'court jesters' they were sometimes called.[12] He was rude to men, like Casey and Evatt, whose accomplishments rivalled his own,[13] and he had little interest in encouraging younger, up-and-coming politicians.[14] Despite having himself first been a cabinet minister in his late thirties, Menzies' 1958 cabinet included only two men younger than fifty. Alexander Downer reports that, when he challenged Menzies on this, he was told that Macmillan had to wait eight years in the House of Commons before being given a post, so the younger men had little to complain about.[15] Menzies' own impatient ambition in both the Argyle and Lyons cabinets would have been as relevant a comparison, but it was not one Menzies was likely to make. Being a son for Menzies was not a useful, transitory experience, but a wholly humiliating and resented one, so he had no interest in identifying with the sons. Perhaps, too, he feared that the sons would be as ruthless towards those above as he could be. Menzies' identifications were always upwards, with those who had achieved greatness and position, never downwards with the hopefuls and challengers. Where Menzies' position was clearly unassailable, as with his court jesters, or with senior public servants, he could be charming, affable and relaxed; when he felt the need to be on guard, it was a different story.

Menzies is described by some of his colleagues as a skilled listener, in private conference as well as in cabinet.[16] At first glance this may appear to contradict the characterisation I am developing here; however, the skills that are testified to are analytic not empathetic. Menzies was able to get to the core of a problem astonishingly quickly, or succinctly sum up the issues in a cabinet debate, but no one, not even great admirers like Bunting and Hasluck, describes him as a sympathetic listener, someone with whom to discuss a difficult personal problem. To listen empathetically one has to be able to put oneself in the other person's shoes, and this requires a very different stance towards other people from Menzies'.

Perhaps the most damaging of all Menzies' political liabilities was his vindictive wit with which he would belittle and denigrate both friend and foe. Menzies, it was said, would rather lose a friend than a repartee.[17] Already, at Wesley, 'his tongue was derisive. He did not hesitate to throw his weight about, and his common term of scorn for those with whom he disagreed – a thing which frequently happened – was "You're a dag".'[18] Howard Beale describes him as 'having a sort of off-hand contempt... which upset listeners as well as the victim... there was in him a strange compulsion, in certain moods, to wound and humiliate'.[19] This vindictive urge to humiliate was particularly apparent before 1941 and made him many unnecessary enemies.[20] Spender describes a typical incident from this period: One night, having enjoyed Menzies' company, a senator who was generally hostile to him said, 'You were wonderful tonight, Bob... it's a pity you are not always so pleasant... Your great trouble, Bob, is that you don't suffer fools gladly.' Menzies replied, 'And what, pray, do you think I am doing now?' Spender comments, 'Menzies had a chance to build a bridge between himself and the Senator – but he blew it up. He affronted before others, however unwittingly, the dignity of a lesser man, and this was not forgotten. In 1941 this Senator worked unceasingly to displace Menzies.'[21]

Menzies did learn to control his tongue somewhat during the 1940s, but the urge to humiliate did not totally disappear. Alexander Downer, who entered the House of Representatives at the 1949 election, remembers Menzies' ridiculing him for his nervousness when addressing the House and comments that several MPs had similar debasing experiences.[22] Menzies' wit not only made him enemies, it frightened people. Frank Menzies told Kevin Perkins that he and his sons were always afraid he would point out that something they said was foolish, and that if he had been in cabinet he would have been afraid that something he said would be stripped down and shown to be silly or foolish. In the interview he said a number of times, 'I was frightened of him myself.' One wonders how his own sons fared.

Menzies' vindictiveness is usually discussed hand in hand with his wit. While observers admired the wit, they were clearly discomforted by it, recognising the aggression behind the jokes. In humour we play with forbidden desires.[23] Most jokes and witticisms deal with the three taboo topics of sex, death and aggression – dirty jokes, sick jokes and put-down jokes. Menzies' speciality was the put-down in which people are made to look and feel stupid or silly, and are revealed as powerless, particularly in relation to himself.[24] The wit or the joke makes the aggression acceptable, as well as generally disabling the victim.

The central issue of Menzies' wit was that of relative position and power; by putting upstarts in their place he asserted and defended his own dominant position.[25] He also took advantage of it; it is, after all, a brave man who makes the boss look foolish. The example Spender gives is typical. The senator's crime was to assume a position of equality from which he could proffer some friendly advice; he was quickly disabused of this presumption. In asserting his dominance Menzies frequently appealed to broader hierarchies of social value, identifying himself with the dominant social values against some less esteemed group. In a typical jibe at the Country Party he flaunts his superior education: 'My colleague Jack McEwen has been nicknamed "Black

Jack". Now and again I address him as "Black", and occasionally, when in a highbrow mood, I call him *Le Noir*. That's only when I don't want other Country Party men to know what I'm talking about.'[26]

Many of Menzies' jokes appealed to class power, particularly as it expressed itself in educational differences. When asked by a heckler what he was going to do about 'ousing, he reputedly replied, 'Put an "h" in front of it.'[27] Physical characteristics were another common target. Replying to a plump heckler who yelled, 'Come on, Bob! Tell us about inflation and round it off!' he said, 'Stand up and let's have a look at you. At a glance, I wouldn't think you need to be told anything about inflation.' Sometimes Menzies' wit failed and there was just the insult and the assertion of superiority, unsweetened by humour. His brother Frank recalled an election speech of the 1930s when he said of Scullin, how could a grocer from Sebastopol know anything about finance. His father, who was in the audience, and who had himself run a general store, thought this quite out of place.[29] Perhaps he recognised himself as the real target.

Menzies used his wit to defend his assumed elevated status. Because, particularly in his early adult life, it was assumed as much as earned, he defended it vigorously. The suspicion that he was not as clever or in command as he presented himself as being must never be allowed to surface, threats must be anticipated and put down before they even formed; in the words with which he praised the batting of Patsy Hendren, 'His was the defence of the attack.'[30] And the main weapon of his defence was language, supplemented by skill in mimicry and an imposing physical presence. This weapon was chiefly used against immediate competitors and those below – hecklers, ill-prepared ministers, junior party members, inept opponents.

Menzies' relations with those above were more complex. In his imagination he may have been able to sidestep his father's authority, and he worked hard to achieve a social position appropriate to his elevated self as quickly as possible. However, although he was generally very successful at extracting deference for this elevated self from those around him, he still had to deal with those above and with the broader relations of power which sanctioned their authority over him. Gifted and superior though he may have been, he was not born at the top and he had to learn to suffer superiors. How did Menzies relate to his betters?

SUPERIORS

MENZIES HAD great difficulty with his leaders in Australian politics. In both Victorian and federal politics he resigned from cabinet on points of principle in ways that caused political difficulties for the government: in the first case over the government's decision to reopen an inland freezing works to save a sitting member's seat; in the second over the Lyons government's dropping of a national insurance scheme on the eve of its proclamation. In both cases the resignations were justified by appeals to the principles of responsible democratic government; in Melbourne it was the government putting political expediency above its responsibility for the state's finances; in Canberra it was his duty to keep his word to his electorate. Both resignations were preceded by public speeches on the need for leadership. Menzies venerated public office and the responsibilities of state, and he held high standards for the proper conduct of those who chose the most noble of the civil vocations – such high standards, in fact, that many incumbents of high office were inevitably found wanting.

The Nationalist Party members he joined on his election to the Victorian Upper House in 1928 were an undistinguished lot and Menzies lost no time in differentiating himself from them, forming with Wilfred Kent Hughes the Young Nationalists to ginger up the party.[31] In 1929 in an address to a 'Pleasant Sunday Afternoon' at Melbourne's Wesley Church, Menzies took as his theme the gap between the ideal legislator and the candidates preferred by the Victorian voters. The ideal legislator, he said, should have 'a well informed brain', a broad grasp of general principles, the capacity for hard work, and be able to consider the needs of the whole state, not just his constituency. A few Members of Parliament measured up to this ideal, but the majority fell short; they were 'too concerned with the effect of their actions on their constituents and thus forfeited their position as leaders', wasting their time doing 'dogwork' for their constituents in the public departments. All was not lost, however: 'fortunately in British history the men who gave heed to principles had not always been neglected, or we would have been without the great men who have adorned public life'.[32]

Here Menzies honours the offices and institutions of parliamentary democracy while criticising the incumbents. Menzies' own ambition is clearly evident behind the principles, for the implicit argument is that although those already in high office are not up to their grave responsibilities, he is, and he is ready and willing to serve; Menzies had clearly not entered politics to waste himself on 'dogwork' but to contribute to grander, more worthwhile matters. When he won the seat of Kooyong and left state politics for bigger things, the Victorian Premier, Sir Stanley Argyle, is reported to have said to a federal politician, 'Thank God we got rid of him. You're welcome to him.'[33]

There was no long wait on the backbench for Menzies when he entered federal politics, and he was straight away appointed Attorney-General. His relations with Prime Minister Joe Lyons were cordial, but by the late 1930s tensions were obvious. Lyons' health was failing, contributing no doubt to the indecisive leadership of which many were complaining, and he was keen to retire. There were a number of contenders for the leadership, Menzies prominent among them.[34] Peter Heydon, who was his private secretary during a trip to England in early 1938, said of Menzies at the time, 'There is no doubt that at this time one thing dominated Menzies' thinking. He thought he would be a good Prime Minister of Australia, he wanted to be Prime Minister of Australia and all his actions were largely tested against that particular framework of reference.'[35] During this trip, he was hailed in London as 'inevitably' becoming Australia's Prime Minister. Displaying immense self-confidence, he criticised Churchill to a *Sunday Times* reporter for reading his speeches, and made adverse public comments on both English cricket-writers and the poor technical knowledge of the crowd at Lord's.[36] England was beginning to lose some of its imaginary glow and to attract Menzies' more critical, competitive eye.

In October 1938, in circumstances charged with doubts about the Prime Minister's capacities, Menzies made a speech complaining of a lack of leadership in Australian politics. The speech was very general, arguing that Australia needed inspiring leadership to face the dangers of the times.[37] Menzies denied he had been referring to Lyons, but in the circumstances of the time, from such an obviously ambitious man, the denial was not convincing. Joe Lyons' wife Enid, for one, did not believe it: 'The attack on Joe's leadership had for weeks, yes, even months, filled columns of the daily press. He would be a naive person indeed who would expect such a speech at that time to be taken at its face value, and Bob was not noted for naivete.'[38]

This speech was also followed by a principled resignation. Menzies had promised his electorate to support a national insurance scheme and when it was dropped on the eve of its proclamation he announced that he had no option but to resign or break his word. Again he justified his actions in terms of his principles:

> It is clear that I cannot, with self respect, abandon today what I wrote only a few weeks ago. I am bound, not only by my real belief that the best interests of Australia would be served by going on with this scheme, but by my categorical statement to my constituents.
>
> I make no cheap criticism of the position of the Prime Minister or any of my colleagues. In particular, I make no attack on my friend and colleague the Treasurer [Richard Casey], who has worked manfully on this matter. Each of us must determine his own line of action according to his own rights and obligations.[39]

Despite disavowals, his resignation, like his speech on the need for better leadership, was seen by many as a public criticism of Lyons, and when Lyons died of a heart attack a few months later Menzies was accused of having contributed to his death through actions calculated to increase the pressure on a sick man. Enid Lyons, however, saw his resignation differently. The whole period, she wrote, was one of stress, not only for Joe but also for Menzies: 'For Menzies it was a continuing clash between desire and loyalty: the desire of a young ambitious man convinced of his own power to serve his country well, and the loyalty he owed the Leader who had given years of selfless service, but whose capacity for further leadership he genuinely doubted.' She did not accept Menzies' reasons for his resignation, but regarded it as merely a convenient exit from a situation he no longer found bearable. Joe, she said, was relieved.[40]

Menzies' ideals helped him both control and mask the aggression he inevitably felt towards those above him and to attempt to put it to good use. He was not only criticising those above to advance himself, but also advancing the honourable cause of good government in which he truly believed; so although his ideals provided cover and rationalisations for his ambition, they also harnessed that ambition to higher ends. Both resignations could be seen as justified. The Victorian government of William McPherson *was* hopelessly parochial, and its decision to fund a freezing works it had opposed when in opposition *was* motivated by little more than political expediency. The Lyons government *was* politically indecisive. It had put immense effort into the preparation for a national insurance scheme, which it then dropped for no immediately apparent good reason.[41] It was thus easy for Menzies to convince himself that his actions, in both cases, were justified by what he believed. Many of his contemporaries in politics were not convinced, and saw the espousal of ideals as chiefly serving the ambition; only Enid Lyons, watching the competitive world of male politics from the sideline, grasped the tension between his desire (ambition) and his loyalty (ideals).

Menzies' ideals served complex psychological purposes. Yes, they did help him advance himself, but they also helped him hold in check his envy and anger towards anything or anyone who made him feel small. Warren Denning saw in the 'Mona Lisa' of Australian politics 'a curious little pucklike Mr Menzies, an elfin creature of mischief and malice, never able to resist sticking pins in the world's pants, always under temptation to twist the noses of pompous people, or to dance on the prides, the pretensions, and the illusions of nearly everybody who crossed his path.'[42] Most of the time this malicious, derisive self was under control; what's more, he recognised it immediately when he saw it in others and berated it soundly.

Menzies frequently complained about the unfair criticism to which the prominent were subjected; '... the moment a man begins to achieve a position in public life, every little tongue and every little dirty mind begins to look around and try to find something about him; whether he beats his wife, or whether he is a chronic "boozer" '.[43] Such attitudes, he argued, were all too prevalent in democracies: 'To discourage ambition, to envy success, to distrust independent thought, to sneer at and impute false motives to public service – these are the maladies of modern democracy, and of Australian democracy in particular.'[44] The press were particular villains – 'the denigrators' he called them.[45] John Bunting was puzzled by the depths of Menzies' contempt for the press.[46] His dislike of public criticism obviously partly explains such attitudes, but there was more to it than that. Protecting the institutions he revered from the denigrators, he was also protecting them from himself.

Even more sinister threats to society than the press and the ingrates of democracy were those radicals and revolutionaries intent on wrecking society's institutions, the duplicitous communists who masked their destructive intent with soft words of peace. Many trenchant defenders of authority are as ambivalent about it as the radicals who attack it, which is why they are so intransigent in its defence, yielding no ground lest this ambivalence be released. Their ambivalence, however, is dealt with differently. Rather than attacking the institutions in which they, at least at the beginning, had a subordinate place, they elevate them, lifting them as far as they can from the denigrators, including themselves. Ideals can also be idealisations – defences against envy and anger; by idealising an object one can protect it from the rage and anger one feels at the inferiority and dependence to which one is relegated by its superiority.[47] Wrote Goethe, 'Against another's great merits there is no remedy but love.'[48]

Menzies did not become a radical or revolutionary, or even a journalist; rather he devoted his life to the service of two of the dominant institutions of power and authority in the society into which he was born – the law and Parliament. In writings and speeches throughout his life Menzies continually affirmed the wisdom and value of Australia's dominant legal and political institutions – the law, the institutions of responsible parliamentary government, and the British Commonwealth. The 'rule of law' was to him one of the fundamental truths and conditions of democratic rule; he regarded the system of responsible government under the Crown as the best ever devised; and he remained an ardent supporter of the British Commonwealth.[49] His devotion to these institutions was anchored in his devotion to England, the source of all that was valuable in his world. But within his ostentatious identification with authority and veneration of England there was more ambivalence than he cared to admit, more perhaps than he even knew.

THE NARCISSISTIC WOUND OF COLONIAL BIRTH

THE COMMONLY told story of England as the great romance of Menzies' life ignores the competitive, querulous notes that at times broke through the hymns of praise; for Menzies wanted to be recognised at the centre, not just humbly to sing its praises. Menzies idealised England far beyond and far longer than most other Australians of his day;[50] from the point of view of later generations he idealised it to the point of parody, even wanting in the 1960s to name the major unit of Australia's new decimal currency the Royal. In this excessiveness was unconscious purpose; Menzies' idealisation of England was in part a defence against the envy and rage he felt against something which made him feel small.

Menzies' family romance was spun from British literature and British history; these provided the material from which he could construct an imagined world where his elevated self would be among its peers, a world far from the limited, provincial world of Jeparit and far from his father's authority. His natural talents, aided by determination and hard work, could make that romance come true and his true nature would manifest itself in his success. Beyond the boyhood ambition to be Chief Justice of Victoria there was national office in the newly formed Australian government, and beyond that was London, the centre of Empire. A place in English history was the ultimate goal of Menzies' ascent, and in a sense he reached it with his investiture as Lord Warden of the Cinque Ports. In another sense, however, it eluded him, for he never had a position of substantive political power in England. Anthony Trollope's Lady Glencora remarks that to be Prime Minister of England 'is to be the greatest man in the greatest country in the world. Do ever so little and the men who write history must write about you'.[51] But Prime Minister of England Menzies could never be. Menzies' apparently limitless rise had eventually to come up against the intractable fact of his Australianness.

The narcissistic wound of colonial birth is well attested to in the writings of colonials, and Menzies' adult sensitivities to hierarchies of place and power suggest he would have felt it keenly. It can, however, be responded to in different ways. The most common are the defiant denial of the superiority of the metropolis and excessive deference to it, the stances which Arthur Phillips described as the strut and the cultural cringe.[52] Menzies' response was different again. It was twofold: to deny that there was any significant difference between province and metropolis, centre and periphery, at least as far as he is concerned; and to idealise the centre in order to hold it high above the rage he felt against anything which made him feel small and powerless.

In David Malouf's *Johnno*, the narrator expresses a sense of the profound contingency of a birth that has condemned him to the most ordinary place in the world – Arran Avenue, Hamilton, Brisbane, Queensland:

> What an extraordinary thing it is, that I should be here rather than somewhere else. If my father hadn't packed up one day to escape military service under the Turks; if my mother's people, for God knows what reason, hadn't decided to leave their comfortable middle class house at New Cross for the goldfields of Mount Morgan, I wouldn't be an Australian at all. It is practically an accident, an entirely unnecessary fate.[53]

To be Australian – an entirely unnecessary fate. The agents of Menzies' entirely unnecessary fate, James and Kate Menzies, compounded the misfortune of their own colonial births by moving to a place as unpropitious as Jeparit for the birth of their fourth child. Here was something further to add to the resentment against the limits their authority already placed on him.

Menzies never sought to deny his Australianness; rather he sought to minimise its implications by fervently believing in the unity of the British Empire. Allan Dawes titles his manuscript biography of Menzies 'A Young Man from the Provinces' and begins with a quotation from Menzies.

> Neville Chamberlain was a remarkable man. At an annual banquet of the Royal Academy at Burlington House Chamberlain took a text – I almost suspect him of some good sound Presbyterian blood – 'And

a young man came up out of the Provinces!' And what he had to say was so abundantly and magnificently true in Great Britain... that out of the small provincial towns and the remotest hamlets there had come, century after century, a great army of men who served their King and Country in war and peace; and on their contribution to national life rested, essentially, the national character and the national achievement.[54]

Thus Menzies makes the provinces central.

Menzies' was an imperial rather than a colonial personality. All his imagery of Empire, his stress on ties of blood and race, assert the continuities. Australians were simply Britons in another part of the world, 'the boundaries of Great Britain are not on the Kentish coast but at Cape York and Invercargill'.[55] To stress the unity of the Empire made more plausible the ambition to reach high office at the centre. Men from the dominions did occasionally achieve this. From about the turn of the century the United Kingdom began to admit a few men from the settler dominions to the inner corridors of power in London. It was possible for Australians such as Stanley Bruce to be elevated to the British peerage and thus become members of the House of Lords; it was possible for a man from the dominions to become an Empire statesman and serve on the imperial war cabinet, as South African Jan Smuts did in World War I; it was possible for the Australian Richard Casey to represent Britain overseas, both as United Kingdom Minister of State in Cairo and as Governor of Bengal.[56] In an Empire as unified as Menzies wished, bright young men from the provinces would be able to move from the edge to the centre on the basis of their superior talents; his dream was that he was such a man and that he would surely shine at the centre if only he were there. The only reason he wasn't was the accident of his parents' and his remote, colonial birth. In 1940, as Prime Minister of Australia, Menzies was at the centre, and for a few brief months his dream seemed tantalisingly close to coming true.

CHURCHILL AND THE MEANING OF 1941

WAR-TIME LONDON

MENZIES HAD been Prime Minister five months when Hitler invaded Poland and Australia followed Britain into World War II. Australia sent some troops to the Middle East, but for the most part the war in Europe remained remote. Australia's biggest fear was of Japan, and she was relying heavily on the strength of Britain's naval base at Singapore for her defence. The United Australia Party scraped home in the election of 1940, holding onto government with the support of two independents. In January 1941 Menzies set out for England, visiting Australian troops in the Middle East en route. His wife Pattie warned against undertaking the trip in such precarious political circumstances: 'If you feel you must go, you will go. But you will be out of office within six weeks of your return.'[1] Menzies did not return to Australia until the end of May, postponing his decision to leave London three times.

Menzies was popular with the British press. His visit to England had been preceded by acclaim of a sort he never received in Australia, and within two weeks of his arrival there was public speculation about a possible political future for him in Britain, a columnist for the *Sunday Express* suggesting that Australia should 'export Menzies'. His third decision to prolong his visit was greeted by *The Times* with the argument that, although Menzies faced some difficulties in Australia because of his continuing absence, these should not be allowed to outweigh 'the immense advantage of enlisting all the best leadership of the British Empire in the decisive direction of Imperial policy'.[2] Contrary to the patrician air Australians ascribed to him, in England Menzies was seen as 'downright democratic'. A journalist who heard him speak at the Dorchester described him as something new, different, but with a comparatively easy-going manner and aggressively independent:

> ... a solid, challenging, slightly ironical lump of Australia, dumped in the middle of London's West End, attracting admiration because of his obvious independence yet so wholly demonstrating that this independence sprang from a conviction that the Empire had never been more securely united and that just as in a family circle, frankness was welcomed as a tonic.[3]

Menzies impressed himself on the British public through a busy round of speech-making in which he praised them for their courage and told them that in their darkest hour they were not alone, the whole of 'the British Empire beyond the sea was with them'.[4] Slipped into his trip diary, on paper of the Dorchester Hotel where he stayed while in London, are some verses in his hand, reminiscent of the verse he wrote during World War I. Titled 'To England from Australia, You do not fight alone', it reads in part:

> *Not while the wind that sways its gusty way*
> *Across Australia and its sunburnt space*
> *Bears songs and echoes of another day*
> *And hymns the saga of our ancient race*

> Not while the sea that swells along to break
> In foaming white upon our golden sands
> Thunders the names of Nelson and of Drake,
> And all the heroes of their sailor bands,
>
> Not while the tongue we speak, the English tongue,
> That bears its message out of time to time
> Has power to stir the brain and warm the heart
> At each new hearing of the English rhyme.[5]

Menzies toured provincial cities such as Sheffield, Manchester and Bristol, as well as Wales and Ulster, and spoke at various public and private gatherings in London. His speeches were widely reported and he recorded in his diary that during his trip to Birmingham he was recognised wherever he went and autograph books were produced.[6] He undoubtedly noticed the absence of the hecklers and cries of Pig Iron Bob from the crowds. Some of these speeches were published in a small book entitled *To the People of Britain at War from the Prime Minister of Australia*, and five thousand copies were sold by the end of July.[7]

In Menzies' later account of this trip, he stressed that 'the whole reason why I went to England was to discuss the Japanese menace and to urge the strengthening of the defences of Singapore'.[8] His diary of the time, however, reveals very different preoccupations. 'Impression grows,' he wrote on 26 February, 'that best value of this mission is to encourage and lift up the people here. They have had a bad time and want a boost to their spirits.' A month later he noted the purpose of his visit as 'To exchange ideas, to discover ways and means of perfecting our cooperation for the winning of the war; to bring from Australia and her armed forces a message of admiration and love to the people of Great Britain; to take back with me that knowledge and inspiration which must be produced by witnessing the actions, the spirit, of the people here'.⁹ There is no mention here of the purpose he was later to claim as paramount. Lifting the spirits of the people of Great Britain may have been encouraging to the British and deeply satisfying for Menzies, but it was of no use at all to Australia as it worried about the growing militancy of Japan, and it did little to achieve the transfer of industrial capital which he promised Fadden was imminent when he prolonged his stay at the end of March.¹⁰

In London Menzies' ideal self found temporary realisation: he was seen as he most liked to see himself and valued at the centre for the talents he had worked hard to develop in the provinces. The contrast with his far more critical reception in Australia was striking and after shining at a dinner at Claridge's hosted by Lord Beaverbrook (the press magnate and Minister for Aircraft Production), he noted ruefully, 'A prophet is never without honour save in his own country and among his own people.'¹¹ Such success could not help but excite his ambition. The standing ovation he received for his address to the Empire Parliamentary Association prompted the reflection, 'Some of these fellows would not mind my defeat at Canberra if they could get me into the House of Commons. OMNIS IGNOTUS PRO MAGNIFICO.'¹² (The totally unknown may become great.)

Menzies had his home-movie camera with him in London and at some later date edited the film, complete with titles. The film begins with the word 'England' in Gothic letters superimposed on the sort of conventional English village scene which delighted him so much on his first trip – thatched pub beside country lane. It mainly consists of footage of bombsites and of members of the English ruling class. Following the title 'The Rulers of England' is a series of shots of members of the British War Cabinet and of leading Labour politicians, who variously smile or clown for the camera. In one of these Churchill peeps impishly around the corner of a door; another of Churchill with Menzies is coyly titled 'Just to prove I really met him'. At Chequers an armed guard marches into the camera, followed by Menzies strolling nonchalantly down a path smoking a pipe, almost as if he is trying out for the part.[13]

Did Menzies really have a political future in Britain? The historian David Day has argued that the possibility was there in early 1941 as opponents of Churchill among the British ruling elite saw Menzies as a possible challenger. Although Menzies later sang Churchill's praises at every opportunity, in 1941 he was highly critical. Like Menzies' leaders before him, Churchill failed to live up to Menzies' high standards. On his first trip to Britain in 1935 Menzies had been distinctly unimpressed with Churchill, finding that 'the idol has feet of clay' and that his speeches are a constant litany of 'I told you sos'.[14] In 1940, before Churchill became Prime Minister, Menzies described him to Bruce as a 'menace, who stirs up hatreds in a world already seething with them'.[15] His diary of the trip contains similar comments. He criticises him for his apparent enjoyment of hatred; for his captivity to the power of his own oratory; and for his domination of his Cabinet. After attending his first cabinet meeting he records that he was the only one present to put a question; later in the visit, after the disasters of Britain's strategy in Greece and Libya had become apparent, he describes Churchill as 'a dictator' who 'cannot be over ruled' and the Cabinet as 'deplorable – dumb men most of whom disagree with Winston but none of whom dare say so'.[16] Menzies aired his criticisms of Churchill widely. They were shared by many members of the British military and political elite, particularly after British military defeats in Greece and the Middle East. Menzies was sure that he could provide the necessary check in cabinet to Churchill's methods.[17]

The main ground of Menzies' opposition to Churchill was the latter's refusal to give to the Dominions what he, Menzies, regarded as their proper role in the war. He consulted them insufficiently and Menzies feared that Churchill's uncompromising pursuit of total victory against Germany would weaken Britain's ties with its dominions.[18] Not only did it put the defence of the Kentish coast far ahead of the defence of Cape York or Invercargill, but it only seemed possible with substantial help from America, which would further weaken Empire ties. To his mind an Imperial conference was clearly called for, ideally to be followed by the establishment of an Imperial War Cabinet, or at least by the inclusion of a Dominions representative on the British war cabinet. In his opposition to Churchill's priorities, Menzies could not or would not see the English nation at the heart of the British Empire.[19]

Menzies lobbied hard for some form of permanent Dominion representation on the British war cabinet, and for the inclusion of someone on the cabinet prepared to stand up to Churchill.[20] These were both roles he felt he would fill admirably, the first as a prelude to the second. Day suggests that the position of Australian representative on the war cabinet was to be the Trojan Horse whereby Menzies could get within Churchill's citadel to launch a direct attack against him.[21] There was no obvious successor to Churchill, and Menzies expected that once he was a permanent member of the war cabinet he would rapidly become the heir apparent, ready to take over when the war took a turn for the worse and Churchill fell. While these ambitions left little trace on the public record, contemporary observers, both in London and Canberra, recognised them and acknowledged they were possible. Again Menzies' ambitions worked in tandem with his ideals in his challenge to a political superior; in taking on

Churchill he was both protecting his beloved Empire and advancing himself.

Menzies extended his stay in Britain three times, but eventually he had to return to Australia. He had achieved little in terms of the Australian strategic and economic goals which had been the ostensible purpose for his prolonged stay,[22] but on the eve of his departure it is Britain's rather than Australia's problems which are uppermost in his mind. He records in his diary that Beaverbrook 'approves of me, and thinks absurd that I should go back to Australia! I am desperately afraid for the future of Great Britain.'[23] On his way back to Australia he visited Canada and the United States and while there pursued his plans to return to London. He must have been gratified to be hailed by *Time* magazine as 'Mr Churchill's most likely successor if anything happened to the Prime Minister'.[24] He was not, however, successful in winning the Canadian Prime Minister, Mackenzie King, to his cause. King's diary record of the visit is a shrewd assessment of Menzies by another man in the provinces, but one whose identity is more securely grounded in his country of birth. While he was very taken with him, King saw Menzies as 'thinking pretty much of Menzies most of the time' and being too fond of high society and palaces for his own political good. King argued trenchantly and hard-headedly against the Dominion prime ministers spending prolonged periods in London, setting out the multiple political disadvantages for their own countries' prosecution of the war and arguing that their real service to the Empire was to keep their countries united during the war. King sensed the feeling in Menzies 'that he would rather be on the War Cabinet in London than Prime Minister of Australia'.[25]

Menzies returned to Australia empty-handed and none too graciously. The day before he landed he wrote in his diary, 'A sick feeling of repugnance and apprehension grows on me as I near Australia. If only I could creep in quietly to the bosom of my family and rest there.'[26] But he could not. He had been away four months and it was urgent that he resume his national prime ministerial duties. A newsreel of his return shows him uncharacteristically agitated. Clad in an overcoat and looking tired and windswept, he reported the Australian troops' continuing concern for those at home, praised the magnificent people of Great Britain, and then with scorn and anger in his voice told those who had come to welcome him home, 'I come back to Australia with just one sick feeling in my heart – that I must come back to my own country and play politics.'[27] In his return broadcast to the people the next day he repeated the sentiment, saying it is 'diabolical' to have to come back to play politics, however cleanly.[28] Artie Fadden, who had held the fort during his extended stay in London and had come to welcome him home, was left standing at the airport without a word of thanks after Menzies commandeered his car.[29]

RETURN AND RESIGNATION

CHURCHILL WAS a far tougher opponent than any of Menzies' rivals in Australian politics. During the months following his departure from London, Menzies made persistent efforts to return. Churchill, alerted by then to Menzies' ambitions and with Mackenzie King as an ally, blocked all Menzies' moves for an Imperial war conference. Menzies' other option for returning to London was as the Australian Prime Minister, permanently abroad for the duration of the war. If he were in London as Prime Minister he would have been included in the war cabinet. To achieve this, however, he needed the ALP's permission. Curtin could be persuaded to Menzies' plan, but others, including Evatt, could not. In the end all Menzies' schemes for securing a central place for himself in the prosecution of the war ran aground on his political troubles in Australia. After so long away it was imperative that Menzies firmly and decisively reassert his leadership of Australia's war effort, both to quell the critics in his own ranks and to establish the government's dominance over the ALP. But this he failed to do. The impression from contemporary accounts is that Menzies' heart was not in it. Rumours of his plans to return to England undermined the credibility of his calls for a greater war effort, even as his preoccupation with such plans distracted him from that effort.[30]

On 28 August 1941 Menzies announced his resignation as Prime Minister. The reasons he gave were that his unpopularity with large sections of the press and the people, as well as with some sections of the government parties, was a handicap to the effectiveness of the government's war effort. His resignation, he hoped, would 'offer a real prospect of unity in the ranks of the government'.[31] The continuing intrigue and criticism within the government ranks, which had started as soon as he left for Britain and had risen to a chorus of 'We'll never win with Bob', seem to have worn him down, but contemporary observers did not regard Menzies' resignation as inevitable. Percy Spender kept a diary at the time which gives a vivid account of the events. He argues that despite the criticisms, a firm lead from Menzies would have rallied the government behind him.[32] Percy Joske, the independent Arthur Coles, and one of the chief critics, Bill McCall, all see Menzies as having folded too easily before the challenge to his leadership.[33]

Menzies' political fall was greeted with considerable relief by the British cabinet; echoing Stanley Argyle a decade earlier, Lord Cranbourne wrote to a friend that it was better that Menzies was out of the way as his 'intriguing was a constant danger'. Churchill made clear to Fadden that no Australian minister other than the Prime Minister would be admitted to the British war cabinet, thus blocking any hopes Menzies may have had of entering the citadel in some other capacity.[34] For the next six months Menzies continued to try to move to London, though to the more humble position of a member of the House of Commons.[35] Various intermediaries took up his case, such as the British High Commissioner in Canberra who reported to Churchill that, 'Lacking any opportunity in Australia, Menzies desires experience of membership of the House of Commons... Menzies believes that he would be more at home in the House of Commons than he is in the Federal Parliament.' Churchill countered all such moves with the argument that Menzies' talents and knowledge were needed in Australia, conveniently ignoring the fact that relegated to the backbench of a depleted opposition, Menzies had very few opportunities for exercising those talents.[36]

Menzies' loss of the prime ministership was widely attributed to his personality – his air of superiority, his lack of the common touch, his inability to rub shoulders in the party room,[37] and the humiliation of the defeat has been seen as teaching him a necessary lesson in human relations, after which he was a wiser man and a far better politician.[38] Writing in 1972, Spender noted the changes in Menzies' personality after 1941. The smooth, unhindered run in politics and his success in England had gone to his head, and the eight years he spent in opposition made a somewhat different and better man of him – 'kinder, more mature and more humane than he was – and he would need to be!'[39] Menzies' reflections in *Afternoon Light*, though taking a kinder view of his pre-1941 self, follow the same lines, presenting 1941 as a hard but necessary lesson in humility.

> In 1939, when I first became Prime Minister, I had enjoyed a very rapid rise to the top position... There was not much precedent for this kind of advancement, and perhaps some resentment of it. True, I worked hard, though some of the press commentators promoted the usual legend that I was a 'brilliant idler'. But I have worked hard all my life, much harder, I feel sure, than any of the critics.
>
> But with so much to do officially, I do not doubt that my knowledge of people, and how to get along with them and persuade them, lagged behind. I was still in that state of mind in which to be logical is to be right, and to be right is its own justification. I had yet to acquire the common touch, to learn that human beings are delightfully illogical but mostly honest, and to realise that all-black and all-white are not the only hues in the spectrum.[40]

The transformation was not total, however; and Howard Beale reports the anxiety of colleagues in the early days of the Liberal Party lest the 'Old Menzies' reappear.[41]

According to contemporary biographical consensus it was the defeats in the Australian cabinet and in the UAP party room which set in motion the psychological transformation which took place in Menzies during the 1940s and enabled his later political success – the rebuilding of conservative forces into the Liberal Party and his sixteen-year-long reign as Prime Minister. Bill McCall, whose persistent criticism of Menzies precipitated the crisis, was later to boast that he did Menzies 'the greatest service any man ever did him' by putting him in purgatory in 1941.[42] Flattering though it may have been to Bill McCall and his ilk to remember how they taught the 'Big Bloke' a lesson, I think they overestimated their role. Although it is hard from this distance and with the sort of evidence available to be at all sure of Menzies' psychological processes during the 1940s, I want to suggest a very different interpretation of the changes that took place in Menzies after 1941 and which made possible his later political success.

Menzies took from childhood two competing senses of himself – the highly valued self of his mother's doting gaze and the small, insignificant self of his relationship with his father. This latter was formed both from his father's more sceptical attitude towards his son's abilities and from the small boy's experience of his father's objectively much greater power. He also took with him his rage at having to submit to his father's authority. While outwardly he may have submitted, inwardly he refused to do so and hung on to his mother's valuation, sidestepping his father, and at the same time venting his rage, by replacing him in his imagination with one more worthy of his gifted son. An imagined England provided the material for this family romance and became the home of his ideal, elevated self and its noble parents. His deep love for his mother was later to find one of its transformations in his abiding attachment to Queen Elizabeth, while he replaced his father with the great men of English history.

Menzies' elevated self was thus formed from the combination of his mother's adoration and his denial of his father's power. While one face gazed up to the sun of his mother's love, the other looked back to his father's harsh judgement which, never submitted to, remained potent and so had continually to be fought off. Menzies' psychological geography helped him to keep these two selves apart. Australia was the home of his competitive, ambitious, vindictive self, the self intent on disproving his father's valuation by climbing the hierarchies of male power. By contrast the elevated self in its imagined English home could be charming, gracious and benign, with all the confident self-assurance of an ascribed identity and bearing none of the scars of an achieved one. This psychological geography also helped Menzies keep his ideals safe from his ambitions. During the 1930s, when Menzies' ambition threatened to overwhelm his ideals and reduce them to transparent rationalisations of his own desire for power, England helped him keep them safe.

Commentators on Menzies have on the whole been fooled by his ease and success in England, seeing it as his natural home. But it was the natural home only of his self as he wanted it to be. While England remained a distant, imaginary place, it was well beyond the reach of his ambitious, competitive self. On his first trip 'home' in 1935 his experience remained within those bounds, as he recognised what he had long imagined. On his war-time trip it was a different story, and members of the British ruling class glimpsed a Menzies more familiar in Australia – critical, ambitious, scheming and competitive. Few people's family romances threaten to come true, but when they do their strategies start to unravel. In early 1941 Menzies' ambitions caught up with his ideals; as real power in England seemed within his grasp he finally faced the contest his family romance had been designed to avoid – the contest with a much more powerful man.

Churchill was at the pinnacle of Menzies' world and when he lost the contest with him there was no refuge left for his elevated self. The strategy of avoiding defeat at the father's hands by replacing him with one more worthy could no longer work – there was no one beyond Churchill. This was Menzies' first experience of a defeat which could not be sidestepped by recourse to an imagined England where his true worth would be recognised. For Menzies there was no where left to go but back to Australia. He was not English and now he never would be. Menzies' soaring political ambition had left both his father and Australia behind. In sidestepping his father's power he had also sidestepped the fact of his Australian birth, imagining that a child from the outer provinces was really a man of the centre. And so 'with a sick feeling' in his heart he had to come back to his competitive, ambitious self and play politics, recognising as he did so that he was, after all, no better than those he had thought beneath him.

Menzies' decisive defeat, the one which explains the subsequent mellowing of his political personality, was not in Canberra at the hands of his parliamentary colleagues but in London at the hands of Churchill. Although the loss of the Australian prime ministership was publicly and deeply humiliating, it was not as psychologically significant as his defeat in his contest with Churchill. In Australia he was brought down by men he regarded as well beneath him – schemers, whisperers, intriguers – and he already had mechanisms for defending himself against them – moral and intellectual superiority, or complaints about ungrateful and unworthy critics. One of the things which puzzled observers of Menzies' behaviour at the time was his failure to activate such mechanisms to deal with the critics of his leadership. Percy Joske, who maintained that Menzies was never in any real danger, stressed that those who expressed discontent were not members who had any influence either in the party room or in Parliament and were people for whom Menzies had nothing but disdain.[43] Menzies should have been able to deal with them easily. In England, by contrast, Menzies was defeated by a man above him and the way up was forever blocked. This was a new experience and the lessons it taught were far more devastating.[44]

RECOVERY

AFTER HIS resignation, Menzies retired to the backbenches. He resumed some legal work and went for long walks.[45] A quip from the time shows his wit uncharacteristically preoccupied with themes other than relative positions of power. When Curtin referred to members of the opposition preventing the Right Honourable Member for Kooyong from continuing as Prime Minister, Menzies said quietly, 'I wish honourable members would leave me alone. It is a most unpleasant experience to be exhumed.'[46] In early 1942 he began the weekly series of broadcasts from 2UE in Sydney of which 'The Forgotten People' was one. By 1943 he was back again as the leader of the UAP and in 1944 he began what he later regarded as his most important political achievement – rebuilding the conservative forces into the Liberal Party of Australia. Menzies explained his political comeback as a consequence of his combative, ambitious self:

> ... my fall from office under circumstances which enabled quite a few people to write my political obituary had a special effect on a man of contentious capacity and healthy ambition. I refused to accept defeat as permanent. True, for years there were observers who would say to my party and my friends, 'You'll never win with Menzies!' But when such slogans reached my ears, I treated them as a great challenge. My unspoken response was that of the small boy – 'I'll show them!'[47]

This answer, though, belies the changes. For although Menzies was still ambitious, he was now able to harness his ambition to his political ends rather than being driven by it to his political destruction.

The changed balance between Menzies' ambition and his ideals can be seen in his decision to stay with politics, and in his extraordinary fortitude in the face of his humiliating defeat and of the gloating and whispering that accompanied it. From where did Menzies get the strength to go on in politics? Why didn't he retire to the law and resume his legal career, perhaps nursing a scornful vindictiveness towards the country which had rejected him? Although politics clearly served Menzies' grandiose, ambitious self, it was also for him a career of service, propelled by a sense of duty and obligation in a democratic polity. The Menzies family placed great emphasis on service. Isabel Green told Kevin Perkins that her father's last words to her as he lay dying were, 'Don't ever get away from giving public service as long as you can do it.'[48] In one of his 1942 weekly radio broadcasts Menzies despaired of the fact that so few people saw a life devoted to politics as he did.

> I went into politics for the first time fourteen years ago. Many of my friends shrugged their shoulders at what they obviously thought a harmless eccentricity. The most generous unspoken comment was 'Another good man gone wrong!' It was plainly not thought by many that the government of the country was as important as the practice of the law.
>
> During those fourteen years I have, times without number, heard the loud complaint of the business man about the politician. I have, as you have, repeatedly heard the statement that 'What the country needs is a Government of business men.' On scores of occasion I have made the obvious rejoinder, 'All right, what's preventing you? Why not go into Parliament yourself?' And then, as in

the old story, 'they all, with one accord, began to make excuse'. One was too busy – as if only the leisured or the unemployed were needed in Parliament. One would lose too much money – as if serving the people in Parliament ought to be a profitable job. One could not face the bitter criticism and misrepresentation through which the parliamentary candidate so often has to wade – as if only the thick-skinned are fit to devise the laws of the land. And so on. All excuses, masking the fundamental fact that the business of politics was disregarded as fit only for the loudmouthed careerists. It was, and is, very depressing. *What should be, if we understood democracy, the noblest and highest of civil vocations, degraded into something of less importance than the higgling of the market and the acquisition of wealth.* (my italics)

It is as if he is mustering his ideals against the argument that to return to the law would be much more lucrative and cause him far less personal pain. Later in this speech he makes an unusual explicit appeal to his father's political example: 'My own father, who was and is a good democrat, and was for some years a member of the Victorian Parliament, had the excellent habit of always going straight to his electors when he heard they disagreed with his vote in the House.'[49] Decisively defeated at last, Menzies no longer had to maintain the illusion that he could succeed without genuine recognition of his father's qualities and without admitting to himself that he was once impressed by and afraid of him.

I argued earlier that Menzies took on his political philosophy fully formed, dressing himself up in a man's clothes when he was still a boy. He was bright and quick to master the main arguments and images of his selected position. His quickness passed for understanding, and his political precocity served his ambition, but the understanding was borrowed and not connected with his own experience. Once the father's power had finally been admitted, the disguise could be dropped and the political ideas and values so hastily taken on in boyhood at last examined to see what use might be in them for the second half of his life. In the weekly broadcasts begun in 1942, Menzies set about, for the first time, systematically reflecting on his political values and he found, as he told his brother, that there *was* a political philosophy in them.[50] Between 9 January 1942 and 14 April 1944, Menzies made 105 such broadcasts, ranging from comments on the prosecution of the war to reflections on freedom, democracy and the rule of law.[51]

This reworking bore fruit in Menzies' formulation a few years later of the aims and objectives of the newly formed Liberal Party in ways that were consonant with the emerging post-war consensus on the role of the state. Non-labour could no longer rely on its pre-war ideas about the state's minimal involvement in the economy. After the sacrifices of the war, people were unlikely to tolerate a return to the Depression conditions of the early 1930s. They were demanding a greater degree of social and economic security and the new Keynesian economics argued that it was possible for the state to meet those demands if it took on a regulatory economic role. In 1944 the Victorian branch of the business organisation the Institute of Public Affairs produced a document called 'Looking Forward', which argued that business should accept a more interventionist state. Menzies quoted this document in his address to the initial conference in Canberra to discuss the formation of a new non-labour party, arguing that the proper relationship between business and the state was one of partnership, not, as had been thought before the war, one of natural opposition of interests. Private enterprise, he stressed, stood only to gain from state action which secured full employment and social security.[52]

During the 1930s Menzies had espoused an almost laissez-faire view of the role of the state, and his attitude towards those who suffered because of the state's failure to intervene had been harsh. He had opposed providing employment through public works, as well as the introduction of unemployment insurance as means of ameliorating the country's economic problems. The best contribution the government could make was to balance its books and reduce its call on the productive sector of society.[53] In arguing for such orthodox economics, Menzies showed little concern with the plight of the unemployed. In one famous remark on the possibility of Australia repudiating her debt to Britain he said, 'If Australia were to get through her troubles by abating or abandoning her traditional British standards of honesty, of justice, of fair play, of resolute endeavour, it would be better for Australia that every citizen within her boundaries should die of starvation during the next six months.'[54] This is a silly hyperbole, but it indicates a striking insensitivity in Menzies at this time towards the concerns of ordinary people, some of whom were starving.[55] And it is in striking contrast to the compassion and generosity for which his father was known.[56] Menzies at this time was poised to make the shift from state to federal politics. He was mixing with wealthy manufacturers and stockbrokers, identifying himself with the interests of the rich and powerful and speaking on their behalf.[57] In such statements it is Menzies' ambition speaking. As the Depression progressed Menzies did begin to soften his views,[58] and he spoke with a quite different voice in the early 1940s.

Menzies first seems to have seriously thought about the misery of many ordinary people on his war-time trip to

England. He was genuinely moved by the suffering and the fortitude of the British people during the Blitz. Speaking at a state dinner in his honour in Auckland on his way back to Australia, he described these common people who so magnificently withstood the German air raids as if he had never noticed them before.

> You know we British people have not always been enlightened in our understanding of the kind of life that we should give to our fellow citizens. We have not always been prepared to throw down the walls of privilege. We have not always been as shocked as we ought to have been at poverty and injustice and yet, the strange and almost divine thing is, that, in the lanes, the slum streets, the back streets of English cities, you find men and women with, in a sense, nothing to lose, men and women who have been dealt the cruellest injustices by life... These common people – I use the word as one talks of the House of Commons – these common people of our race, little people, not very well fed people, not very well housed people... have proved that of all the generations who have found their place in the history of their race, they are the greatest.[59]

This is a peculiar passage, beginning with its ascription to 'we British people' of views which could hardly be held by them all, especially those British people who are the subject of his newfound compassion. He repeats the theme when he lands in Australia, describing the strain of the air raids on people whose only ambition is to live peaceably in their homes. 'I am not talking about great people, people of great authority, but about simple, plain people, people who are not known to the world as individuals and who have had such a raw deal in the past ten or twelve years.'[60] One can only read statements like these as some sort of apology on Menzies' part for his past indifference to the plight of the poor and powerless, the 'little people', an indifference from which he has now, in an almost divine way, been released. His recognition of the humanity of the obscure people of the back lanes of Great Britain is a precursor to his recognition of the humanity of the forgotten people in the backblocks of Australia – the nameless, unadvertised people in their frugal homes. It is significant, however, that this recognition begins in Britain. Britain is the location of Menzies' ideals. Apart from the episode with Churchill, his vindictive, ambitious competitive self remains in Australia where the working class and their claims for social justice generally excited his aggression rather than his sympathy. In England a more benign self was able to recognise suffering and identify with an image of social harmony in which even the obscure had a place.

After 1941 part of that benign self came back to Australia. His visit to the Australian troops in the Middle East on the way over helped him to see a place for this self in Australia. The Australian soldiers responded to him not as a sectional, political leader, but as a symbol of unity, 'a messenger of Australia' and, he told an audience on his return, 'I was never so moved in my life'.[61] 'The Forgotten People' speech is the most explicit expression of the new relationship Menzies developed at this time with his past and with Australia. Churchill had commented to Mackenzie King that Menzies loathed his own people and that one could not hope to be prime minister of a people one did not like.[62] In 'The Forgotten People' Menzies was constructing a constituency for himself which he could like, confessing in the title to his now abandoned family romance as he returned to his origins to give new purpose and direction to his political career. The extent to which Menzies drew in this speech on his memory of his parents and his childhood home was only possible because defeat forced him at last to remember and acknowledge his origins.[63] On the brink of being forgotten himself, Menzies remembered those whom he had forgotten as his ambition and talent bore him ever upward. Menzies no doubt still regarded himself as his parents' greatest contribution to the human race, but now he determined to serve rather than abandon them. Henceforth his political career was based on the representation of rather than the flight from his origins, and he could speak for and to the Australian middle class with conviction.

Thus he embarked on the formation of a new political party to provide a viable non-labour party for his new constituency. Again the break with the pattern of his past political career is evident. In the past Menzies competed for power in already existing organisations where the way ahead was as clear as the next rung on the ladder, till his elevated self reached its proper place at the top; after 1943 he was building an organisation, not simply climbing one, and so elevating his constituency along with himself. And when that party was settled into its long period of government, he took a strong personal interest in government policy towards the educational institutions which had been crucial to the achievement of his own boyhood ambitions – independent schools and the universities.[64] Introducing the Murray Report on Australian Universities into Federal Parliament, Menzies told the House that this was 'a special night in my political life'. Later he described how deep his emotions had been that night.[65] Although Menzies still found it difficult, if not impossible, to be generous and encouraging to younger versions of himself who provided a direct challenge, he was able to build up the institutions which would enable them, like him, to succeed.

Menzies' preoccupation with his own position and dominance did not disappear after 1941, but some of it became more firmly attached to political objects beyond himself – to the Liberal Party and to Australia. His elevated self no longer tried to flee its colonial birthplace but determined instead to raise it up to an appropriate level.[66] This is most clearly seen in the strong personal interest he took in the development of Canberra during his second prime ministership. When Menzies returned to office in 1949, Canberra was a rather ramshackle town. In 1957 he set up the National Capital Development Commission to oversee Canberra's development, keeping as much as possible to the lines of Walter Burley Griffin's original plan. Menzies was particularly insistent that the lake, which was a central feature of Griffin's plan, be created. On his first trip overseas, Menzies had remarked on the contribution water made to the national capitals of Canada and the United States, and on the blunder which had been made in choosing a site with no water for Canberra.[67] Now he was Prime Minister he could rectify the blunder. Menzies wanted Canberra to be a 'worthy capital; something that the Australian people would come to admire and respect; something that would be a focal point for national pride and sentiment'.[68]

LORD WARDEN OF THE CINQUE PORTS

MENZIES CHANGED during the 1940s, but he did not change completely. Resigned to having risen as far as he could, he settled into his long Australian prime ministership, tough with his political opponents, wary of rivals and still adoring of England, now generally represented by either Churchill or the Queen. Anecdotes of Churchill abound in Menzies' speeches and writing after 1941, with Churchill always presented as the exemplar of whichever human virtue Menzies was advocating at the time – the proper attitude towards war-time enemies, the importance of a sense of humour, a statesman's need for a sense of history.[69] His admiration of Churchill was so great that it even led him to revise his opinion of the wisdom of politicians reading their speeches.

> I remember, many years ago, when Ramsay MacDonald was Prime Minister, sitting in the gallery of the House of Commons, looking down on Churchill, who was then in the political wilderness... He was speaking, i.e., he was reading his typed speech... This disappointed me, for I had never heard Churchill speak before. But I suddenly realised the superb art with which he could read. He would pause, chuckle, change the tempo and inflexion, and then deliver the carefully prepared phrase as if it were literally a brilliant impromptu.[70]

In his diary at the time Menzies described Churchill's delivery as 'hesitating'.[71] Anecdotes about Churchill's wisdom allow Menzies to remember the heights to which he nearly rose and to accept, again, the inevitability of his defeat: 'Against another's great merits there is no remedy but love.' Even so, in his imagination at least, the distance between them was perhaps not so great. Jottings for a piece on journalists, headed 'The Denigrators', bracket 'Churchill' with 'Me' as targets of the journalists' denigration.[72]

In his last years, Menzies' own capacities for denigration seem to have resurged with a vengeance; his successors in the Liberal Party failed to live up to his high standards of statesmanship just as their predecessors had failed before them. 'A contemptible little squirt', 'conceited little booby', 'a very stupid fellow', 'a mischievous destroyer' are the sort of phrases he used to describe his ex-colleagues in an interview with David McNicoll of the *Bulletin*.[73] There is no wit here, no attempt to disguise the aggression and contempt. It was perhaps a little unfair of McNicoll to have published remarks Menzies made in confidence, but, says McNicoll, 'he would often use language like this if he was among people he knew and trusted'; and they do give us insight into Menzies' continuing preoccupation with issues of male dominance and his bitterness at being forced by age to retire at last from the fray. Menzies did not shed his competitive, vindictive self as he drew towards death, but carried it as an increasing burden which not all the honours he had received seemed, finally, to have been able to ease.[74]

After his retirement, Menzies' family romance still had one episode left to run, when his aspiration to be one with the great men of England finally seemed realised at last in his investiture as Lord Warden of the Cinque Ports. The Cinque Ports are five ports on the coast of Kent and Sussex which, from the Middle Ages, were expected to furnish the defence of England against invasion and to provide the chief ports of the navy. It is an ancient office, rich in historical associations but without power in the modern world. Reportedly, Attlee had wanted the position to round off his own career and had remarked that he could not understand why Menzies had accepted it, since it could mean little to him.[75] How little the centre understands the provinces.

Dressed in an admiral's uniform, Menzies noted at his investiture that his was the first appointment to the position 'of a man from the outer Commonwealth'. As he was installed into an office that went back to Alfred he dwelt on the sense of history which he believed was essential for all statesmen, indeed for all citizens – the realisation that the spirit of the past lives with us still. This spirit, he said, could well be summed up in the words of Scott's archer in *Ivanhoe*: 'My grandsire drew a stout bow at the battle of Hastings. I trust not to dishonour his name'. He concludes: 'I can not pretend for one moment that I am as fit for it [this high office] as the Churchills or the Wellingtons or the Pitts, that would be ridiculous. I am certainly not as fit for this office as they were; but, after all, a man's reach should exceed his grasp or what's a heaven for?'[76]

So Menzies' family romance seemed to have come true with his installation into an office held by some of the men about whom he read as a boy in Jeparit. But it was installation into an office that no longer had any real power and to which, even in its much reduced contemporary role, Menzies had only a remote relationship. Menzies had never commanded a ship, let alone a fleet; he had not commanded Britain at war and his command of Australia at war was not a success. Assuming the office of Lord Warden of the Cinque Ports, he wore the borrowed robes of naval command without having experienced the substance of the role. This was a fitting end to Menzies' family romance, for the romance is a tale designed to evade certain uncomfortable facts of existence, and this evasion continued to exact its costs.

CORRESPONDENCES

THE TENSION between ideals and ambition is endemic to politics. To be taken as public representatives, aspiring leaders must hitch their ambition to group goals and ideals, claiming to represent the interests and values of others, even as they advance themselves. The affinity between politics and theatre has long been recognised and this affinity lies not just in the degree of personal exhibitionism involved, but in the perception that the drama on the political stage involves a degree of illusion, and that aspiring politicians must possess a certain capacity for self-deception and imposture. The illusion, at bottom, is that politicians really care more about the people on whose behalf they speak than they do about themselves. So, in 1942, Menzies had to convince both the Australian middle class and himself that he was defending their worth, not because he was in danger of being forgotten, but because they were.

The form taken by the tension between ideals and ambition will vary between political groups. Until recently individual ambition has been allowed more scope in non-labour politics, with its dependence on strong leaders to give cohesion and direction to the party, than in labour politics where the ideal leader is only as strong as the movement he leads. Non-labour parties are subject to periods of intense rivalry in between strong leaders, as in the dying days of the UAP government or in the Liberal Party following Menzies' retirement. Within the parties themselves, the tension between individual ideals and ambitions expresses itself as one between the desire to win and hold government and the values and ideals which are to be furthered by this end. This has been a greater tension in the ALP than in the non-labour parties, for whom winning and keeping control of government has always been the major objective and who have thus been less troubled by the inevitable compromises of power.

The psychological tension between interests and ideals has a correlative in the tensions between interests and legitimations in the broader polity. The predecessors of the Liberal Party, the UAP and the Nationalists, both suffered from being too close to the financial interests which backed them, their parliamentarians at times seeming little more than puppets for the powerful interests pulling the strings. By the late 1930s, when Menzies resigned over the Lyons government's abandonment of its National Insurance Scheme, the UAP was virtually paralysed by its subordination to its supporters.[1] When he formed the Liberal Party, Menzies was determined that the new party would be financially independent, keeping the powerful interests of capital at arm's length: rank and file finance, not large donations from businessmen, must be the monetary basis of a democratic organisation, he said.[2] The new party had to be able to present itself to the electorate as a mass-based party representing particular political ideals and values, not just a parliamentary party serving the interests of the rich and powerful. Much of Menzies' effort in forming the new party went into articulating a philosophy for the party which would provide it with a unity and purpose based on a 'genuine community of thought', a set of principles which the ambitious non-labour politician could serve. Menzies' personal and political achievement in his second prime ministership was that, in finding a balance between his own ambitions and ideals, he brought a temporary balance to the tensions between interests and legitimations in non-labour politics, thus enabling non-labour to hitch its historic role as the defender of the inequalities on which capitalism depends to ideals and values of broad public appeal. Since Menzies, the Liberal Party has, for the most part, lost that balance; by the early 1990s, it seemed little more than the proponent of one set of ideas about the proper way to manage a declining economy.

Menzies advanced the cause of Australia's middle class in ways which flattered them, speaking to them not of their threatened material interests but of the threatened ideals and values they represented – hard work, independence, sacrifice for their children and an interest in culture when the day's work is done. These virtues were defined against the other of non-labour politics – the collectivist traditions of the union movement and the ALP whose stress on the interdependence of people was scorned by those with the resources to survive alone. The values Menzies stressed had, from the beginning, a defensive, combative edge and could easily broaden their target from the labour movement to anything that was different or ambiguous; so Menzies could as confidently attack modernist painting as communism and receive considerable public support in both cases.

At the heart of Menzies' political rhetoric were three defended, bounded spaces: the homes of the forgotten people of Australia, whose walls kept at bay not only the demanding cries of the less fortunate and the alienating experiences of modernity, but deep unease about their place on the globe; the island continent of Australia, whose exits and entrances were watched vigilantly to protect the country from unwanted foreign elements; and the competitive selves of legitimate political conflict, whose attention was turned away from the doubts and rewards of the inner life to the all-absorbing game of winning and losing. In each the energy was in the boundaries, and the protected centre atrophied.

Menzies' valorisation of the competitive selves of legitimate political conflict was reflected in his own construction of himself as a combative, public man, and in his own atrophied centre. Menzies' inner emptiness was the result of his avoidance of the truth of the Oedipus complex that a boy learns the substance of manhood in an acknowledged, ambivalent encounter with his father. Refusing to acknowledge his father's power and his own relative incapacities, Menzies became committed too young to a political position and a public self he then had to devote considerable energy to defending. At the outset Menzies' political ideas served his ambition, allowing him to imagine that he owed his father nothing; hence he had little interest in examining them critically in the light of changing experience. His political self was constructed around a denial of experience and an imagined England filled the void.

So too for the people and the country he led. The defended island continent of Australia and the homes of the middle class were also built on denial – the historic denial of the prior occupancy of the Australian continent by the people who became known as the Australian Aborigines, and of the brutality and lawlessness with which their land had been taken. White Australia's continuing fear of invasion must be seen as a massive collective projection of the knowledge of white Australia's origins. As Bernard Smith argued in his Boyer lectures, in order to survive, a culture must have the ethical self-confidence to be able to justify itself both to itself and to others.[3] Middle-class Australia's shallow, derivative culture has in part been a consequence of the wilful and continuing denial of its debt to the Aborigines, and its refusal to think about the nightmare on which the Australian dream has depended. Since Menzies' day, more Australians have faced the truth of the country's past, and creative cultural life has correspondingly flourished for both black and white Australians; but powerful voices continue to ridicule those who speak of white Australians' shared guilt; and, despite promises, there has been no official political recognition of the Aborigines' prior occupancy. Menzies' refusal to acknowledge his father's power created in him the gap between knowledge and experience which enabled him so persuasively to represent the denials of Australian culture and politics in the middle decades of this century.

NOTES

THE WORDS OF MR MENZIES
1 *The Listener-In*, 24-30 January 1942.
2 *Sydney Morning Herald*, 10 January 1942. A selection of these speeches was published under the title *The Forgotten People and Other Studies in Democracy* by Angus & Robertson, Sydney, in 1943. The speech 'The Forgotten People' was printed and circulated as a political pamphlet by Robertson and Mullens of Melbourne shortly after it was delivered.
3 See Don Rawson, *Australia Votes*, p. 65, for this description of Menzies' voice.
4 Frank Menzies to Kevin Perkins, interview.
5 *Commonwealth Parliamentary Debates*, vol. 159, 20 April 1939, pp. 14-17.
6 Accounts of these events are given by various of the participants: Percy Spender, *Politics and a Man*, chapters 4-11; Arthur Fadden, *They Called Me Artie*; Earle Page, *Truant Surgeon*, chapters 29-31; Robert Menzies, *Afternoon Light*, pp. 52-61.
7 Alan Reid, 'Prime Ministers I have known', *Bulletin Centenary Issue*, 29 January 1980, pp. 365-6.
8 For Menzies' own account of these events see *Afternoon Light*, chapter 12; also Graeme Starr, *The Liberal Party of Australia*, chapter 2.
9 PMG estimates of number of sets cited in Lesley Johnson, *The Unseen Voice*, p. 83; discussion of advertising of radio, p. 87; estimates of radio audience from Mick Counihan, 'The Formation of a Broadcasting Audience: Australian Radio in the Twenties', *Meanjin*, vol. 41, no. 2, (June, 1982), p. 196.
10 Lesley Johnson, *The Unseen Voice*, pp. 192-3.
11 Ibid., p. 74.
12 *Labor Daily*, 2 July 1938, cited ibid., p. 116.
13 Ibid., p. 192.
14 Allan Martin, 'The Master's Voice? R.G. Menzies and Public Speaking', paper given at La Trobe University History Department, 8 November 1991.
15 See the astonishingly unilluminating study of this speech by Colin Hughes and John Western, *The Prime Minister's Policy Speech*.
16 *Age*, 13 November 1963, cited in Hughes and Western, p. 5.
17 Diary, 4 July 1935.
18 His papers in the National Library of Australia contain numerous examples of rough notes prepared for public speeches. Some are only a couple of points on the back of an envelope. MS 4936, series 6, NLA.
19 Paul Hasluck, *Sir Robert Menzies*, p. 15.
20 Ray Robinson, *The Wit of Sir Robert Menzies*, p. 11.
21 Hughes and Western, *The Prime Minister's Policy Speech*, p. 30.

22 R.G. Menzies, 'Politics as an Art', *Speech is of Time*, pp. 183-92.
23 R.G. Menzies, *Afternoon Light*, pp. 198, 122, 130.
24 R.G. Menzies, 'Politics as an Art', *Speech is of Time*, p. 189.
25 Ibid., p. 187.
26 R.G. Menzies, 'Speech and Speakers', The George Adlington Syme Oration, *The Australian and New Zealand Journal of Surgery*, vol. 33, no. 3, (Feb 1964), p. 164. Corroborating descriptions of the way Menzies went about preparing his speeches can be found in John Bunting, *R.G. Menzies*, pp. 49-50 and Paul Hasluck, *Sir Robert Menzies*, pp. 14-15.
27 Edgar Holt, *Politics is People*, p. 124.
28. Isabel Green to Kevin Perkins, interview.

THE FORGOTTEN PEOPLE
1 During the twentieth century the main imperative shaping non-labour rhetoric has been the political and ideological strength of the labour movement. Throughout this book I am using the term non-labour to refer to both liberal and conservative strands in non-labour thinking and leaving open the question of the tension between these two traditions of non-labour thought.
2 See William E. Connolly, *The Terms of Political Discourse*, for an elaboration of this argument.
3 Antonio Gramsci, *Selections from the Prison Notebooks*, especially pp. 321-77.
4 For discussion of the debates in Marxism on this question see Stuart Hall, 'The rediscovery of ideology: return of the repressed in media studies' in M. Gurevitch, Tony Bennett, James Curran and Janet Woollacott (eds), *Culture, Society and the Media*; Richard Johnson, 'Histories of Culture/Theories of Ideology: Notes on an Impasse', in Michelle Barrett et al. (eds), *Ideology and Cultural Production*, pp. 49-77; Centre for Contemporary Cultural Studies, *On Ideology*, part one.
5 Peter Loveday, 'The Liberals' Image of their Party', in Cameron Hazlehurst (ed.), *Australian Conservatism*, p. 258.
6 Joint Opposition Policy Speech and Supplementary Statements, 1949, p. 6.
7 L.F. Crisp, *The Australian Federal Labor Party, 1901-1951*, chapter XIV.
8 I am here drawing on the insights of French anthropologist Claude Levi Strauss into the way opposition structures systems of classification. Levi Strauss is interested in oppositions such as male:female; nature:culture; raw:cooked, which can be regarded as universal, but his general argument is useful when dealing with more historically specific oppositions. See in particular, *Structural Anthropology*, especially chapter XI.
9 Peter Loveday, 'The Liberals' Image of their Party', pp. 244-5.

10 For a very good account of this position as a personally held belief see Paul Hasluck, *Shades of Darkness*.
11 *The United Australia Review*, 20 April 1933, p. 9, cited in Loveday, 'The Liberals' Image of their Party', p. 243.
12 R.G. Menzies to Ken Taylor, interview.
13 Interview with Jennifer Cashmore, *Australian Society*, April 1988, p. 41.
14 See Tim Rowse, *Australian Liberalism and National Character*, pp. 196-203 for a discussion of the use of the term middle class by Australian social scientists in the 1940s to the early 1960s. Rowse similarly argues that the term is used as a consensual term opposed to the very idea of class opposition and that it is essentially a moral category.
15 R.G. Menzies, *Speech is of Time*, p. 194.
16 This understanding of modernity is most developed in the work of Max Weber. In what follows, I am drawing in particular on his work on bureaucracy as the characteristic organisational form of modernity, and on the work of Jürgen Habermas who has developed Weber's concept of rationalisation in terms of a contrast between the modes of communication appropriate to the spheres governed by technical rationality and those governed by the consensual norms of face-to-face interaction. H.H. Gerth & C. Wright Mills, *From Max Weber*, chapter VIII; Jürgen Habermas, *Towards a Rational Society*, chapters 4 and 6.
17 *Commonwealth Parliamentary Debates*, 27 April 1950, vol. 207, p. 2000.
18 Raymond Williams, *The Country and the City*. Williams has looked at the way the opposition between the country and the city has structured so much of English society and political thought.
19 *The Woman*, 20 April 1933.
20 Don Aitkin, *Stability and Change in Australian Politics*, p. 332.
21 Maurice Duverger's classic study, *The Political Role of Women* (1950), explained the tendency of women to support conservative parties in this way. For the application of this type of argument to Australian women's conservatism, see Stephen Alomes, Mark Dober and Donna Hellier 'The Social Context of Postwar Conservatism' in Ann Curthoys and John Merritt (eds) *Australia's First Cold War*, Vol. 1.
22 Beatrix Campbell, *Iron Ladies*; Marion Simms, 'Conservative Feminism: A Case Study of Feminist Ideology', *Women's Studies: International Quarterly* 3 (1979), pp. 305-18; Patricia Raselli, 'The Australian Women's National League: Always a Bridesmaid', BA Hons Thesis, Political Science Department, University of Melbourne, 1975.
23 Alan Davies, *Private Politics*, p. 12.
24 Enid Lyons, *So We Take Comfort*, pp. 144-5.
25 Peter Tiver, *Liberal Party*, pp. 34-5.
26 Graeme Starr, *The Liberal Party of Australia*, p. 82.

27 Joint Opposition Policy Speech, 1946, p. 4.
28 Joint Opposition Speech and Supplementary Statements, 1949.
29 Joseph Benedict Chifley, *Things Worth Fighting For*, p. 75.
30 Policy Speech for the 1954 Federal Election, pp. 11-12.
31 Max Weber, *The Protestant Ethic and the Spirit of Capitalism*.
32 H.R. Jackson, *Churches and People in Australia and New Zealand*, p. 147.
33 Kevin Perkins, *Menzies*, p. 10.
34 Joint Opposition Policy Speech, 1946.
35 John Bunting, *Sir Robert Menzies*, p. 21.
36 See for example, his resignation speech, *Age*, 21 January 1966; interview with John Hamilton, *Age*, 20 December 1969; *Afternoon Light*, p. 316.
37 H.R. Jackson, *Churches and People in Australia and New Zealand*, p. 125.
38 Brian Lewis, *Sunday at Kooyong Road*, p. 34.
39 Brian Lewis, *Our War*, pp. 288-91.
40 Max Weber, *The Protestant Ethic*, pp. 121ff.
41 Helmut Schoek, *Envy*; A.F. Davies, *Skills, Outlooks and Passions*, pp. 346-60.
42 Stuart Macintyre, *The Oxford History of Australia, Volume 4, 1901-1942*, p. 49.
43 Ibid., pp. 48-51, 278.
44 Menzies is still smarting here from the recent attacks on him; that his dedication to public service was misunderstood is a frequent complaint in his speeches of this period.
45 Max Scheler, *Ressentiment* (1912); Svend Ranulf, *Moral Indignation and Middle Class Psychology* (1938).
46 Joint Opposition Policy Speech, 1946, p. 8.
47 Ibid., p. 10.
48 Federal Election Policy Speech, 1954, p. 21.
49 In contrasting these two positions I am drawing on the work of Graham Little who, starting from our human dilemma both to relate to other people and to have a sense of ourselves as separate and independent, has developed a powerful psychoanalytic framework to display the psychological structures underlying different sets of political and social beliefs. He argues that one can solve the dilemma of self and other by opting for the self, or for the other, or by trying to hold self and other together. Little emphasises that each of these solutions is only partial: that in emphasising certain human needs and capacities others are downplayed; that each has its characteristic weaknesses, blindnesses and ways of failing; and that each is motivated as much by its fears of the emotional experiences the other celebrates as by the conviction of its own virtues. Graham Little, *Political Ensembles*; see also Judith Brett, 'A Psychosocial Approach to Politics', *Arena*, no. 72, (1985), pp. 133-44.

THE COMMUNISTS

1. Robin Gollan, *Revolutionaries and Reformists*, p. 45.
2. *Argus*, 7 September 1939.
3. Don Watson, *Brian Fitzpatrick*, p. 69.
4. Paul Hasluck, *The Government and the People 1939-1941*, Australians in the War of 1939-45, series 4, vol. 1, p. 588.
5. Percy Joske, *Sir Robert Menzies*, p. 169.
6. *Sydney Morning Herald*, 16 February 1946.
7. Joint Opposition Policy Speech and Supplementary Statements, 1949, p. 14.
8. Robin Gollan, *Revolutionaries and Reformists*, pp. 7-8.
9. Alistair Davidson, *The Communist Party of Australia*, pp. 82, 87-91.
10. Alistair Davidson, *The Communist Party of Australia*, pp. 120, 139.
11. *Sydney Morning Herald*, 18 January 1949.
12. Robert Murray, *The Split*, p. 79.
13. *Commonwealth Parliamentary Debates*, 27 April 1950, vol. 207, p. 1995.
14. Robert Murray has a detailed description of the ALP's response to the legislation in chapter 6 of *The Split*.
15. Frank Cain and Frank Farrell, 'Menzies' War on the Communist Party, 1949-51' in Ann Curthoys and John Merritt (eds), *Australia's First Cold War, 1945-1953*, vol. 1, *Society, Communism and Culture*, pp. 109-34. The most complete account of the referendum is in Leicester Webb's *Communism and Democracy in Australia*.
16. The text of the Communist Party Dissolution Act is in Leicester Webb, *Communism and Democracy*, pp. 186-95.
17. *Commonwealth Parliamentary Debates*, 9 May 1950, vol. 207, p. 2271.
18. The Movement, for example, initially argued against the legislation on the grounds that banning would simply increase the popularity of the party, as it had done in the early years of the war, and would end the isolation into which the party was being driven in the union movement. Once the Bill was introduced, however, the Movement supported the ban. Robert Murray, *The Split*, p. 80.
19. *Commonwealth Parliamentary Debates*, 9 May 1950, vol. 207, p. 2270.
20. Ibid., 9 May 1950, vol. 207, pp. 2267-8.
21. Leicester Webb, *Communism and Democracy in Australia*, p. 58.
22. Mary Douglas, *Purity and Danger*, p. 114.
23. *Commonwealth Parliamentary Debates*, 14 November 1934, vol. 145, p. 256.
24. Accounts of Kisch's visit to Australia can be found in Don Watson, *Brian Fitzpatrick*, pp. 64-7; Manning Clark, *A History of Australia*, vol. VI, pp. 459, 463-7, 469-72, 474-7, 481-2; R. Gollan, *Revolutionaries and Reformists*, pp. 44-8; and in Egon Kisch, *Australian Landfall*.
25. *Commonwealth Parliamentary Debates*, 14 November 1934, vol. 145, p. 257.

26 Ibid., p. 264.
27 Ibid., p. 269.
28 Eric Campbell, *The Rallying Point*, p. 67.
29 Ibid., p. 81.
30 Michael Cathcart, *Defending the National Tuckshop*, p. 76. There are many similarities between Cathcart's analysis of conservative ideology and my own. Both focus on the way it divided society into two groups – Australian and alien, loyal centre and disloyal margin – and on the symbolic strategies used to persuade of this distinction.
31 Mary Douglas, *Purity and Danger*, chapter 7.
32 Don Watson, *Brian Fitzpatrick*, pp. 60-2; Manning Clark, *A History of Australia*, vol. VI, pp. 239-43.
33 *Commonwealth Parliamentary Debates*, 25 June 1925, vol. 110, p. 461.
34 Ibid.
35 See for example, Jack Beasley during debate on Kisch, *Commonwealth Parliamentary Debates*, 14 November 1934, vol. 145, p. 259.
36 *Commonwealth Parliamentary Debates*, 9 May 1950, vol. 207, p. 2268.
37 Alistair Davidson, *The Communist Party of Australia*, p. 53.
38 Richard Hall, *The Secret State*. Inspector Browne of the Australian intelligence service who was investigating the activities of the secret armies reported to his superiors on a number of occasions that they posed a threat to civil peace. Michael Cathcart, *Defending the National Tuckshop*, pp. 2, 49, 61ff.
39 Don Watson, *Brian Fitzpatrick*, pp. 60-2; Stuart Macintyre, *Oxford History*, pp. 307-8; Manning Clark, *A History of Australia*, vol. VI, pp. 418-19; Frank Cain, *The Origins of Political Surveillance in Australia*, pp. 245ff.
40 Peter Coleman, *Obscenity, Blasphemy and Sedition*, p. 83.
41 Don Watson, *Brian Fitzpatrick*, p. 69.
42 *Commonwealth Parliamentary Debates*, 20 May 1932, vol. 134, p. 1143.
43 Douglas Cole, '"The Crimson Thread of Kinship": Ethnic Ideas in Australia, 1870-1914', *Historical Studies*, 14, 56 (April 1971), pp. 511-25.
44 David Bowman, 'Can the ASIO Revolution Last?', *Australian Society*, November 1989, pp. 23-6; Richard Hall, 'Menzies's Literary Lie', *Age Monthly Review*, 3, 9 (January 1984), pp. 3-4.
45 For an introduction to Melanie Klein's work see, Hanna Segal, *Introduction to the Work of Melanie Klein* and Juliet Mitchell, *The Selected Melanie Klein*.
46 Klein calls this position the depressive. Its links with the popular meaning of depression are hard to see at first because of the wide meaning Klein is giving the term, but if it is remembered that the core of depression is guilty self-accusation the link is clearer. Where the paranoid schizoid position deals with frustration by turning anger outwards, seeing the fault in the world not the self, the depressive turns it inward, seeing the

cause of the problem in the self not the world. This can result in the painful state of guilt-ridden lassitude and sense of worthlessness called depression in everyday language.
47 Alan Davies, *Skills, Outlooks and Passions*, pp. 368-74.
48 Richard Hofstadter, *The Paranoid Style in American Politics and Other Essays*.
49 Although the ceremony of the scapegoat is most associated with small tribal communities like the ancient Jews, Kenneth Burke has argued that the use of a victim to enact redemption is one of the great social dramas whose form still determines how we play our roles in modern society. Kenneth Burke, 'On Human Behaviour Considered Dramatistically' in *Permanence and Change*. See also A.F. Davies, *Skills, Outlooks and Passions*, pp. 334ff.
50 'Ideology as a Cultural System', in Clifford Geertz, *The Interpretation of Culture*.
51 Joint Opposition Policy Speech and Supplementary Statements, 1949, p. 15.
52 *Commonwealth Parliamentary Debates*, 9 May 1950, vol. 207, p. 2280.
53 Percy Spender, *Politics and a Man*.
54 Menzies' Second Reading Speech for the Communist Party Dissolution Bill was made on 27 April, 1950. *Commonwealth Parliamentary Debates*, vol. 207, pp. 1994-2007.
55 Ibid., pp. 1998-9.
56 Ibid., p. 2000.
57 Ibid., p. 2000.
58 Ibid., p. 1999.
59 Ibid., p. 2003.
60 Ibid., p. 2001.
61 Ibid., p. 1998.
62 These notes had somehow become separated in Menzies' papers in the NLA. Pages 1-14 are in series 20, box 436, folder 7; the remainder is in series 6, box 253, folder 20.
63 ABC Broadcast, 26 April 1939, reported in *Argus*, 27 April 1939. This description of himself was proffered by Menzies on succeeding Lyons as Prime Minister in response to accusations of being aloof and superior.
64 *The Forgotten People and Other Studies in Democracy*, chapters II and III.
65 J.S. Mill, 'Essay on Liberty' (1859) in *Three Essays*, p. 83.
66 *Commonwealth Parliamentary Debates*, 14 September 1937, vol. 154, p. 980.
67 *The Forgotten People and Other Studies in Democracy*, chapter X.
68 James Alexander, 'The Psychology of Bitterness', *International Journal of Psychoanalysis*, vol. 41, (1960), pp. 514-20; see also A.F. Davies, *Skills, Outlooks and Passions*, pp. 329ff.
69 R.G. Menzies, *Afternoon Light*, p. 319.

70 R.G. Menzies, *The Forgotten People*, p. 27.
71 Diary, 24 February 1935.
72 Jean Spender, *Ambassador's Wife*, p. 76.
73 Foreword to R.S. Whitington, *The Frank Packer Story*, MS 4936, series 10, box 358.
74 Alan Watt, *Australian Diplomat*, p. 172.
75 *The BHP Recreation Review*, 30 March 1927. A copy of this is in Menzies' papers, box 251. Many years later he rewrote the trial scene 'in the light of modern legal concepts' for the literary magazine, *Southerly*, vol. 17, no. 2, (1956), pp. 65-6.

ENGLAND

1 *Melbourne University Magazine*, vol. 7, no. 2, (1913), p. 57.
2 This was reported to me by the late Professor Vincent Buckley who was present and who also knew the passage from Wordsworth by heart.
3 *Melbourne University Magazine*, vol. 8, no. 3, pp. 84-5.
4 Arthur Phillips, *The Australian Tradition*, p. 58. The essay 'The Cultural Cringe' was originally published in *Meanjin*, vol. 9, no. 4, (1950).
5 R.G. Menzies, *Speech is of Time*, pp. 18-19.
6 Diary, 6 March 1935.
7 Diary, 21 March 1935.
8 Diary, 24 March 1935.
9 Diary, 14 April 1935.
10 Diary, 20 April 1935.
11 Diary, 11 May 1935.
12 Diary, 25 March 1935.
13 Diary, 10 May 1935.
14 Diary, 4 July 1935.
15 *The Times*, 5 July 1935.
16 *The Times*, 5 July 1935.
17 Diary, 11 May 1935.
18 Diary, 14 May 1935.
19 Diary, 20 April 1935.
20 Diary, 7 June 1935.
21 Diary, 15 June 1935.
22 Diary, 21 July 1935.
23 For the following interpretation of the political strategy of Baldwin's rhetoric I am indebted to Bill Schwartz's essay 'The Language of Constitutionalism: Baldwinite Conservatism' in *Formations of Nations and People*, pp. 1-18.
24 *Afternoon Light*, pp. 96-9.

25 *On England*, p. 16, cited in Bill Schwartz, 'The Language of Constitutionalism', p. 16.
26 See for example, 'The English Tradition', in *Speech is of Time*.
27 'The Oldest Book with the Newest Message', speech on the occasion of the Centenary Thanksgiving Meeting of the British and Foreign Bible Society, Victoria, 15 July 1940, MS 4936, series 6, box 252, folder 6.
28 W.J. Hudson, *Blind Loyalty*, pp. 7-15.
29 Weston Bate, *Lucky City*.
30 Geoffrey Blainey, James Morrissey and S.E.K. Hulme, *Wesley College*, p. 103.
31 Geoffrey Blainey, *A Centenary History of the University of Melbourne*, p. 98.
32 R.G. Menzies, ' "Not to Yield": A Study of the British Problem', dictated en route to England, June 1948. MS 4936, series 10, box 359.
33 For example, the long passage at the end of 'The British Commonwealth of Nations in International Affairs' (Roy Milne Memorial Lecture, Adelaide, 26 June 1950), on what the Commonwealth means to him. *Speech is of Time*, pp. 18-20.
34 'The Crown and the Commonwealth', dated 8 February 1952; MS 4936, series 10, box 356.
35 *Rotarian*, (Chicago), November 1953, MS 4936, series 10, box 356.
36 Article for *Sydney Morning Herald*, on occasion of Queen Elizabeth's visit. MS 4936, series 10, box 356; manuscript dated 24 January 1954.
37 Edward Shils and Michael Young, 'The Meaning of the Coronation', *Sociological Review*, (i), vol. 1, no. 2, (1953), pp. 63-81.
38 Edward Shils, *Centre and Periphery*.
39 Edward Shils, *Centre and Periphery*, p. 7.
40 Diary, 3 June 1935.
41 Here we see the link between the conservative social theorist Edward Shils, with his legacy of Emile Durkheim's emphasis on the need for common secular symbols to establish social solidarity in the modern world, and the conservative politician Robert Menzies, with his interest in combating the communal language of labour. It is not surprising that their ideas about the coronation are so similar.
42 *The Times*, 5 July 1935.
43 Diary, 4 July 1935, 5 July 1935.
44 Diary, 26 June 1935.
45 Diary, 8 July 1935.
46 Diary, 3 April 1935.
47 Diary, 6 May 1935.
48 Diary, 2 May 1935.
49 'Australia's Place in the Empire', delivered 9 April 1935, printed in *International Affairs*, July-August 1935, copy in MS 4936, series 10, box 251, folder 3, pp. 1, 4.

50 See Diary, 5 May 1935.
51 'Australia's Place in the Empire', p. 9.
52 These speeches were collected in *To the People of Britain at War from the Prime Minister of Australia*.
53 David Day, *Menzies and Churchill at War*.
54 See diary entries for 29 July, 18 August 1948.
55 R.G. Menzies, '"Not to Yield": A Study of the British Problem', dictated en route to England, June 1948. MS 4936, series 10, box 359, chapter VI.
56 David Ascoli to Menzies, 9 August 1968, MS 4936, series 10, box 366.
57 A.F. Davies, *The Human Element*, p. 98.

INLAND BORN

1 Cameron Hazlehurst, 'Young Menzies', in Cameron Hazlehurst (ed.), *Australian Conservatism*, p.3.
2 R.G. Menzies, 'A Few Thoughts About Engineers', *Journal of the Institution of Engineers, Australia*, vol. 11, December 1939, p. 442, cited in Cameron Hazlehurst (ed.), *Australian Conservatism*, p. 3.
3 'Freedom in Modern Society', in R.G. Menzies, *Speech is of Time*, pp. 220-1. A footnote by Menzies to this speech in its published version says the record of how and to what audience the speech was delivered has been mislaid. Percy Joske cites the speech as given when he was a member of the Victorian Legislative Council. A manuscript of the speech in series 6, box 251 of Menzies' papers in the NLA is dated either 1935 or 1936. This could be a retyped version of a speech given earlier, but it seems that the speech was written sometime in the 1930s.
4 R.G. Menzies, *Afternoon Light*, p. 8.
5 R.G. Menzies to Ken Taylor, interview.
6 Isabel Green to Kevin Perkins, interview.
7 Kevin Perkins, *Menzies*, p. 7; F. Raven, *The History of the Menzies Family in Jeparit*.
8 R.G. Menzies, *Speech is of Time*, p. 18.
9 Les Blake, *Wimmera*, p. 12.
10 Terri G. Allen, *Wotjobaluk*, p. 5; Terri G. Allen, *Wyperfeld*, p. 1.
11 Aldo Massola, *Bunjil's Cave*, p. 3.
12 Terri G. Allen, *Wotjobaluk*, pp. 18-20.
13 Les Blake, *Wimmera*, pp. 66ff.
14 R.G. Menzies, *Afternoon Light*, pp. 7-8.

15 This was probably *Sarcocornia quinqueflora* (glasswort), a highly salt-resistant succulent which is edible to cattle.
16 Ronald Seth, *R.G. Menzies*, pp. 20-1.

17 R.G. Menzies, *Afternoon Light*, p. 8.
18 R.G. Menzies, *Afternoon Light*, p. 9; Ronald Seth, *R.G. Menzies*, p. 18; Kevin Perkins, *Menzies*, pp. 10-11; Percy Joske, *Sir Robert Menzies*, p. 4.
19 Speech at the unveiling of the Jeparit memorial to Sir Robert Menzies, 18 September 1966, MS 4936, series 6, box 284, NLA.
20 Cameron Hazlehurst, 'Young Menzies', p. 5.
21 Les Blake, *Wimmera*, pp. 15, 32; Josef Vondra, *German Speaking Settlers in Australia*, pp. 33-4.
22 Speech at unveiling of monument in Jeparit, 18 September 1966, MS 4936, series 6, box 284; manuscript biography by Allan Dawes, MS 4936, series 10, box 354, chapter 2.
23 Bernard Smith, *The Spectre of Truganini*, p. 18.
24 Kevin Perkins, *Menzies*, p.9.
25 Terri Allen, *Wotjoballuk*.
26 R.G. Menzies to Ken Taylor, interview.
27 Bernard Smith, *The Spectre of Truganini*, pp. 15ff.
28 Introduction to volume on Australasia, Oceania and the Antarctic for a seven series volume of social studies called 'Lands and People'. MS 4936, series 10, box 359, NLA.
29 Draft of entry for 1972 *Encyclopedia Britannica Book of the Year*, MS 4936, series 10, box 356, NLA.
30 Bernard Smith, *The Spectre of Truganini*, p. 28.
31 'A Century of Australian Song', Part II, *The Melbourne University Magazine*, vol. 12, no. 2, August 1918, p. 58.
32 Both poems, in all their brutality, can be found in *The Poetical Works of Brunton Stephens*, Cornstalk Publishing Company, Sydney, 1925. An interview Menzies gave towards the end of his life to Francis McNicoll and held in the oral history section of the National Library of Australia (TRC 1169/349) shows that the attitudes he displays here remained in his attitude to the Aborigines. The interview is not dated, but it takes place during the period of the Whitlam government while Billie Snedden was Leader of the Opposition.
33 The way the arguments of 'The Forgotten People' can be directed against Aborigines was seen in a statement made by Andrew Peacock in his first term as Liberal opposition leader. Arguing against Aboriginal claims for land rights, he invokes the symbols of the home and of self-renunciation to deny that there is anything special about Aborigines' relationship with the land.

> I understand the relationship between people and land. I well understand that Aborigines have an affinity with land, but so do other Australians. I have it myself with my farm in Victoria, and

it's wrong to believe that only one section of Australia has a special affinity with the land. What Australian who has saved and gone without over 30 years to own his or her own home doesn't have an affinity with that land. (*Age*, 30 July 1984).

34 Bernard Smith, *The Spectre of Truganini*, pp. 21-2.
35 Ibid., p. 16.
36 Ibid., p. 10.
37 Ibid., p. 44.

KNOWLEDGE, CULTURE, EXPERIENCE

1 R.G. Menzies, *Afternoon Light*, chapter 9. On the effect of Menzies' loyalty to Britain on his prosecution of Australia's interests during the first years of World War II, see David Day, *Menzies and Churchill at War*; David Day, *The Great Betrayal: Britain, Australia and the Onset of the Pacific War*. On Menzies' involvement in the Suez Crisis see W.J. Hudson, *Blind Loyalty: Australia and the Suez Crisis, 1956*; and A.L. Martin, 'R.G. Menzies and the Suez Crisis', *Australian Historical Studies*, vol. 23, no. 92, (April 1989), pp. 163-85.
2 *Melbourne University Magazine*, vol. IX, no. 1, (June 1915), pp. 5-6.
3 *Melbourne University Magazine*, vol. XI, no. 2, (August 1917), p. 57. The 'Shop' was a student name for Melbourne University.
4 Cameron Hazlehurst, 'The Young Menzies', p. 6.
5 R.G. Menzies, *Speech is of Time*, p. 209.
6 Diary, 6 March 1935.
7 Diary, 13, 14, 15 March 1935.
8 A.L. Martin, 'R.G. Menzies and the Suez Crisis', p. 168.
9 Walter Crocker, Diaries, 5 July 1959, Barr-Smith Library, University of Adelaide, South Australia; cited in Meg Gurry, 'Leadership and Bilateral Relations: Menzies and Nehru, Australia and India, 1949-1964', unpublished paper, La Trobe University.
10 Alexander Downer, *Six Prime Ministers*, p. 43.
11 R.G. Menzies, *Afternoon Light*, p. 6.
12 Interview with Barry Jones, 6 February 1968, MS 4936, series 6, box 171, NLA.
13 See for example, Donald Horne, *The Lucky Country*, 'The Age of Menzies'.
14 Richard Haese, *Rebels and Precursors*, chapter 2, and Humphrey McQueen, *Black Swan of Trespass*, pp. 26-7, both have accounts of the attempt to establish the academy.
15 *Argus*, 28 April 1937.

16 *Age*, 28 April 1937.
17 Adrian Lawlor, *Arquebus*.
18 Norman Macgeorge's Letter to the Editor, *Argus*, 1 May 1937; Menzies' reply, *Argus*, 3 May 1937.
19 Adrian Lawlor, *Arquebus*, p. 23.
20 *Herald*, 3 May, 1937.
21 *Herald*, 6 May, 1937.
22 *Herald*, 4 May, 1937.
23 *Herald*, 6 May, 1937.
24 S. Ure Smith to Norman Carter, 8 February 1938, cited in H. McQueen, *The Black Swan of Trespass*, p. 27.
25 R.G. Menzies, *The Forgotten People and Other Studies in Democracy*, pp. 6-7.
26 Kevin Perkins, *Menzies*, p. 28.
27 Geoffrey Blainey, James Morrissey and S.E.K. Hulme, *Wesley College*, p. 155.
28 Percy Joske, *Sir Robert Menzies*, p. 8.
29 John Bunting, *R.G. Menzies*, p. 114; Paul Hasluck, *Sir Robert Menzies*, p. 30.
30 'De Natura', *Melbourne University Magazine*, vol. 8, no. 3, (November 1914), pp. 84-5.
31 'A Century of Australian Song', Part I, II and III, *Melbourne University Magazine*, vol. 12, no. 1, (May 1918), pp. 8-11; vol. 12, no. 2, (August 1918), pp. 57-9; vol. 12, no. 3, (October 1918), pp. 105-7.
32 'Club Fever', dated 6 August 1926, MS 4936, series 10, box 355; John Bunting, *R.G. Menzies*, pp. 206-12.
33 Barry Andrews, 'The Federal Government as Literary Patron', *Meanjin*, vol. 41, no. 1, (March 1982), p. 8.
34 Allan Ashbolt, 'The Great Literary Witch-hunt' in A. Curthoys and J. Merritt (eds), *Australia's First Cold War*, p. 161.
35 'Australian Letter', *Landfall*, vol. 7, no. 4, (1953), p. 281.
36 R.G. Menzies, *Afternoon Light*, p. 131.
37 *Commonwealth Parliamentary Debates*, vol. 218, 28 August 1952, pp. 717-29; 4 September 1952, pp. 1031-41.
38 Richard Hall, 'Menzies' Literary Lie', *The Age Monthly Review*, vol. 3, no. 9, (January 1984), pp. 3-4.
39 Allan Ashbolt, 'The Great Literary Witch-hunt', p. 181. See also Lynne Strahan's *Just City and the Mirrors*.
40 Allan Dawes, 'R.G. Menzies: An Interim Report'.
41 Kevin Perkins, p. 227.
42 R.G. Menzies, 'The Place of a University in the Modern Community', delivered at the Annual Commencement of the Canberra University College, 1939, pp. 16-18.
43 Hazel Craig to Robert Kennedy, 2 December 1962, MS 4936, series 10,

box 362.
44 MS 4936, series 10, box 365, NLA.
45 R.G. Menzies, *Afternoon Light*, p. 4.
46 Cited in Humphrey McQueen, *From Gallipoli to Petrov*, p. 171.
47 Paul Hasluck, *Sir Robert Menzies*, pp. 27-8.
48 Percy Spender, *Politics and a Man*, p. 153.
49 Ibid., pp. 153-4.
50 Howard Beale, *This Inch of Time*, p. 105.
51 Alexander Downer, *Six Prime Ministers*, p. 17.
52 John Bunting, *R.G. Menzies*, p. 38.

FATHERS
1 R.G. Menzies, *Afternoon Light*, p. 318.
2 R.G. Menzies, *Speech is of Time*, pp. 186-7.
3 See for example, R.G. Menzies, *Afternoon Light*, p. 317; speech made on his resignation from prime ministership, 20 January 1966, MS 4936, series 6, box 170, NLA.
4 R.G. Menzies, *Afternoon Light*, p. 57.
5 The most unambivalent accounts of Menzies' personality in these terms are by Paul Hasluck, *Sir Robert Menzies* and John Bunting, *R.G. Menzies*.
6 For an extreme example of this sort of assessment see Humphrey McQueen, 'Menzies' in *From Gallipoli to Petrov*. The television mini-series 'The True Believers' (broadcast on the ABC during July and August 1988 and scripted by ALP supporter Bob Ellis) also presented Menzies as vain, cynical and manipulative, in contrast to the warmth and humility of the ALP leader Ben Chifley.
7 Cited in Cameron Hazlehurst, *Menzies Observed*, pp. 311-12; see also Warwick Fairfax, 'The Bewildering Mr Menzies', *SMH*, 17 August 1943, reprinted in Cameron Hazlehurst, *Menzies Observed*, pp. 266-70.
8 Alan Reid, 'Prime Ministers I have known', *Bulletin*, Centenary Issue, 29 January, 1980.
9 This interpretation is indebted to Heinz Kohut's work on narcissism and self-psychology, as developed in his two books, *The Analysis of the Self* and *The Restoration of the Self*. In particular see chapter 4 of *The Restoration of the Self* on 'The Bipolar Self'.
10 Menzies' own account of his parents and childhood in 'A Portrait of my Parents' in *Afternoon Light* is obviously a key source. Its comments and anecdotes are prefigured in both Seth's and Perkins' biographies. The characterisation of the parents and of life in Jeparit in Ronald Seth's *R.G. Menzies* are very close to Menzies' own in *Afternoon Light*. Seth had a two-hour interview with Menzies when he was in London for the

Commonwealth Prime Ministers Conference in 1960 and 'several hours' with Frank who was also in London at the same time. Kevin Perkins was not granted an interview by Menzies when he was researching *Menzies*, but he did interview Frank and Isabel. He very generously permitted me to listen to his recordings of these interviews. Percy Joske's biography, *Sir Robert Menzies*, was written after *Afternoon Light* and primarily relies on it for its very scanty treatment of the childhood. Cameron Hazlehurst has compiled further sources relating to Menzies' childhood in *Menzies Observed* and has written a reflective essay on the young Menzies in *Australian Conservatism* in which he sifts through some of the myths about Menzies' early years.

Menzies' papers in the NLA contain a draft manuscript of a partial biography by Allan Dawes ('R.G. Menzies of Australia: An Interim Report', MS 4936, series 10, box 354). The draft has been read and corrected by Menzies, so I am assuming that, even if he was not the actual source of all of its material, and he clearly was of much of it, he was happy to regard it as an accurate account of his experience of his childhood and youth. What is at stake here is not just what really happened but what Menzies remembered as happening, or wanted to remember as happening. Frank Menzies makes mention of the Dawes' biography in his interview with Kevin Perkins. He says it was written in 1950 and 1951 and that Menzies gave Dawes access to all his diaries and records. Dawes only completed a small part of what had been anticipated by Menzies, and the work was never published.

Recorded interview sources I have used which contain material on Menzies' childhood and family relations are Kevin Perkins' interviews with Frank and Isabel Menzies, an interview by Francis McNicoll with Frank Menzies some time in the early 1970s (Oral History Collection, NLA, TRC 1169/350), and an interview by Ken Taylor with Menzies himself recorded on 25 February 1969. A copy of this is also held in the Oral History Collection of the NLA, TRC 1169/294-5.

11 Cameron Hazlehurst, 'Young Menzies', p. 19.
12 In their interviews with Kevin Perkins both Frank and Isabel describe Bob as very close to his mother; Frank says, 'we always regarded him as a Sampson'.
13 Susan Priestley, *Warracknabeal*, p. 118.
14 R.G. Menzies, *Afternoon Light*, p. 6.
15 Ronald Seth, *R.G. Menzies*, p. 16.
16 Ibid., p. 10.
17 Susan Priestley, *Warracknabeal*, p. 119.
18 Ronald Seth, *R.G. Menzies*, p. 13.

19 Allan Dawes, 'R.G. Menzies of Australia: An Interim Report', MS 4936, series 10, box 354, p. 26.
20 Menzies' descriptions of his parents are from *Afternoon Light*, pp. 11-12.
21 Both Frank and Isabel recall the physical punishment. Frank Menzies interview with Francis McNicoll; Isabel Green interview with Kevin Perkins.
22 R.G. Menzies, *Afternoon Light*, p. 9.
23 Menzies to Ken Taylor, interview. Menzies was wont to claim that he was the only member of the Victorian Bar never to have had a row with a particularly irascible judge because 'when the judge's temper was beginning to rise he looked "exceedingly like my father, and knowing the signs of the rising tide I was able to avoid it welling over"'. Percy Joske, *Sir Robert Menzies*, p. 5.
24 Cameron Hazlehurst, *Menzies Observed*, p. 19.
25 Isabel Green to Kevin Perkins, interview.
26 Ronald Seth, *R.G. Menzies*, p. 57. In Allan Dawes' manuscript James says, 'You know, my dear, I have been underestimating Robert.' Dawes comments, 'That was very good. It almost revolutionised his outlook on his third son's talents.'
    Menzies was one of five children and his father's reserve towards him may well have been partly motivated by his consideration of the claims of the other children. Robert's brother, Frank, was Crown Solicitor of Victoria for many years and Dawes reports that it was James Menzies' habit when anyone enquired after his 'distinguished son' to reply 'which one?'
27 See footnote 10.
28 Frank Menzies to Francis McNicoll, interview.
29 Ibid.
30 Isabel Green to Kevin Perkins, interview.
31 Allan Dawes, 'R.G. Menzies of Australia: An Interim Report', p. 26.
32 Speech at unveiling of spire in Jeparit, 19 September 1966, MS 4936, series 6, box 284, NLA.
33 Isabel Green to Kevin Perkins, interview.
34 R.G. Menzies, *Afternoon Light*, p. 316. This story appears earlier in an article on Menzies when he entered Victorian politics. He told the journalist sent to interview him of the phrenologist's prediction. *Table Talk*, 25 April 1929.
35 Ronald Seth, *R.G. Menzies*, pp. 4-6.
36 Frank Menzies to Kevin Perkins, interview.
37 Ronald Seth, *R.G. Menzies*, p. 32.
38 Ibid., p. 33; Cameron Hazlehurst, 'Young Menzies', p. 5.
39 Allan Dawes, 'R.G. Menzies: An Interim Report', pp. 51-2.

40 Percy Joske, *Sir Robert Menzies*, p. 8.
41 For the details of Menzies' secondary education, see Cameron Hazlehurst, *Menzies Observed*, pp. 16-20.
42 Isabel Menzies to Allan Dawes, 'R.G. Menzies: An Interim Report', p. 69.
43 *Melbourne University Magazine*, vol. 17, no. 3, (November 1913), p. 152.
44 Sigmund Freud, 'Family Romance', *The Standard Edition of the Complete Psychological Works of Sigmund Freud*, vol. 9. For a suggestive discussion of the varieties of family romance phantasies see Marthe Robert, *Origins of the Novel*, pp. 21-31.
45 Sigmund Freud, 'Family Romance', p. 237.
46 Ibid., pp. 240-1.
47 Marthe Robert, *The Origins of the Novel*, pp. 27-9.
48 Sigmund Freud, 'Family Romance', p. 229.
49 Allan Dawes, 'R.G. Menzies of Australia: An Interim Report', pp. 31-2.
50 Diary, 11 July 1935.
51 *Sydney Morning Herald*, 24 January 1954.
52 Marthe Robert, *The Origins of the Novel*, p. 29.
53 Frank Menzies to Francis McNicoll, interview.
54 Kevin Perkins, *Menzies*, p. 156.
55 Ibid., p. 10; Allan Dawes, 'R.G. Menzies of Australia: An Interim Report', pp. 29-32; Frank Menzies to Kevin Perkins, interview.
56 Cameron Hazlehurst, *Menzies Observed*, p. 17.
57 Geoffrey Blainey, James Morrissey and S.E.K. Hulme, *Wesley College: The First Hundred Years*, pp. 75-9 and chapters 5, 6 and 7; Brian Lewis, *Our War*, chapter 14.
58 Blainey, Morrissey and Hulme, *Wesley College*, p. 118.
59 R.G. Menzies, 'Politics as an Art' in *Speech is of Time*, pp. 187, 189.
60 M.H. Ellis, 'The Mind of R.G. Menzies: A Personal Appraisal', *Bulletin*, 22 March 1961.
61 Isabel Green to Kevin Perkins, interview; R.G. Menzies, *Afternoon Light*, p. 67; note also a comment by Jim Cairns on talking with Menzies shortly before his retirement: 'What came out of the discussion I had with him was that he cared very much for what history was going to say about him, and that he was a bit worried about it'. Kevin Perkins, *Menzies*, p. 241.
62 Further evidence for this argument would come from an examination of Menzies' relations with his sons when he himself must occupy the father's position. Menzies had two sons, Kenneth and Ian, who were born early in his marriage. There is little on the public record about Menzies' family life, but what there is suggests that his relations with his sons were not close. He certainly did not reproduce in his own family the well-knit family of his own childhood. During his sons' childhoods

when he was making his name in the law he worked eighty hours a week according to his own estimation (*Afternoon Light*, p. 316), and when he entered federal politics the two boys were sent to boarding school. I expect that when more is known about Menzies' relations with his sons it will confirm the characterisation I am developing here of a man who failed to identify sufficiently with the position of the father to allow himself to relax for long enough from the competitive assertion of his masculinity to be an attentive, loving father himself. His relations with his daughter, Heather, were much happier. Downer, who expresses puzzlement at Menzies' distant relations with his sons, describes Heather as 'the principal joy in his life' in the period in which he knew him. (Alexander Downer, *Six Prime Ministers*, pp. 54-5.)

63 Paul Hasluck writes of him that as tradition was his guide 'he did not do much that was wrong, but he was slow to do anything that was novel'. *Sir Robert Menzies*, pp. 23-4.

THE ELEVATED SELF

1 Brian Lewis, *Our War*, p. 261.
2 Edgar Holt, *Politics is People*, pp. 101-2. John Bunting also describes the transformation of the private into the public man: 'the public face was there in an instant, whenever his mind told him it was needed. That perhaps was most of the time'. *R.G. Menzies*, p. 47; Percy Spender comments that everything Menzies did in public was a performance. *Politics and a Man*, p. 154.
3 For example, Percy Spender, *Politics and a Man*, p. 152.
4 Cited in Cameron Hazlehurst, *Menzies Observed*, p. 19.
5 Brian Lewis, *Our War*, pp. 263-4.
6 Cameron Hazlehurst, *Menzies Observed*, p. 20; See also, Percy Spender – 'Menzies regarded himself as a superior being. His great fault was that he could not conceal this regard for himself from others.' *Politics and a Man*, p. 152; Brian Penton – 'too proudly he wore the mantle of the superior man', cited in Cameron Hazlehurst, *Menzies Observed*, p. 186.
7 Arthur Fadden, *They Called Me Artie*, p. 110.
8 Enid Lyons, *Among the Carrion Crows*, p. 54.
9 Judge J.G. Norris, cited in Cameron Hazlehurst, *Menzies Observed*, p. 37.
10 For example, see Casey to Bruce, 17 November 1937, cited in Cameron Hazlehurst, *Menzies Observed*, pp. 128-9; Percy Spender, *Politics and a Man*, pp. 155-6; Alexander Downer, *Six Prime Ministers*, pp. 1-2.
11 Edgar Holt, *Politics is People*, p. 109; Howard Beale, *This Inch of Time*, p. 110; Paul Hasluck, *Sir Robert Menzies*, pp. 16-17.

12 Percy Spender, *Politics and a Man*, pp. 152-4; Alexander Downer, *Six Prime Ministers*, p. 22; Frank Menzies to Kevin Perkins, interview; *National Times*, 22-28 May 1978; Warwick Fairfax, *SMH*, 17 August 1943, cited in Cameron Hazlehurst, *Menzies Observed*, p. 269; Donald Horne, *The Lucky Country*, p. 183.

13 Alexander Downer, *Six Prime Ministers*, p. 16; Percy Spender, *Politics and a Man*, p. 72; Howard Beale, *This Inch of Time*, pp. 101-2.

14 Howard Beale, *This Inch of Time*, p. 105; Alexander Downer, *Six Prime Ministers*, p. 26. John Bunting gives a slightly different picture of Menzies' relations with younger men, describing very warm relations between Menzies and his senior public servants. *R.G. Menzies*, chapter 6. Such men, however, posed no direct challenge to Menzies, for in the Westminster system the political leader is clearly in charge. They were known as Menzies' 'Boys' and he regularly addressed even as senior a man as Bunting as 'lad'.

15 Alexander Downer, *Six Prime Ministers*, p. 26.

16 Ibid., p. 15; John Bunting, *R.G. Menzies*, p. 33; Paul Hasluck, *Sir Robert Menzies*, p. 7.

17 R.H. Croll, *Collections and Recollections*, p. 173.

18 Percy Joske, *Sir Robert Menzies*, p. 7.

19 Howard Beale, *This Inch of Time*, p. 106; see also Warren Denning, cited in Cameron Hazlehurst, *Menzies Observed*, pp. 313-14. Karen Horney suggests that the pursuit in adults of vindictive triumph through inflicting humiliation on others is motivated by the need to revenge humiliations suffered in childhood. *Neurosis and Human Growth*, pp. 197ff. In some ways Menzies fits Horney's portrait of 'the arrogant vindictive', but his self-esteem is far more buoyant. As well as the humiliation he suffered from submission to his father's authority, he may have suffered from older siblings in his position as the fourth child, but I have found no direct evidence of this. Perhaps his eyes were so fixed on his father that the older siblings did not register.

20 See, for example, comments cited in Cameron Hazlehurst, *Menzies Observed*, pp. 80, 168, 312-13; and Percy Spender, *Politics and a Man*, pp. 154-5.

21 Percy Spender, *Politics and a Man*, p. 154.

22 Alexander Downer, *Six Prime Ministers*, p. 7; see also Billy Snedden, *An Unlikely Liberal*, p. 57. Spender reports that in cabinet Menzies would at times use sarcasm and penetrating questions against the muddled or ill-prepared: 'Men are men and do not like to be made to appear foolish or unprepared, no matter how foolish or unprepared they might be.' Percy Spender, *Politics and a Man*, p. 155. Beale reports anxiety in the newly founded Liberal Party about the reappearance of the old Menzies. Howard Beale, *This Inch of Time*, p. 109.

23 Sigmund Freud, *Jokes and Their Relation to the Unconscious* (1908), *Standard Edition*, vol. 8.
24 Bruce Watson, 'Wit and Politics: A Study of Whitlam and Menzies', *Melbourne Journal of Politics*, vol. 13, (1981), pp. 32-4. Watson analyses examples of Menzies' wit published in *The Wit of Sir Robert Menzies*, compiled by Robert Robinson. John Bunting says Menzies had no taste for the bawdy. *Sir Robert Menzies*, p. 157.
25 Bruce Watson draws an interesting comparison here with Whitlam, whose sense of superiority focused on his own uniqueness, often softened by a touch of self-mocking. Whitlam was untroubled by comparisons as he was sure he was above them. Menzies, by comparison, always asserted his superiority vis-a-vis someone else and seemed to derive pleasure from the assertion of comparative advantage. Bruce Watson, 'Wit and Politics', *Melbourne Journal of Politics*, vol. 13, (1981), pp. 32-44.
26 Robert Robinson, *The Wit of Sir Robert Menzies*, p. 65.
27 I say 'reputedly' because in correspondence with the publisher of the book in 1966 Menzies says he cannot remember making this remark, thinks it sounds bad, and requests that it be taken out. The compiler does not give the source, but it sounds very typical of Menzies, and was probably made many years before. Menzies to Leslie Frewin, 17 March 1966 and 4 April 1966, MS 4936, series 10, box 365.
28 Robert Robinson, *The Wit of Sir Robert Menzies*, p. 21.
29 Frank Menzies to Francis McNicoll, interview.
30 Cited in Cameron Hazlehurst, *Menzies Observed*, p. 97.
31 Ibid., p. 47-69; Michael Kino, 'The Forgotten Menzies: Robert Gordon Menzies 1894-1934 and Victorian Politics', BA Hons Thesis, Monash University.
32 *Argus*, 6 May 1929.
33 Don Whitington, *Twelfth Man?*, p. 82.
34 Cameron Hazlehurst, *Menzies Observed*, pp. 149-57.
35 Cited in Cameron Hazlehurst, *Menzies Observed*, p. 136.
36 Cameron Hazlehurst, *Menzies Observed*, pp. 131-2.
37 *Sydney Morning Herald*, 25 October 1938.
38 Enid Lyons, *Among the Carrion Crows*, pp. 62-3.
39 Cited in Kevin Perkins, p. 70.
40 Enid Lyons, *Among the Carrion Crows*, p. 65.
41 W.J. Hudson, *Casey*, p. 104.
42 Cited in Cameron Hazlehurst, *Menzies Observed*, p. 313.
43 Speech delivered in Goulborn, 15 June 1937; cited in Cameron Hazlehurst, *Menzies Observed*, pp. 148-9.
44 R.G. Menzies, *The Forgotten People*, p. 6; see also p. 175.

45 The title Menzies gave to some jottings on journalists made after his retirement. MS 4936, series 10, box 358, NLA. Menzies particularly felt he had been misrepresented in the Sydney press, and his papers also contain a facetious *Sydney Morning Herald* obituary from some time in the early 1960s cataloguing the misrepresentations. MS 4936, series 10, box 355, NLA.
46 John Bunting, *R.G. Menzies*, p. 61.
47 Melanie Klein, *Envy and Gratitude and Other Works*, pp. 192-3.
48 Cited in Max Scheler, *Ressentiment*, p. 53.
49 These beliefs of Menzies were repeated so often it is not possible to give exhaustive evidence. On the rule of law, see Paul Hasluck, *Sir Robert Menzies*; on role of Crown see R.G. Menzies, *Afternoon Light*, chapter 10, 'Looking around at eighty', 12 December 1974, MS 4936, series 10, box 357, NLA; on the role of the Commonwealth see R.G. Menzies, *Speech is of Time*, Part One and *Afternoon Light*, chapters 9 and 10.
50 W.J. Hudson comments that of his generation, who all carried colonial deference to England, 'Few were as romantic as Menzies'. *Blind Loyalty*, p. 31.
51 Anthony Trollope, *The Prime Minister*, vol. II, p. 311.
52 Arthur Phillips, 'The Cultural Cringe', *Meanjin*, vol. 9, no. 4, (1950).
53 David Malouf, *Johnno*, p. 52.
54 Allan Dawes, 'R.G. Menzies of Australia: An Interim Report', p. 17. Dawes gives no reference for this quote and I have been unable to locate its source; it is, however, in a copy which Menzies has read and corrected.
55 R.G. Menzies, 'Not to Yield', chapter IV, MS 4936, series 10, box 359, NLA.
56 W.J. Hudson, *Blind Loyalty*, pp. 31-2; *Casey*, pp. 131-4 and chapter 8.

CHURCHILL AND THE MEANING OF 1941

1 R.G. Menzies, *Afternoon Light*, p.19.
2 David Day, *Menzies and Churchill at War*, pp. 47, 71; *The Times*, 16 April 1941, cited in Day, p. 130.
3 Tahu Hole, *Anzacs into Battle*, cited in Cameron Hazlehurst, *Menzies Observed*, pp. 214-15.
4 R.G. Menzies, *To the People of Great Britain at War from the Prime Minister of Australia*, p. 14.
5 Diary for 1941.
6 Diary, 12 April 1941.
7 Cameron Hazlehurst, *Menzies Observed*, p. 218.
8 R.G. Menzies, *Afternoon Light*, p. 20.

9   Diary, on page opposite entry for 21 March 1941.
10 David Day, *Menzies and Churchill at War*, p. 99.
11 Diary, 6 March 1941.
12 Diary, 11 March 1941.
13 'England: Menzies War-time Tour', Home movie, AVC 006284, VA 050675-005, National Film and Sound Archive, Canberra.
14 Diary, 2 May 1935.
15 Menzies to Bruce, 22 February 1940, cited in David Day, *Menzies and Churchill at War*, p. 16.
16 Diary, 22 February; 2 March; 24 February; 14 April 1941.
17 David Day, *Menzies and Churchill at War*, chapters 10 and 11.
18 Ibid., p. 39.
19 See Benedict Anderson, *Imagined Communities*, pp. 102ff. for discussion of the tension between national and imperial ideologies in the old imperial centres.
20 David Day, *Menzies and Churchill at War*, chapters 10 and 11.
21 Ibid., p. 151.
22 Ibid., p. 191.
23 Diary, 1 and 2 May 1941.
24 *Time*, New York, 5 May 1941, cited in David Day, *Menzies and Churchill at War*, p. 175.
25 Mackenzie King's Diary, 7 May 1941, cited in Cameron Hazlehurst, *Menzies Observed*, pp. 224-9.
26 Diary, 23 May 1941.
27 Movietone News 1941. This scene is included in two documentaries on Menzies I have viewed: 'A Profile of Robert Menzies', TVW7 Perth, 1972, Australian Film and Sound Archive; and 'The Ming Dynasty', a Hindsight programmed hosted by Geraldine Doogue and shown on the ABC in 1991.
28 *Age*, 26 May 1941.
29 Arthur Fadden, *They Called Me Artie*, p. 60.
30 David Day, *Menzies and Churchill at War*, chapter 14.
31 Press statement, cited in R.G. Menzies, *Afternoon Light*, p. 54.
32 Percy Spender, *Politics and a Man*, pp. 160ff.
33 Percy Joske, *Sir Robert Menzies*, p. 122; Kevin Perkins, *Menzies*, pp. 138-9, 140. In chapter 12 Perkins tells the story from the point of view of Bill McCall, one of Menzies' loudest critics.
34 David Day, *Menzies and Churchill at War*, pp. 229-30.
35 Ibid., chapter 15.
36 Ibid., pp. 243, 246.
37 Cameron Hazlehurst, *Menzies Observed*, p. 249; Percy Spender, *Politics and a Man*, p. 152; Kevin Perkins, *Menzies*, p. 149.

38 This interpretation was put forward as early as 1943 by Warwick Fairfax, writing in the *Sydney Morning Herald*, cited in Cameron Hazlehurst, *Menzies Observed*, p. 269.
39 Percy Spender, *Politics and a Man*, p. 152.
40 R.G. Menzies, *Afternoon Light*, p. 57.
41 Howard Beale, *This Inch of Time*, p. 109.
42 Kevin Perkins, *Menzies*, p. 149.
43 Percy Joske, *Sir Robert Menzies*, p. 122.
44 There was, perhaps, another dimension as well to the changes which took place in Menzies at this time. He was approaching fifty and so well past the mid-point of life when a man realises he has stopped growing up and started to grow old. The final limit of all may have tolled its sombre knell, helping him to recognise the finitude of his possible achievements. In his famous essay 'Death and the Midlife Crisis' Eliot Jacques argues that the recognition in mid-adulthood of the inevitability of death and the finitude of what one can accomplish precipitates a psychological crisis. Successfully weathered it can usher in the mature, sculpted creativity of later life. *International Journal of Psychoanalysis*, vol. 46, no. 4, (1965), pp. 502-14.
45 Cameron Hazlehurst, *Menzies Observed*, p. 257; Kevin Perkins, *Menzies*, p. 148.
46 Cited in Kevin Perkins, *Menzies*, p. 148.
47 R.G. Menzies, *Afternoon Light*, p. 57.
48 Isabel Green to Kevin Perkins, interview. (Reported by Perkins in *Menzies*, p. 156.)
49 R.G. Menzies, 'The Sickness of Democracy', *The Forgotten People*, pp.175, 178.
50 Frank Menzies to Kevin Perkins, interview.
51 Some of these broadcasts were published in mid-1943 in *The Forgotten People and Other Studies in Democracy*. The complete series can be found in Menzies' papers, MS 4936, series 6, box 256, folders 31-3, NLA. A glimpse of Menzies' activities at this time is revealed by a slip of newspaper used as a bookmark in the pocket edition of Edmund Burke in his library at Melbourne University. The newspaper fragment advertises a band concert at the Adelaide Town Hall on 18 December 1942. In rethinking his political philosophy Menzies was doing some reading. Burke's discussion of the role of political parties in 'Thoughts on the Present Discontents' is particularly heavily marked. Also marked is Burke's advice to men in public life as to how to live a good life.
52 Graeme Starr, *The Liberal Party of Australia*, pp. 93-4; Marion Simms, *A Liberal Nation*, pp. 14-20.
53 Michael Kino, 'The Forgotten Menzies', chapter 3.
54 'Politics and the Church', *Argus*, 4 May 1931.

55 Cameron Hazlehurst records two further examples of Menzies' striking inability to identify with problems of ordinary people. When he was Minister for the Railways in the Victorian government he was involved with a strike in the Wonthaggi coal mine in response to the government's attempts to cut wages. The miners reported that they had never known a minister more callously indifferent to the hardships and sufferings of others. *The Labor Call*, 31 May 1934, cited in *Menzies Observed*, p. 79. Nor was his indifference exclusive to the working class. As Attorney-General in the Victorian government he prepared a report on the law relating to solicitors who misuse client's funds – the funds of the thrifty middle class he was later to praise. Hazlehurst comments on the report that it overlooked the one class of persons whom it might have been expected to be protecting – the solicitors' clients. *Menzies Observed*, p. 81.

56 Menzies' parents were generous with the extension of credit towards the struggling wheat farmers in Jeparit. R.G. Menzies, *Afternoon Light*, p. 8; Isabel Green to Kevin Perkins, interview. Frank Menzies comments that his father had suggested to Bob that he go into the Labor Party, his father having a great deal of sympathy for the working man. Frank Menzies to Francis McNicoll, interview. Both Isabel and Frank comment that James was particularly noted for his generosity and compassion.

57 Cameron Hazlehurst notes the coincidence at this time between Menzies' attitudes and those of significant Melbourne commercial and financial interests. There were times, he says, when parts of his speeches seemed to be compiled from stockbrokers' newsletters. *Menzies Observed*, p. 71.

58 Michael Kino, 'The Forgotten Menzies', p. 64.

59 Speech at Grand Hotel, Auckland, 22 May 1941, MS 4936, series 6, box 252, folder 11.

60 Movietone News, shown in 'A Profile of Robert Menzies', TVW7 Perth, 1972, National Film and Sound Archive.

61 Speech at Sydney Town Hall, 26 May 1941. MS 4936, series 6, box 252.

62 Mackenzie King Diary, 23 August 1941, cited, David Day, *Menzies and Churchill at War*, p. 226.

63 Processes of mourning may have aided this. James Menzies died in 1945 and Kate in 1946.

64 Bob Bessant, 'Robert Gordon Menzies and Education in Australia', *Melbourne Studies in Education*, 1977, pp. 75-101.

65 R.G. Menzies, *The Measure of the Years*, p. 86.

66 See Vamik D. Volkan, 'Narcissistic Personality Organisation and Reparative Leadership', *The International Journal of Psychoanalysis*, vol. 30, no. 2, (April 1980), pp. 131-52, for a very suggestive discussion of two different types of narcissistic leaders – one destructive, the other

reparative. Where the destructive narcissistic leader maintains his sense of specialness and power by increasing the distance between himself and others, the reparative leader determines to raise the group up to a level appropriate to his own elevated self.

67 Diary, 2, 7 and 8 August 1935.
68 R.G. Menzies, *The Measure of the Years*, chapter 16.
69 For Menzies' attitude towards Churchill in this period see particularly *Afternoon Light*, chapter 4.
70 R.G. Menzies, 'Speech and Speakers', The George Adlington Syme Oration, *The Australian and New Zealand Journal of Surgery*, vol. 33, no. 3, (February 1964), p. 163.
71 Diary, 2 May 1935.
72 This manuscript is undated but was written after Menzies retired. MS 4936, series 10, box 358, NLA.
73 David McNicoll, *Luck's a Fortune*, chapter 19. Extracts of this interview were published in the *Age*, 28 November 1979. The interview reported here was recorded by McNicoll on 3 April 1974. Material of a similar sort can be found on tapes of interviews Menzies recorded with his chosen biographer, Francis McNicoll, who, coincidentally, is David McNicoll's sister-in-law. TRC 1169/349, Oral History Collection, NLA.
74 Angus McIntyre, *Ageing and Political Leadership*, explores the various ways in which those who have enjoyed political power respond to their ageing and impending death.
75 Percy Joske, *Sir Robert Menzies*, pp. 347-53.
76 Transcript of speech at Dover College, 20 July 1966. MS 4936, series 6, box 258, NLA.

CORRESPONDENCES

1 Stuart Macintyre, *The Oxford History of Australia*, p. 303.
2 R.G. Menzies, *Afternoon Light*, p. 292; Menzies' address to the Canberra Conference, 13 October 1944, Graeme Starr, *The Liberal Party of Australia*, p. 75.
3 Bernard Smith, *The Spectre of Truganini*, p. 10.

BIBLIOGRAPHY

THE PRIMARY sources for this book are Robert Menzies' speeches and writings, both published and unpublished. The unpublished are to be found in his papers in the National Library of Australia, MS 4936 in series 6 (speeches), series 10 (writings) and in series 13 (diaries of his early overseas trips). Published sources used are:

—'A Century of Australian Song', (in three parts), *The Melbourne University Magazine*, vol. 12, no. 1-3, 1917.
—*The Rule of Law During War*, Bowen Prize Essay, 1917, Charles Maxwell Law Booksellers, Melbourne, 1917.
—'The Place of a University in the Modern Community', address delivered at Canberra University College, 1939. Melbourne University Press, Melbourne, 1939.
—'A Few Thoughts About Engineers', *Journal of the Institution of Engineers, Australia*, vol. 11, December 1939.
—*To the People of Britain at War from the Prime Minister of Australia*, Longmans, London, 1941.
—*The Forgotten People and Other Studies in Democracy*, Angus & Robertson, Sydney, 1943.
—Joint Opposition Policy Speech, 1946. Liberal Party of Australia, Sydney, 1946.
—Joint Opposition Policy Speech and Supplementary Statements, 1949. Liberal Party of Australia, Sydney, 1949.
—Federal Election Policy Speech, 1954, Liberal Party of Australia, Canberra, 1954.
—*Speech is of Time: Selected Speeches and Writings*, Cassell, London, 1958.
—'Speech and Speakers', The George Adlington Syme Oration, *The Australian and New Zealand Journal of Surgery*, vol. 33, no. 3, (February 1964), pp. 161-8.
—*Afternoon Light*, Cassell, Melbourne, 1967.
—*Central Power in the Australian Commonwealth: An Examination of the Growth of Commonwealth Power in the Australian Federation*, Cassell, London, 1967.
—*The Measure of the Years*, Cassell, Melbourne, 1970.

BOOKS, ARTICLES, THESES

Aitkin, Don. *Stability and Change in Australian Politics*, Australian National University Press, Canberra, 1977.

Alexander, James. 'The Psychology of Bitterness', *International Journal of Psychoanalysis*, vol. 41, no. 4, 1960, pp. 514-20.

Allen, Terri G. *Wyperfeld*, roneo publication, Hopetoun, Victoria, 1975.
— *Wotjobaluk: Aborigines of the Wimmera River System*, roneo publication, Hopetoun, Victoria, 1974.
Anderson, Benedict. *Imagined Communities: Reflections on the Origins and Spread of Nationalism*, Verso, London, 1983.
Andrew, Barry. 'The Federal Government as a Literary Patron', *Meanjin*, vol. 41, no. 1, March 1982, pp. 3-19.
Bate, Weston. *Lucky City – The First Generation at Ballarat 1851-1901*, Melbourne University Press, 1979.
Beale, Howard. *This Inch of Time: Memoirs of Politics and Diplomacy*, Melbourne University Press, Melbourne, 1977.
Bessant, Bob. 'Robert Gordon Menzies and Education in Australia', in *Melbourne Studies in Education*, 1977, pp. 75-101.
Blainey, Geoffrey. *A Centenary History of Melbourne University*, Melbourne University Press, Melbourne, 1957.
Blainey, Geoffrey; Morrissey, James and Hulme, S.E.K. *Wesley College: The First Hundred Years*, Wesley College Melbourne, in association with Robertson and Mullens, Melbourne, 1967.
Blake, Les. *Wimmera*, Cyprus Publications, Melbourne, 1973.
Bolton, Geoffrey. *The Oxford History of Australia*, vol. 5, 1942-1988, Oxford University Press, Melbourne, 1990.
Bowman, David. 'Can the ASIO Revolution Last?', *Australian Society*, November 1989, pp. 23-6.
Brett, Judith. 'A Psychosocial Approach to Politics', *Arena*, 72, 1985, pp. 133-44.
Bunting, John. *R.G.Menzies: A Portrait*, Susan Haynes/Allen & Unwin, Sydney, 1988.
Burke, Kenneth. *Permanence and Change*, Hermes, Los Altos, California, 1930.
Cain, Frank. *The Origins of Political Surveillance in Australia*, Angus & Robertson, Sydney, 1983.
Campbell, Eric. *The Rallying Point: My Story of the New Guard*, Melbourne University Press, Melbourne, 1965.
Campbell, Beatrix. *Iron Ladies: Why do Women Vote Tory?*, Virago, London, 1987.
Cathcart, Michael. *Defending the National Tuckshop: Australia's Secret Army Intrigue of 1931*, McPhee Gribble, Melbourne, 1988.
Centre for Contemporary Cultural Studies, *On Ideology*, Hutchinson, London, 1977.
Chifley, Joseph. *Things Worth Fighting For: Speeches by Joseph Benedict Chifley*. Melbourne University Press, Melbourne, 1952.
Clark, Manning. *The History of Australia*, vol. VI, Melbourne University Press, Melbourne, 1987.

Cole, Douglas. ' "The Crimson Thread of Kinship": Ethnic Ideas in Australia, 1870-1914'. *Historical Studies*, vol. 14, no. 56, April 1971, pp. 511-25.

Coleman, Peter. *Obscenity, Blasphemy and Sedition: One Hundred Years of Censorship in Australia*, revised edition, Angus & Robertson, Sydney, 1974.

Connolly, William E. *The Terms of Political Discourse*, Princeton University Press, Princeton, New Jersey, 1983.

Counihan, Mick. 'The Formation of a Broadcasting Audience: Australian Radio in the Twenties', *Meanjin*, vol. 42, no. 2, June 1982, pp. 196-208.

Cowen, Zelman. *Menzies Remembered*, the first Menzies Lecture, 23 June 1986, Sir Robert Menzies Centre for Australian Studies, Institute of Commonwealth Studies, University of London.

Crisp, L.F. *The Australian Federal Labor Party, 1901-1951*, Hale & Iremonger, Sydney, 1978.

Croll, R.H. *Collections and Recollections*, Robertson & Mullens, Melbourne, 1939.

Curthoys, Ann and Merritt, John (eds). *Australia's First Cold War*, vol. 1, 'Society, Communism and Culture', Allen & Unwin, Sydney, 1984.

Davidson, Alistair. *The Communist Party of Australia: A Short History*, Hoover Institute Press, Stanford, California, 1969.

Davies, A.F. *Private Politics*, Melbourne University Press, Melbourne, 1966.

— *Skills, Outlooks and Passions: A Psychoanalytic Contribution to the Study of Politics*, Cambridge University Press, Cambridge, 1980.

— *The Human Element: Three Essays in Political Psychology*, McPhee Gribble, Melbourne, 1988.

Dawes, Allan. 'R.G. Menzies: An Interim Report', incomplete manuscript biography of Menzies, MS 4936, series 10, box 354, NLA.

Day, David. *Menzies and Churchill at War*, Angus & Robertson, Sydney, 1986.

— *The Great Betrayal: Britain, Australia and the Onset of the Pacific War 1939-1942*, Angus & Robertson, Sydney, 1988.

Douglas, Mary. *Purity and Danger: An Analysis of the Concepts of Pollution and Taboo*. Routlege & Kegan Paul, London, 1966.

Downer, Alexander. *Six Prime Ministers*, Hill of Content, Melbourne, 1982.

Duncan, H.D. *Communication and the Social Order*, Oxford University Press, Oxford, 1968.

Duverger, Maurice. *The Political Role of Women*, Unesco Press, Paris, 1950.

Edwards, P.G. 'S.M. Bruce, R.G. Menzies and Australia: War Aims and Peace Aims, 1939-1940'. *Historical Studies*, vol. 17, no. 66, April 1976, pp. 1-14.

Ellis, M.H. 'The Mind of R.G. Menzies: A Personal Appraisal', *Bulletin*, March 1961.

Fadden, Arthur. *They Called Me Artie: The Memoirs of Sir Arthur Fadden*, Jacaranda Press, Brisbane, 1969.

Freud, Sigmund. *Jokes and Their Relation to the Unconscious, The Standard Edition of the Complete Psychological Works of Sigmund Freud*, translated by James Strachey, (1905), vol. 8, Hogarth Press, London, 1960.
— 'Family Romances', (1908), *Standard Edition*, vol. 9.
Geertz, Clifford. *The Interpretation of Culture*, Basic Books, New York, 1973.
Gerth, H.H. and Mills, C. Wright. *From Max Weber: Essays in Sociology*, Routledge & Kegan Paul, London, 1948.
Gollan, Robin. *Revolutionaries and Reformists: Communism and the Australian Labour Movement 1920-1955*, Australian National University Press, Canberra, 1975.
Gramsci, Antonio. *Selections from the Prison Notebooks*, Lawrence & Wishart, London, 1971.
Habermas, Jürgen. *Towards a Rational Society*, Heinemann, London, 1971.
Haese, Richard. *Rebels and Precursors: The Revolutionary Years of Australian Art*, Allen Lane, Melbourne, 1981.
Hall, Richard. 'Menzies's Literary Lie', *Age Monthly Review*, vol. 3, no. 9, January 1984, pp. 3-4.
— *The Secret State: Australia's Spy Industry*, Cassell, Sydney, 1978.
Hall, Stuart. 'The Rediscovery of Ideology: The Return of the Repressed in Media Studies', in Michael Gurevitch, Tony Bennett, James Curran and Janet Woollacott (eds), *Culture, Society and the Media*, Methuen, London, 1982.
Harries, Owen. 'The Menzies Foreign Policy: A Study in Realism', *Quadrant*, December 1983, pp. 23-33.
Hasluck, Paul. *The Government and the People 1939-1941*, Australian War Memorial, Canberra, 1952.
— *Sir Robert Menzies* (Daniel Mannix Memorial Lecture, 1979), Melbourne University Press, Melbourne, 1980.
— *Shades of Darkness: Aboriginal Affairs, 1925-1965*, Melbourne University Press, Melbourne, 1988.
Hazlehurst, Cameron. *Menzies Observed*, Allen & Unwin, Sydney, 1979.
Hazlehurst, Cameron (ed.), *Australian Conservatism: Essays in Twentieth Century Political History*, Australian National University Press, Canberra, 1979.
Henderson, Peter. *Privilege and Pleasure*, Methuen & Haynes, Sydney, 1986.
Hofstadter, Richard. *The Paranoid Style in American Politics and Other Essays*, Alfred Knopf, New York, 1965.
Holt, Edgar. *Politics is People: The Men of the Menzies Era*, Angus & Robertson, Sydney, 1969.
Horne, Donald. *The Lucky Country: Australia in the Sixties*, Penguin, Ringwood, Victoria, 1964.
Horney, Karen. *Neurosis and Human Growth*, W.W. Norton, New York, 1950.
Howard, Frederick. *Kent Hughes: A Biography*, Macmillan, Melbourne, 1972.

Hudson, W.J. *Casey*, Oxford University Press, Melbourne, 1986.
— *Blind Loyalty: Australia and the Suez Crisis*, Melbourne University Press, Melbourne, 1989.
Hughes, Colin and Western, John. *The Prime Minister's Policy Speech: A Case Study in Televised Politics*, Australian National University Press, Canberra, 1966.
Jackson, H.R. *Churches and People in Australia and New Zealand*, Allen & Unwin, Sydney, 1987.
Jacques, Eliot. 'Death and the Mid-life Crisis', *International Journal of Psychoanalysis*, vol. 46, no. 4, 1965, pp. 502-14.
Johnson, Lesley. *The Unseen Voice: A Cultural Study of Early Australian Radio*, Routledge, London, 1988.
Johnson, R. 'Histories of Culture/Theories of Ideology: Notes on an Impasse', in Michelle Barrett et al. (ed.), *Ideology and Cultural Production*, Croom Helm, London, 1979.
Joske, Sir Percy. *Sir Robert Menzies: 1894-1978: A New, Informal Memoir*, Angus & Robertson, Sydney, 1978.
Kino, Michael. 'The Forgotten Menzies', BA Honours Thesis, Politics Department, Monash University, 1975.
Kisch, Egon. *Australian Landfall* (1937), Australian Book Society, Sydney, 1969.
Klein, Melanie. *Love, Guilt and Reparation and Other Works: 1921-1945*, Hogarth Press and Institute of Psychoanalysis, London, 1975.
— *Envy and Gratitude and Other Works: 1946-1963*, Hogarth Press and Institute of Psychoanalysis, London, 1975.
Kohut, Heinz. *The Analysis of the Self*, International Universities Press, New York, 1971.
— *The Restoration of the Self*, International Universities Press, New York, 1977.
Kramnick, Isaac. *The Rage of Edmund Burke: Portrait of an Ambivalent Conservative*, Basic Books, New York, 1977.
Latham, Earl (ed.). *The Meaning of McCarthyism: Problems in American Civilisation*, D.C. Heath & Co., Boston, 1965.
Lawlor, Adrian. *Arquebus*, Ruskin Press, Melbourne, 1937.
Levi-Strauss, Claude. *Structural Anthropology*, Basic Books, New York, 1963.
Lewis, Brian. *Sunday at Kooyong Road*, Hutchinson, Melbourne, 1976.
— *Our War: A View of World War I From Inside an Australian Family*, Melbourne University Press, Melbourne, 1980.
Little, Graham. *Strong Leadership: Thatcher, Reagan and an Eminent Person*, Oxford University Press, Melbourne, 1988.
— *Political Ensembles: A Psychosocial Approach to Politics*, Oxford University Press, Melbourne, 1985.
Lyons, Enid. *So We Take Comfort*, Heinemann, London, 1965.
— *Among the Carrion Crows*, Rigby, Adelaide, 1972.

McIntyre, Angus. *Aging and Political Leadership*, Oxford University Press, Melbourne, 1988.
Macintyre, Stuart. *The Oxford History of Australia*, vol. 4, 1901-1942, Oxford University Press, Melbourne, 1986.
McNicoll, David. *Luck's a Fortune*, Wildcat Press, Sydney, 1979.
McQueen, Humphrey. *The Black Swan of Trespass: The Emergence of Modernist Painting in Australia*, Alternative Publishing Cooperative Ltd., Sydney, 1979.
— *Gallipoli to Petrov: Arguing with Australian History*, Allen & Unwin, Sydney, 1984.
Malouf, David. *Johnno*, University of Queensland Press, Brisbane, 1975.
Martin, A.L. 'The Master's Voice? R.G. Menzies and Public Speaking', paper given at La Trobe University History Department, 8 November 1991.
— 'R.G. Menzies and the Suez Crisis', *Australian Historical Studies*, vol. 23, no. 92, April 1989, pp. 163-85.
Manne, Robert. *The Petrov Affair: Politics of Espionage*, Pergamon, Sydney, 1987.
Massola, Aldo. *Bunjil's Cave: Myths, Legends and Superstitions of the Aborigines of South-East Australia*, Landsdowne Press, Melbourne, 1968.
Mill, John Stuart. *Three Essays*, Oxford University Press, Oxford, 1975.
Mitchell, Juliet. *The Selected Melanie Klein*, Hogarth Press, London, 1986.
Murray, Robert. *The Split: Australian Labor in the Fifties*, Cheshire, Melbourne, 1970.
Page, Earle. *Truant Surgeon: The Inside Story of Forty Years of Australian Political Life*, Angus & Robertson, Sydney, 1963.
Palmer, Vance. 'Australian Letter', *Landfall*, vol. 7, no. 4, 1953.
Perkins, Kevin. *Menzies: Last of the Queen's Men*, Rigby, Adelaide, 1968.
Phillips, Arthur. *The Australian Tradition*, F.W. Cheshire, Melbourne, 1958.
Priestley, Susan. *Warracknabeal: A Wimmera Centenary History*, Jacaranda Press, Brisbane, 1967.
Ranulf, Svend. *Moral Indignation and Middle Class Psychology* (1938), Schocken Books, New York, 1964.
Raselli, Patricia. 'The Australian Women's National League: Always a Bridesmaid', BA Honours Thesis, Political Science Department, University of Melbourne, 1975.
Raven, Fred. *The History of the Menzies Family in Jeparit*, Jeparit Chamber of Commerce, 1966.
Rawson, Don. *Australia Votes: The 1958 Federal Election*, Melbourne University Press, Melbourne, 1961.
Reid, Alan. 'Prime Ministers I Have Known', *Bulletin Centenary Issue*, 29 January 1980, pp. 365-6.
Robert, Marthe. *The Origins of the Novel*, Harvester Press, Brighton, UK, 1980.

Robinson, Ray. *The Wit of Sir Robert Menzies*, Leslie Frewin, London, 1966.
Rowse, Tim. *Australian Liberalism and National Character*, Kibble Books, Malmsbury, Victoria, 1978.
Scheler, Max. *Ressentiment* (1912), edited by Lewis Coser, Free Press, New York, 1961.
Schoek, Helmut. *Envy: A Theory of Social Behaviour*, Secker and Warburg, London, 1969.
Schwartz, Bill. 'The Language of Constitutionalism: Baldwinite Conservatism', in *Formations of Nation and People*, Routledge & Kegan Paul, London, 1984.
Segal, Hanna. *Introduction to the Work of Melanie Klein*, Hogarth Press, London, 1973.
Seth, Ronald. *R.G. Menzies*, Cassell, London, 1960.
Shils, Edward. *Center and Periphery: Essays in Macrosociology*, University of Chicago Press, Chicago, 1975.
Shils, Edward and Young, Michael. 'The Meaning of the Coronation', *Sociological Review*, vol. 1, no. 2, 1953, pp. 63-81.
Simms, Marian. *A Liberal Nation: The Liberal Party and Australian Politics*, Hale & Iremonger, Sydney, 1982.
— 'Conservative Feminism: A Case Study of Feminist Ideology', *Women's Studies: International Quarterly*, 3, 1979, pp. 305-18.
Smith, Bernard. *The Spectre of Truganini*, 1980 Boyer Lectures, Australian Broadcasting Commission, 1980.
Snedden, Billie Mackie and Schedvin, M. Bernie. *Billy Snedden: An Unlikely Liberal*, Macmillan, Melbourne, 1990.
Spender, Jean. *Ambassador's Wife: A Woman's View of Life in Politics, Diplomacy and International Law*, Angus & Robertson, Sydney, 1968.
Spender, Percy. *Politics and a Man*, Collins, Sydney, 1972.
Starr, Graeme. *The Liberal Party of Australia: A Documentary History*, Drummond/Heineman, Richmond, Victoria, 1980.
Strahan, Lynne. *Just City and the Mirrors: Meanjin Quarterly and the Intellectual Front, 1940-1965*, Oxford University Press, Melbourne, 1984.
Tampfke, Jürgen and Doxford, Colin. *Australia Willkommen: A History of the Germans in Australia*, New South Wales University Press, Sydney, 1980.
Tiver, Peter. *The Liberal Party: Principles and Performance*, Jacaranda Press, Brisbane, 1978.
Trengrove, Alan. *Menzies: A Pictorial Biography*, Nelson, Melbourne, 1978.
Volkan, Vamik D. 'Narcissistic Personality Organisation and Reparative Leadership', *The International Journal of Psychoanalysis*, vol. 30, no. 2, April 1980, pp. 131-52.
Vondra, Josef, *German Speaking Settlers in Australia*, Cavalier Press, Melbourne, 1981.

Walter, James and Head, Brian. *Intellectual Movements and Australian Society*, Oxford University Press, Melbourne, 1988.

Watt, Alan. *Australian Diplomat*, Angus & Robertson, Sydney, 1968.

Watson, Bruce. 'Wit and Politics: A Study of Whitlam and Menzies', *Melbourne Journal of Politics*, vol. 13, 1981, pp. 32-44.

Watson, Don. *Brian Fitzpatrick: A Radical Life*, Hale & Iremonger, Sydney, 1979.

Watson, George. *The English Ideology: Studies in the Language of Victorian Politics*, Allen Lane, London, 1973.

Webb, Leicester. *Communism and Democracy in Australia: A Survey of the 1951 Referendum*, Cheshire, Melbourne, 1954.

Weber, Max. *The Protestant Ethic and the Spirit of Capitalism*, translated by Talcott Parsons, Allen & Unwin, London, 1930.

White, Richard. *Inventing Australia: Images and Identity 1688-1980*, Allen & Unwin, Sydney, 1981.

Whitington, Don. *Twelfth Man?*, Jacaranda Press, Brisbane, 1972.

Williams, Raymond. *The Country and the City*, Chatto & Windus, London, 1973.

TAPE-RECORDINGS

Robert Menzies to Ken Taylor, recorded for ABC, 25 February 1969, copy held in Oral History Collection NLA, TRC 1169/294-295.

Robert Menzies to Francis McNicoll (1973-4), Oral History Collection, NLA, TRC 1169/349.

Frank Menzies to Francis McNicoll (early 1970s?), Oral History Collection, NLA, TRC 1169/350.

Frank Menzies to Kevin Perkins, 1967, in Kevin Perkins' possession.

Isabel Green (née Menzies) to Kevin Perkins, 1967, in Kevin Perkins' possession.

INDEX

Aborigines/Kooris: white settler attitudes towards, 168, 171-2, 273-4; Menzies' attitude towards, 166-70; *see also* Jeparit, Wotjaballuk tribe
Adamson, L.A., 187, 210, 220-1
Afternoon Light, 117, 142, 153-4, 158, 161, 163, 178, 191, 194-5, 202-5, 253
aggression, 116-17, 231; Menzies and, 114-20, 230-1, 237-8
Alexander, James, 115
ambition, Menzies and, 16, 70, 121, 155, 201, 209-12, 240, 249-50, 256, 257, 258-9
anti-communism (Australian): in 1920s and 1930s, 86-92; and paranoia, 92-4; compared with United States, 97-8; and scapegoating, 98, 118, *see also* communism, Communist Party Dissolution Bill
Argyle, Sir Stanley, 229, 234, 252
Asians, Menzies and, 124, 177
Attlee, Clement, 268
Australian Labor Party: 2, 31; war-time government, 15, 17-19; and communism, 74, 76, 78, 80, 89, 105; and socialism, 35-6, 74; as bearers of mechanical imagery of social change, 47; association with bureaucracy, 48-9; ambitions and ideals, 271, 272
Australian Security Intelligence Organisation (ASIO), 93
Australian Women's National League, 52, 53, 56, 57

Baldwin, Stanley, 22, 138, 140-3

Ballarat, 41, 144, 159, 166
Beale, Howard, 230 254
Beaverbrook, Lord, 247, 250
Bell, George, 183, 184
Bent, Thomas, 216
bitterness, 115-16, 118-19
Black, Eugene, 187
Blair, Dorothy, 202, 205, 227-8.
British and Foreign Bible Society of Victoria, 143
British Empire/Commonwealth, Menzies and, 134, 144-7, 153-5, 174-5, 239-43, 245, 249
Brooke, Rupert, 137
Bruce, Stanley, 88-9, 242
Bunting, John, 1, 63, 187, 198, 238
Burdett, Basil, 183
bureaucracy, hostility to, 48-9
Burke, Edmund, 20, 138, 221, 297n51
Burns, Robert, 51, 62, 134, 158

Cairns, Jim, 291n61
Cameron, Archie, 84
Campbell, Eric, 86, 93
Canberra, Menzies' interest in, 266
Cashmore, Jennifer, 42
Cathcart, Michael, 86
Casey, Richard, 133, 177, 229, 242, 326
censorship, 75, 87, 90
Central Power in the Commonwealth, 194
Chamberlain, Neville, 241
Chifley, Joseph Benedict, 22, 42; 1949 policy speech, 58; response to Communist Party Dissolution Bill, 79-80, 89; and Commonwealth Literary Fund, 191

308

Churchill, Winston, 115, 151, 222, 248, 252-3; Menzies' conflict with, 153, 249-51; Menzies' criticism of, 151, 235, 248; Menzies' defeat by, 251-3, 256-7; Menzies' praise of, 266-7
civil liberties, Menzies and, 74-5, 81-2, 99, 108, 109-12, 125, 177
Clark, Manning, 195-6
class, as essentially contested concept, 32; Menzies' rejection of class-based political language, 38-46; *see also* middle class, working class
Coleman, Peter, 90
Coles, Arthur, 252, 254
Commonwealth Literary Fund (CLF), Menzies and, 191-3; Chifley and, 191
communism and communists, 47, 74, 85-6, 88, 92-3, 118-20, 192-3; Menzies and, 77, 84, 108, 118-20, 149, 192-3; *see also* anti-communism, Communist Party Dissolution Bill, Communist Party of Australia
Communist Party Dissolution Bill, 77-81; Menzies' Second Reading speech, 49, 77, 102-8, 121; *see also* Chifley, Percy Spender
Communist Party of Australia, 74, 75, 76-7, 80-2, 84, 89, 93-4, 105
Conservative Party (British), 141
Country Party, 16, 31, 75, 81, 156, 231
Cranbourne, Lord, 252
Crocker, Walter, 177
Cromwell, Oliver, 138, 142
cultural cringe, 133, 134, 240
curiosity, Menzies' lack of, 176-7
Curtin, John, 16, 251, 258

Davies, Alan, 154
Dawes, Allan, 165, 206, 207, 210, 241
Day, David, 248, 249
'Democracy and Management', 43
Denning, Warren, 200, 237
Depression, the, 17, 58, 89, 261, 262
depressive position, 95-6
discourse, *see* ideology
Dobell, William, portrait of Menzies, 195
Douglas, Mary, 82, 87
Downer, Alexander, 198, 229, 230
'The Drover's Wife', 162
Duffy, Gavan, 206
duplicity, as inevitable characteristic of politics and politicians, 25, 108, 270; Menzies and, 102-8, 118-19, 120, 122

Ebenezer Mission, 166
education, Menzies' attitude towards, 69, 228, 232, 265
Elizabeth II, Menzies and, 2, 147, 216-17, 255, 266
Ellis, M.H., 221
Empire Parliamentary Association, 20, 138, 150, 247
England, Menzies and, 113-14, 130, 132-5, 140-55, 239-43, 245-8, 255-6, 263-4; Menzies' trip to (1935), 133, 135-40, 149, 150-3, 176-7, 256, 266; (1938), 235; (1941), 16, 153, 244-51, 256, 262-4; (1948), 145; *see also* British Empire/Commonwealth
envy, 65-6, 116, 118-19, 237, 240
Evatt, H.V., 83, 229, 251

Fadden, Arthur, 16, 75, 228, 247, 251, 253
family romance, 212-18, 222-3, 225, 240, 256, 268-9

310 Index

'Freedom of Speech and Expression', 108-12
'The Forgotten People', 3-4, 15, 26-7, 31-73, 157-9, 172-3, 185-6, 258, 264-5
Fox, Charles, 221
Freud, Sigmund, 212, 213, 215, 216, 218, 225
Frost, Robert, 72-3
frugality, 59-60, 61-2, 64, 163

Geertz, Clifford, 100
George V, 133, 134
George VI, 146
Goethe, Johann Wolfgang von, 238
Germans, meet Kisch's boat, 89; as settlers in Wimmera, 165, 173, 176
Gollan, Robin, 74
Gordon, General Charles, 159
Gorton, John, 192
Gramsci, Antonia, 33, 38
Granchester, 137
Gray's Inn, 138, 151
great men, Menzies and, 216, 218-19, 221-3, 225-6, 255
Green, Isabel (née Menzies), 24, 163, 202, 205, 206, 207, 218, 259

Hall, Richard, 89, 192
Hampden, John, 136-7, 221
Harpur, Charles, 189
Hasluck, Paul, 189, 196-7, 277n10
Hastings, Warren, 136, 137, 152
'Hatred as an Instrument of War Policy', 114-16
Hazlehurst, Cameron, 156, 165, 176
hecklers, Menzies and, 21, 232
Henderson, Heather (née Menzies), 292n62
Heydon, Peter, 235
Hofstadter, Richard, 97-8

Holt, Edgar, 24, 226
home: as site of individuality, 46-9; and women, 38, 51-6; and frugality, 45, 59; *see also* middle class, working class, Protestantism, individualism, Menzies' childhood
Horne, Donald, 2, 174
Hughes, Wilfred Kent, 234
Hughes, William (Billy) Morris, 16, 17

ideals, 199, 201, 270-1; Menzies and, 201, 237-8, 249-50, 256, 259-60
idealisations, 238
ideology, 33-4, 99-100, 116
Immigration Act, 83, 88, 90
individualism, 71-3, 149, 154-5; *see also* home, liberalism, Protestantism
Institute of Public Affairs, 261

Jeparit, 132, 156; in Menzies' childhood, 158, 159-61, 173, 216, 240, 241; Aborigines in vicinity of, 166; memorial spire to Menzies, 163-4, 211-12
Jones, Barry, 178
Joske, Percy, 252, 257
journalists, Menzies and, 238-9, 267

Kendall, Henry, 132, 188-9
King, Mackenzies, 250, 251, 264
Kisch, Egon, 82-5
Klein, Melanie, 94-6
Kohut, Heinz, 288n9
Korean War, 76

Latham, John, 40
law, Menzies and, 21, 117, 124, 144, 206, 211, 228, 239
Lawler, Adrian, 182

Lazarus, Clem, 176
leaders, Menzies and, 233-7
Levi-Strauss, Claude, 276n8
Lewis, Brian, 63-4, 227
Lewis, Phyllis, 64, 227
liberalism, 33, 47, 71-2
Liberal Party of Australia, 3, 4, 254, 270; philosophy, 34-5; and women, 56-7; formation, 17, 258, 261, 265, 266, 271-2
literature and poetry, Menzies' attitude towards, 130-2, 139, 165, 187-95
Little, Graham, 278n49
Lord Warden of the Cinque Ports, Menzies as, 240, 267
Lyons, Enid, 53, 54-5, 228, 235, 236, 237
Lyons, Joseph, 16, 22, 54-5, 89, 90, 211, 229, 235, 236

Macbeth, 107, 121-3
McCall, Bill, 252
MacDonald, Ramsay, 151
McEwan, Jack, 231
Macgeorge, Norman, 182
Macintyre, Stuart, 66
McNicoll, David, 267-8
McPherson, William, 237
Malouf, David, 241
margins and boundaries, 87-8, 124-5, 172-3, 272-3
Marxism, 33, 42, 47, 50-1, 148-9, 154-5
masculinity, 116-18, 119-21, 123-4
Meanjin, 192
The Measure of the Years, 194
Melbourne University Magazine, 131, 175, 178, 188, 210
Menzies, Frank, 163, 201, 206-7, 209, 218, 228, 231
Menzies, Ian, 292n62
Menzies, James, 159, 203-8, 210, 218, 232, 241, 259, 260, 262
Menzies, Kate (née Sampson), 159, 202-3, 205-9, 241
Menzies, Kenneth, 292n62
Menzies, Pattie, 203, 204
Menzies, Robert: Australians' attitudes towards, 1-3, 25, 200; as Attorney-General, 1-2, 74, 75, 82, 83-4, 90, 234; *see also* Royal Academy of Australian Art; books in childhood, 134, 144, 159, 163-5, 218-19; change after 1941, 4, 16-17, 253-4, 266; childhood, 41, 159-65, 218-19, 289n10; as club man, 20, 190; economic attitudes, 261, 262; education of, 208-10; attitude to education, 69, 228, 232, 265; and friends, 197-8; home movies, 247-8; library, 121, 129-30; and parents, 201-9, 212, 218, 225-6, 255-6, 265; politics as vocation, 23, 35, 199, 259-60; and political colleagues, 229-30, 265; precocious formation of political views, 178, 181-2, 223-4, 260-1, 273-4; as public man, 181, 196-8, 224, 226; and public speaking, 19-21, 195, 220-1; return to Australia (1941), 250-1, 256-7; resignations, 233, 235-6, 252-3; voice of, 15; as war-time Prime Minister, 16, 75, *see also* trip to England, 1941; wit of, 230-2, 258. *See also under relevant individual entries.*
The Merchant of Venice (Portia), 124, 217

312 Index

middle class; defined by exclusion, 39-40, 120; as moral category, 41-4; association with pre-modern life, 51; psychology of, 64-8, 70-1; and England, 143, 163, 174; and art, 185-6; Menzies as representative of, 4, 272
Mill, John Stuart, 109-12
monarchy, Menzies and, 146-8, 217, 239
Morrison, John, 192
Murray Report, 265

Nehru, Jawaharlal, 124
Neilson, John Shaw, 189
New Guard, *see* secret armies
nostalgia for England, 171-2
'Not to Yield', 145-6, 153

O'Dowd, Bernard, 189
Oedipus complex, 213-14, 222-3, 273
oppositions (binary), 36-8, 45-6, 120
Overland, 192

Packer, Frank, 123
Page, Earle, 16
Palmer, Vance, 191
paranoia: paranoid schizoid position, 95-6, 97; in politics, 96-7; *see also* anti-communism
parliament, Menzies and, 20, 113, 117, 136, 138-9, 239
parliamentary privilege, Menzies and, 113
party conflict in Australia, 31, 36-8
Peacock, Andrew, 285n33
Penton, Brian, 292n6
To the People of Britain at War from the Prime Minister of Australia, 246
Petrov, Vladmir, 2
Phillips, Arthur, 133, 134, 240

policy speeches, federal elections: (1946), 57, 62-3, 68; (1949), 35, 58-9, 76; (1954), 60-1, 70; (1963), 21
political language, 25-6, 31-5, 99-100; Menzies' skill with and attitude towards, 3, 19-25, 49-50, 108, 150-1
'Politics as an Art', 21-3
Presbyterians, *see* Protestantism
Protestantism, 59-64, 68

racism, 91-2, 119, 120, 166, 167-8, 171
radio, 18-19; Menzies and, 15, 18-19, 258-9, 261
Ranulf, Svend, 66, 67
Reagan, Ronald, 25
Reid, Alan, 16, 200
Robert, Marthe, 215
Roosevelt, Franklin, 19
Royal Academy of Australian Art, Menzies and, 179-85
Russell, Bertrand, 43

Sampson, John, 178, 202, 207
Sampson, Sydney, 202-3
Santamaria, B.A., 76
Savage Club, 189-90
Scheler, Max, 66, 67
Scullin, James, 232
Seamen's strike (1925), 88
secret armies, 86, 89
Sharkey, Lance, 105
Shils, Edward, 148
Smith, Bernard, 165, 171-2, 273
Smith, Sydney Ure, 185
Smuts, Jan, 242
Social Darwinism, 168, 170
socialism, Australian Labor Party and, 35-6, 74; Menzies and, 62-3, 68-71

sociology, 47, 50-1, 70
Soviet Union, 76-7, 97
Speech is of Time, 176
Spender, Jean, 123
Spender, Percy, and anti-communism, 101-2; on Menzies, 197, 230, 252, 253
sport, Menzies and, 117, 187, 227
Stalin, Joseph, 77, 90, 103
Stephens, James Brunton, 00
Suez crisis, Menzies and, 177-8

television, Menzies and, 19
Thatcher, Margaret, 25
Trollope, Anthony, 240

United Australia Party, 16, 17, 244, 254, 270-1
University of Melbourne, 121, 129, 130, 144; Menzies at, 175-6, 188-9, 210-11, 228

Victorian Artists' Society, *see* Royal Academy of Australian Art
Victorian Book Censorship League, 90
vindictiveness, Menzies and, 230, 255, 267-8

Walpole, Robert, 137, 221
Waten, Judah, 192
Weber, Max, 61, 64, 277n16

welfare state, Menzies and, 40, 65, 68
Wentworth, W.C., 192
Wesley Church, Melbourne, 234
Wesley College, Menzies at, 64, 144, 165, 187, 210, 219-21, 230
White Australia Policy, 83, 90-1, 169
White, Thomas (Tommy) W., 84, 90-1, 119
Wimmera, 160-1
women: radio boon to, 18, 52; in non-labour politics, 52-3, 56-7; and socialism, 71; Menzies attitude to, 56-9, 120-4, 217-18; *see also* Australian Women's National League, home, Enid Lyons
Wordsworth, William, 129-32, 134, 137
work, as dull and anonymous, 46; labour's hold on symbol of, 60-2; Menzies and, 63, 199; *see also* Protestantism
working class, as lacking individuality (including exclusion from image of home), 43-6, 48, 120; as more open to sociological understanding, 50-1; and communists, 105
World War I, Menzies and, 228
Wotjoballuk tribe, 160, 165-6, 173